PERSONAL WATER VEHICLE
SE   JAL

VM 348.5 .P47 1988

(FIRST EDITION)

FAZER	**WETBIKE**
SCAT HOVERCRAFT	
FUNJET BOATS	**WETJET**
SURF-JET	
JET SKI	**YAMAHA**

Published by
INTERTEC PUBLISHING CORPORATION
P.O. BOX 12901, OVERLAND PARK, KS 66212

Cover photograph courtesy of:

Kawasaki Motors Corp., U.S.A.
9950 Jeronimo Road
Irvine, CA 92718-2016

D1709345

8-95   # 22544648

CONTENTS

FUNDAMENTALS SECTION

SERVICE SECTION

DUAL DIMENSIONS

This service manual provides specifications in both the Metric (SI) and U.S. Customary systems of measurement. The first specification is given in the measuring system used during manufacture, while the second specification (given in parenthesis) is the converted measurement. For instance, a specification of "0.28 mm (0.011 inch)" would indicate that the equipment was manufactured using the metric system of measurement and the U.S. equivalent of 0.28 mm is 0.011 inch.

Intertec Publishing thanks the following firms for their cooperation and technical assistance:

Kawasaki Motors Corporation, U.S.A., Irvine, California

Progressive Power Corporation, Janesville, Wisconsin

UltraNautics, Oxnard, California

Shawnee Kawasaki Honda, Shawnee, Kansas

Wetjet International Ltd., Paynesville, Minnesota

Yamaha Motor Corporation U.S.A., Cypress, California

DESIGN FUNDAMENTALS

OPERATING PRINCIPLES

ENGINE TYPES

The engines used to power personal water vehicles and many other items of power equipment in use today are basically similar. All are technically known as "Internal Combustion Reciprocating Engines."

The source of power is heat formed by the burning of a combustible mixture, usually petroleum products and air. In a reciprocating engine, this burning takes place in a closed cylinder containing a piston. Expansion resulting from the heat of combustion applies pressure on the piston to turn a shaft by means of a crank and connecting rod.

The fuel:air mixture may be ignited by means of an electric spark (Otto Cycle Engine) or by heat formed from compression of air in the engine cylinder (Diesel Cycle Engine). The complete series of events which must take place in order for the engine to run may occur in one revolution of the crankshaft (two strokes of the piston in cylinder) which is referred to as a "Two-Stroke Cycle Engine," or in two revolutions of the crankshaft (four strokes of the piston in cylinder) which is referred to as a "Four-Stroke Cycle Engine."

OTTO CYCLE. In a spark ignited engine, a series of five events is required in order for the engine to provide power. This series of events is called the "Cycle" (or "Work Cycle") and is repeated in each cylinder of the engine as long as work is being done. This series of events which comprise the "Cycle" is as follows:

1. The mixture of fuel and air is pushed into the cylinder by atmospheric pressure when the pressure within the engine cylinder is reduced by the piston moving downward in the cylinder (or by applying pressure to the fuel:air mixture as by crankcase compression in the crankcase of a "Two-Stroke Cycle Engine" which is described in a later paragraph).

2. The mixture of fuel and air is compressed by the piston moving upward in the cylinder.

3. The compressed fuel:air mixture is ignited by a timed electric spark.

4. The burning fuel:air mixture expands forcing the piston downward in the cylinder thus converting the chemical energy generated by combustion into mechanical power.

5. The gaseous products formed by the burned fuel:air mixture are exhausted from the cylinder so a new "Cycle" can begin.

The above described five events which comprise the work cycle of an engine are commonly referred to as (1), INTAKE; (2), COMPRESSION; (3), IGNITION; (4), EXPANSION (POWER); and (5), EXHAUST.

TWO-STROKE CYCLE. Two-stroke cycle engines may be of the Otto Cycle (spark ignition) or Diesel Cycle (compression ignition) type. However, since the two-stroke cycle engines listed in the repair section of this manual are all of the Otto Cycle type, operation of two-stroke Diesel Cycle engines will not be discussed in this section.

In two-stroke cycle engines, the piston is used as a sliding valve for the cylinder intake and exhaust ports. The intake and exhaust ports are both open when the piston is at the bottom of its

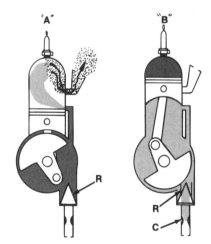

Fig. 1-1—Schematic diagram of a two-stroke cycle engine operating on the Otto Cycle (spark ignition). View "B" shows piston near top of upward stroke and atmospheric pressure is forcing air through carburetor (C), where fuel is mixed with the air, and the fuel:air mixture enters crankcase through open reed valve (R). In view "A," piston is near bottom of downward stroke and has opened the cylinder exhaust and intake ports; fuel:air mixture in crankcase has been compressed by downward stroke of engine and flows into cylinder through open port. Incoming mixture helps clean burned exhaust gases from cylinder.

downward stroke (bottom dead center or "BDC"). The exhaust port is open to atmospheric pressure; therefore, the fuel:air mixture must be elevated to a higher than atmospheric pressure in order for the mixture to enter the cylinder. As the crankshaft is turned from BDC and the piston starts on its upward stroke, the intake and exhaust ports are closed and the fuel:air mixture in the cylinder is compressed. When the piston is at or near the top of its upward stroke (top dead center or "TDC"), an electric spark across the electrode gap of the spark plug ignites the fuel:air mixture. As the crankshaft turns past TDC and the piston starts on its downward stroke, the rapidly burning fuel:air mixture expands and forces the piston downward. As the piston nears bottom of its downward stroke, the cylinder exhaust port is opened and the burned gaseous products from combustion of the fuel:air mixture flows out the open port. Slightly further downward travel of the piston opens the cylinder intake port and a fresh charge of fuel:air mixture is forced into the cylinder. Since the exhaust port remains open, the incoming flow of fuel:air mixture helps clean (scavenge) any remaining burned gaseous products from the cylinder. As the crankshaft turns past BDC and the piston starts on its upward stroke, the cylinder intake and exhaust ports are closed and a new cycle begins.

Since the fuel:air mixture must be elevated to a higher than atmospheric pressure to enter the cylinder of a two-stroke cycle engine, a compressor pump must be used. Coincidentally, downward movement of the piston decreases the volume of the engine crankcase. Thus, a compressor pump is made available by sealing the engine crankcase and connecting the carburetor to a port in the crankcase. When the piston moves upward, volume of the crankcase is increased which lowers pressure within the crankcase to below atmospheric. Air will then be forced through the carburetor, where fuel is mixed with the air, and on into the engine crankcase. In order for downward movement of the piston to compress the fuel:air mixture in the crankcase, a valve must be provided to close the carburetor to crankcase port.

Three different types of valves are used. In Fig. 1-1, a reed type inlet valve is shown in the schematic diagram of the two-stroke cycle engine. Reeds (R) are forced open by atmospheric pressure as shown in view "B" when the piston is on its upward stroke and pressure in the crankcase is below atmospheric. When the piston reaches TDC, the reeds close as shown in view "A" and fuel:air mixture is trapped in the crankcase to be compressed by downward movement of the piston. In Fig. 1-2, a schematic diagram of a two-stroke cycle engine is shown in which the piston is utilized as a sliding carburetor—crankcase port (third port) valve. In Fig. 1-3, a schematic diagram of a two-stroke cycle engine is shown in which a slotted disc (rotary valve) attached to the engine crankshaft opens the carburetor-crankcase port when the piston is on its upward stroke. In each of the three basic designs shown, a transfer port (TP—Fig. 1-2) connects the crankcase compression chamber to the cylinder; the transfer port is the cylinder intake port through which the compressed fuel:air mixture in the crankcase is transferred to the cylinder when the piston is at bottom of stroke as shown in view "A."

Due to rapid movement of the fuel:air mixture through the crankcase, the crankcase cannot be used as a lubricating oil sump because the oil would be carried into the cylinder. Lubrication is accomplished by mixing a small amount of oil with the fuel or by a separate oil metering system. In either case, the engine lubricating oil is carried through the crankcase and eventually is forced into the combustion chamber where it is burned. Where an oil metering system is used, ratio of oil to fuel by volume is varied by throttle opening and engine speed. When oil is pre-mixed with the fuel, manufacturer's recommended fuel:oil ratio should be strictly observed.

FOUR-STROKE CYCLE. In a four-stroke cycle engine operating on the Otto Cycle (spark ignition), the five events of the cycle take place in four strokes of the piston, or in two revolutions of the engine crankshaft. Thus, a power stroke occurs only on alternate downward strokes of the piston.

In view "A" of Fig. 1-4, the piston is on the first downward stroke of the cycle. The mechanically operated intake valve has opened the intake port and, as the downward movement of the piston has reduced the air pressure in the cyclinder to below atmospheric pressure, air is forced through the carburetor, where fuel is mixed with the air, and into the cylinder through the open intake port. The intake valve remains open and the fuel:air mixture continues to flow into the cylinder until the piston reaches the bottom of its downward stroke. As the piston starts on its first upward stroke, the mechanically operated intake valve closes and, since the exhaust valve is closed, the fuel:air mixture is compressed as in view "B."

Just before the piston reaches the top of its first upward stroke, a spark at the spark plug electrodes ignites the compressed fuel:air mixture. As the engine crankshaft turns past top center, the burning fuel:air mixture expands rapidly and forces the piston downward on its power stroke as shown in view "C." As the piston reaches the bottom of the power stroke, the mechanically operated exhaust valve starts to open and as the pressure of the burned fuel:air mixture is higher than atmospheric pressure, it starts to flow out the open exhaust port. As the engine crankshaft turns past bottom center, the exhaust valve is almost completely open and remains open during the upward stroke of the piston as shown in view "D." Upward movement of the piston pushes the remaining burned fuel:air

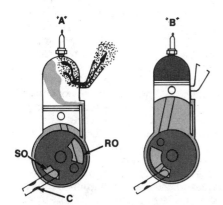

Fig. 1-2—Schematic diagram of two-stroke cycle engine operating on Otto Cycle. Engine differs from that shown in Fig. 1-1 in that piston is utilized as a sliding valve to open and close intake (carburetor to crankcase) port (IP) instead of using reed valve (R—Fig. 1-1).

C. Carburetor
EX. Exhaust port
IP. Intake port (carburetor to crankcase)
TP. Transfer port (crankcase to cylinder)

Fig. 1-3—Schematic diagram of two-stroke cycle engine similar to those shown in Figs. 1-1 and 1-2 except that a rotary carburetor to crankcase port valve is used. Disc driven by crankshaft has rotating opening (RO) which uncovers stationary opening (SO) in crankcase when piston is on upward stroke. Carburetor is (C).

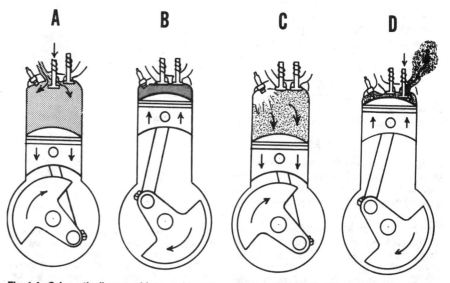

Fig. 1-4—Schematic diagram of four-stroke cycle engine operating on the Otto (spark ignition) cycle. In view "A," piston is on first downward (intake) stroke and atmospheric pressure is forcing fuel:air mixture from carburetor into cylinder through the open intake valve. In view "B," both valves are closed and piston is on its first upward stroke compressing the fuel:air mixture in cylinder. In view "C," spark across electrodes of spark plug has ignited fuel:air mixture and heat of combustion rapidly expands the burning gaseous mixture forcing the piston on its second downward (expansion or power) stroke. In view "D," exhaust valve is open and piston is on its second upward (exhaust) stroke forces the burned mixture from cylinder. A new cycle then starts as in view "A."

mixture out of the exhaust port. Just before the piston reaches the top of its second upward or exhaust stroke, the intake valve opens and the exhaust valve closes. The cycle is completed as the crankshaft turns past top center and a new cycle begins as the piston starts downward as shown in view "A."

In a four-stroke cycle engine operating on the Diesel Cycle, the sequence of events of the cycle is similar to that described for operation on the Otto Cycle, but with the following exceptions: On the intake stroke, air only is taken into the cylinder. On the compression stroke, the air is highly compressed which raises the temperature of the air. Just before the piston reaches top dead center, fuel is injected into the cylinder and is ignited by the heated, compressed air. The remainder of the cycle is similar to that of the Otto Cycle.

CARBURETORS

The function of the carburetor is to atomize the fuel and mix it with the air flowing into the engine. The carburetor must also meter the fuel to provide the proper fuel:air ratio for the different engine operating conditions, and the proper density of total charge to satisfy the power and speed requirements.

A gasoline:air mixture is normally combustible between the limits of 25 parts air to 1 part fuel, and 8 parts air to 1 part fuel. Because much of the fuel will not vaporize when the engine is cold, a rich mixture is required for cold starting. The exact ratio will depend on the temperature and the volatility (ability to vaporize) of the fuel.

Carburetor design is based on the venturi principle which simply means that a gas or liquid flowing through a necked-down section (venturi) in a passage undergoes an increase in velocity (speed) and a decrease in pressure as compared to the velocity and pressure in full size sections of the passage. The principle is illustrated in Fig. 1-6, which shows air passing through a carburetor venturi. The figures given for air speeds and vacuum are approximate for a typical wide-open throttle operating condition. Due to low pressure (high vacuum) in the venturi, fuel is forced out through the fuel nozzle by the at-

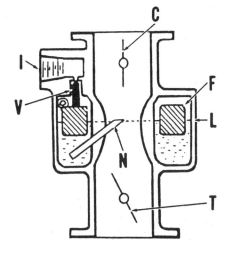

Fig. 1-7—Drawing showing basic float type carburetor design. Fuel must be delivered under pressure either by gravity or by use of fuel pump, to the carburetor fuel inlet (I). Fuel level (L) operates float (F) to open and close inlet valve (V) to control amount of fuel entering carburetor. Also shown are the fuel nozzle (N), throttle (T) and choke (C).

mospheric pressure (0 vacuum) on the fuel; as fuel is emitted from the nozzle, it is atomized by the high velocity air flow and mixes with the air.

Although some carburetors may be very basic, the varying requirements of personal water vehicle engines make it necessary to incorporate features to provide variable fuel:air ratios for different operating conditions. These design features will be described in the following paragraphs which outline the different carburetor types.

FLOAT TYPE CARBURETOR. The principle of float type carburetor operation is illustrated in Fig. 1-7. Fuel is delivered at inlet (I) by a fuel lift pump. Fuel flows into the open inlet valve (V) until fuel level (L) in bowl lifts float against fuel valve needle and closes the valve. As fuel is emitted from the nozzle (N) when engine is running, fuel level will drop, lowering the float and allowing valve to open so fuel will enter the carburetor to meet the requirements of the engine.

In Fig. 1-8, a cut-away view of a float type carburetor is shown. Atmospheric pressure is maintained in fuel bowl through passage (20) which opens into carburetor air horn ahead of the choke plate (21). Fuel level is maintained at just below level or opening (O) in nozzle (22) by float (19) actuating inlet valve needle (8). Float height can be adjusted by bending float tang (5).

When engine is running at slow idle speed (throttle plate nearly closed as indicated by dotted lines in Fig. 1-8), air pressure above throttle plate is low and atmospheric pressure in fuel bowl forces fuel up through the nozzle and out

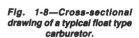

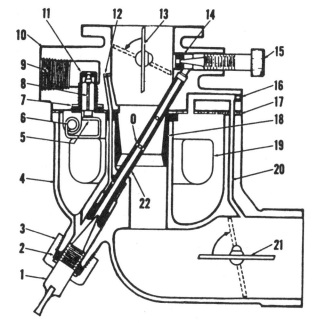

Fig. 1-8—Cross-sectional drawing of a typical float type carburetor.

0. Orifice
1. Main fuel needle
2. Packing
3. Packing nut
4. Carburetor bowl
5. Float tang
6. Float hinge pin
7. Gasket
8. Inlet valve
9. Fuel inlet
10. Carburetor body
11. Inlet valve seat
12. Vent
13. Throttle plate
14. Idle orifice
15. Idle fuel needle
16. Plug
17. Gasket
18. Venturi
19. Float
20. Fuel bowl vent
21. Choke
22. Fuel nozzle

Fig. 1-6—Drawing illustrating the venturi principle upon which carburetor design is based. Figures at left are inches of mercury vacuum and those at right are air speeds in feet per second that are typical of conditions found in a carburetor operating at wide open throttle. Zero vacuum in fuel nozzle corresponds to atmospheric pressure.

through orifice in seat (14) where it mixes with air passing the throttle plate. The idle fuel mixture is adjustable by turning needle (15) in or out as required. Idle speed is adjustable by turning the throttle stop screw (not shown) in or out to control amount of air passing the throttle plate.

When throttle plate is opened to increase engine speed, velocity of air flow through venturi (18) increases, air pressure at venturi decreases and fuel will flow from openings (O) in nozzle instead of through orifice in idle seat (14). When engine is running at high speed, pressure in nozzle (22) is less than at vent (12) opening in carburetor throat above venturi. Thus, air will enter vent and travel down the vent into the nozzle and mix with the fuel in the nozzle. This is referred to as air bleeding and is illustrated in Fig. 1-9.

DIAPHRAGM TYPE CARBURETOR.
Refer to Fig. 1-10 for cross-sectional drawing showing basic design of a diaphragm type carburetor. Fuel is delivered to inlet (I) under pressure from a fuel pump. Atmospheric pressure is maintained on lower side of diaphragm (D) through vent hole (V). When choke plate (C) is closed and engine is cranked, or when engine is running, pressure at orifice (O) is less than atmospheric pressure, this low pressure, or vacuum, is transmitted to fuel chamber (F) above diaphragm through nozzle channel (N). The higher (atmospheric) pressure at lower side of diaphragm will then push the diaphragm upward compressing spring (S) and allowing inlet valve (IV) to open and fuel will flow into the fuel chamber.

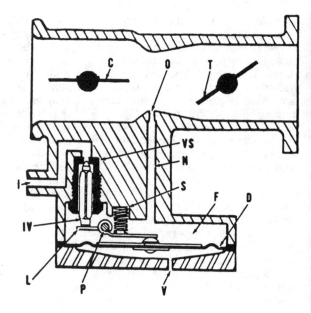

Fig. 1-10—Cross-section drawing of basic design diaphragm type carburetor. Atmospheric pressure actuates diaphragm (D).

C. Choke
D. Diaphragm
F. Fuel chamber
I. Fuel inlet
IV. Inlet valve needle
L. Lever
N. Nozzle
O. Orifice
P. Pivot pin
S. Spring
T. Throttle
V. Vent
VS. Valve seat

Some diaphragm type carburetors are equipped with an integral fuel pump. Although design of the pump may vary as to type of check valves, etc., all operate on the principle shown in Fig. 1-11. A channel (C) (or pulsation passage) connects one side of the diaphragm to the engine crankcase. When engine piston is on upward stroke, vacuum (V) (lower than atmospheric pressure) is present in channel; thus atmospheric pressure on fuel forces inlet valve (B) open and fuel flows into chamber below the diaphragm as shown in middle view. When piston is on downward stroke, pressure (P) (higher than atmospheric pressure) is present in channel (C); thus, the pressure forces the diaphragm downward closing the inlet valve (B) and causes the fuel to flow

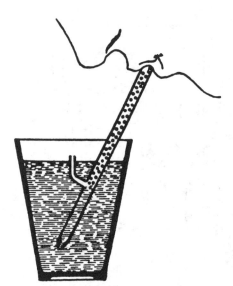

Fig. 1-9—Illustration of air bleed principle explained in text.

Fig. 1-11—Operating principle of diaphragm type fuel pump is illustrated in above drawings. Pump valves (A & B) are usually a part of diaphragm (D). Pump inlet is (I) and outlet is (O). Chamber above diaphragm is connected to engine crankcase by passage (C). When piston is on upward stroke, vacuum (V) at crankcase passage allows atmospheric pressure to force fuel into pump fuel chamber as shown in middle drawing. When piston is on downward stroke, pressure (P) expands diaphragm downward forcing fuel out of pump as shown in lower drawing.

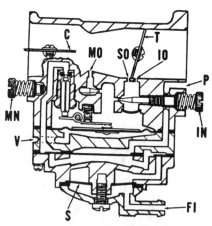

Fig. 1-12—Cross-sectional view of a popular make diaphragm type carburetor with integral fuel pump. Refer to Fig. 1-10 for view of basic diaphragm carburetor and to Fig. 1-11 for views showing operation of the fuel pump.

C. Choke
FI. Fuel inlet
IN. Idle fuel adjusting needle
IO. Idle orifice
MN. Main fuel adjusting needle
MO. Main orifice
P. Pulsation channel (fuel pump)
S. Screen
SO. Secondary orifice
T. Throttle
V. Vent (atmospheric to carburetor diaphragm)

out by the outlet valve (A) as shown in lower view.

In Fig. 1-12, a cross-sectional view of a popular make diaphragm type carburetor, with integral diaphragm type pump, is shown.

VARIABLE VENTURI (SLIDE) CARBURETOR. A typical slide type carburetor is shown schematically in Fig. 1-13. The throttle slide (TS) serves the double purpose of engine speed control and variable venturi. When the slide is completely open, the small step in the throttle bore serves as a large diameter venturi for high speed. As the slide is lowered, the venturi size is decreased as shown in Fig. 1-14. Decreasing the venturi size slows the speed by decreasing the amount of fuel and air mixture that can be drawn into the engine and also

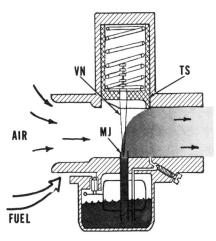

Fig. 1-13—View of variable venturi, slide type throttle valve. Throttle slide (TS) is in the fully raised high speed position. Valve needle (VN) is raised allowing main jet (MJ) to be completely open.

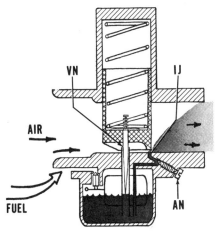

Fig. 1-14—With throttle slide lowered to idle speed position, only a small amount of air is allowed to pass. The valve needle (VN) is lowered, closing the main jet and fuel is drawn from the idle jet (IJ). Idle mixture adjustment needle (AN) controls fuel:air ratio.

increases the vacuum at the venturi fuel nozzle. A valve needle attached to the throttle slide is incorporated to lower the amount of fuel drawn in by the high vacuum created by the small venturi. An idle jet is sometimes installed as shown in Fig. 1-14 to provide an additional mixture adjustment for low speed settings. Idle speed is controlled by stopping the throttle slide before it completely closes the throttle bore. If the valve needle is raised in the throttle slide, it will increase the fuel flow from the main nozzle at intermediate throttle settings. If a larger carburetor of this same type is installed, it is possible that low speed (part throttle) operation will function normally, but at full throttle the venturi will be too large to provide the correct fuel:air mixture.

Some carburetors utilize a vacuum controlled, variable venturi as shown in Fig. 1-15. These models use a disc type throttle plate which controls the amount of fuel:air mixture available to the engine. When the engine is running at slow speed (throttle nearly closed) the venturi piston is lowered as shown in Fig. 1-15. As the throttle disc is opened (Figs. 1-16 and 1-17) the vacuum at the venturi is transferred into chamber (V) via port (P) and atmospheric pressure is admitted under venturi piston via port (A). The high pressure below the venturi and low pressure above causes the piston to raise as shown in Figs. 1-16 and 1-17. As with the slide type variable venturi, a valve needle is attached to the venturi to limit the amount of fuel drawn from the main nozzle at low speed. An idle mixture jet (IJ-Fig. 1-15) and intermediate jet (IM—Fig. 1-16) are provided to correct the fuel to air ratio throughout the entire speed range. It is extremely important that the venturi

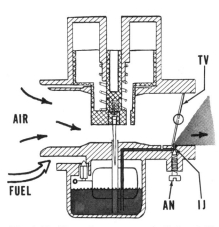

Fig. 1-15—View of vacuum controlled variable venturi type carburetor with throttle valve (TV) nearly closed. Idle mixture adjustment needle (AN) is shown. Fuel is discharged from idle jet (IJ).

piston is free to move easily in its bore and that it fits tightly enough to seal the different pressures. Idle speed is controlled by stopping the throttle disc before it closes the throttle bore.

STARTING ENRICHMENT

The ratio of fuel to air must be much richer when starting in cold weather than when running at full open throttle. Two methods of obtaining a rich starting mixture are commonly used.

CHOKE PLATE. Fig. 1-18 shows a typical choke plate installation in relation to the carburetor venturi.

At cranking speeds, air flows through the carburetor venturi at a slow speed; thus, the pressure in the venturi does not usually decrease to the extent that atmospheric pressure on the fuel will force enough fuel from the nozzle. If the

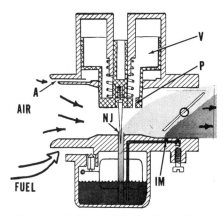

Fig. 1-16—At intermediate throttle setting, atmospheric air pressure is allowed to enter port (A) under the venturi piston and venturi vacuum is transferred to top of piston (V) via port (P). The vacuum above the piston and atmospheric pressure below, causes the venturi piston to raise. Fuel is discharged at partially open needle jet (NJ) and intermediate jet (IM).

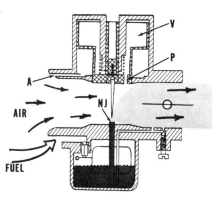

Fig. 1-17—As engine speed and throttle opening are increased, vacuum at venturi port (P) and above venturi piston (V) increases until venturi is completely open. Needle jet (NJ) is completely open.

choke plate is closed as shown by the broken line, air cannot enter into the carburetor and pressure in the carburetor decreases greatly as the engine is turned at cranking speed. Fuel is then forced from the fuel nozzle. In manufacturing the carburetor choke plate or disc, a small hole or notch is cut in the plate so that some air can flow through the plate when it is in closed position to provide air for the starting fuel:air mixture. In some instances after starting a cold engine, it is advantageous to leave the choke plate in a partly closed position as the restriction of air flow will decrease the air pressure in carburetor venturi, thus causing more fuel to flow from the nozzle resulting in a richer fuel:air mixture. The choke plate or disc should be in fully open position for normal engine operation.

STARTING VALVE. Fig. 1-19 shows a simplified starting system typical of the type found in many carburetors. A combination of two principles is utilized to enrich the fuel:air mixture. First, the passage is normally less restricted (larger) than the normal idle passage and second, the starting port is located between the throttle slide and engine. With the starting port (P) located as shown, closing the throttle slide in-

creases the vacuum at the starting port in much the same way as the choke plate previously described. It is obvious that this rich mixture should not normally be used, so a shut-off valve is incorporated in the system. The starter jet shut-off valve (SV) is sometimes actuated by a control on the carburetor; however, is often remote controlled by a lever via a control cable.

REED VALVES

The inlet reed (or leaf) valve is essentially a check valve which permits the fuel:air mixture to move in only one direction through the engine. It traps the fuel charge in the crankcase, permitting the inlet pressure to be raised high enough to allow a full charge to enter the cylinder against the remaining exhaust pressure during the short period of time the transfer ports are open. The ideal design for the valve is one which offers the least possible resistance to the flow of gases entering the crankcase, but completely seals off any flow back through the carburetor during the downward stroke of the piston.

IGNITION SYSTEM

In a magneto ignition system, the force contained in a permanent magnet is converted to electrical energy. A brief description of the operating principle is as follows.

When an electrical current passes through a conductor a magnetic field builds up around the wire.

When a magnetic field cuts across the path of a conductor an electric current is induced into the conductor.

When the conductor is straight or the magnetic field constant, nothing much happens, but experimenters have found

that if the wire (conductor) is coiled, the minute current can be multiplied until its effect is significant.

The effect of the magnetic lines of force can be utilized by moving the conductor through the magnetic field, moving the field across the conductor or causing the field to collapse by interrupting the production of electrically induced magnetism.

Fig. 1-21 shows a typical magneto flywheel with magnets in place. North-South magnets are alternately placed around the flywheel rim. The lines of force are dispersed as they flow through the air but are concentrated in flywheel rim as they complete the field.

When the laminated magneto armature containing the coils is placed inside the flywheel, the magnetic field is concentrated in the armature as shown in Fig. 1-22. As the flywheel turns and the magnets change position with relation to the coil (Fig. 1-23), the lines of force change direction as they pass through the coil as shown, resulting in the buildup of a pulsating alternating

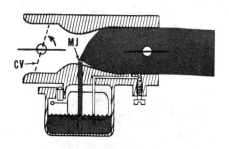

Fig. 1-18—As choke valve (CV) is closed as shown by the broken lines, vacuum is increased at main jet (MJ).

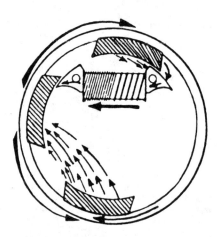

Fig. 1-22—As flywheel turns, magnetic field is concentrated in ignition coil pole shoe flowing from right to left leg.

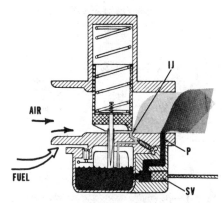

Fig. 1-19—View of simplified starting valve enrichment method. With starting valve (SV) open, the normal idle mixture supplied by idle jet (IJ) is further enriched by starting port (P).

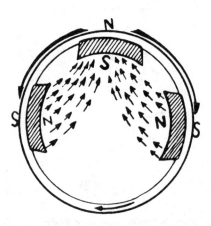

Fig. 1-21—A magnetic field is concentrated when passing through iron and dispersed when passing through air as indicated by arrows.

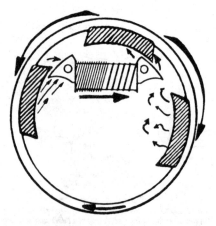

Fig. 1-23—As flywheel continues to turn, magnetic field in pole shoe is reversed causing a current to flow in ignition primary wire.

current in the ignition primary winding as shown in Fig. 1-24. This electrical current generates its own magnetic field which surrounds the many fine windings of the ignition coil secondary circuit. In order to generate the high-voltage secondary current which forms the spark, the breaker points open, interrupting the primary current at a predetermined time. Point opening (or timing) must occur when the engine piston is in the proper position for best performance. Point opening must also be timed to occur when the alternating primary voltage is at its peak or the secondary voltage will be weak and spark plug may not fire. It is impossible or impractical in the average shop to measure the alternating primary current relative to flywheel position, so the proper timing for peak voltage is determined by design engineers and becomes a service specification variously referred to as **Edge Gap, Break Away Gap** or **Pole Shoe Break.** Fig. 1-25 shows a typical method of measurement between leading edge of pole shoe laminations and trailing edge of magnets.

The conventional flywheel magneto encloses the primary and secondary ignition windings in a single package as shown in Fig. 1-26. A second system known as **Energy Transfer** uses a remote ignition coil similar to that used in a battery ignition system, and the coil next to the magnets is used simply as a generating coil. A typical energy transfer system is illustrated schematically in Fig. 1-27.

In most of the units used on personal water vehicles, a second generating coil is added to provide electrical power for lights or other accessories, or to charge a battery. The generating system has been omitted from this discussion for clarity but is covered separately in a later section.

Another type of ignition system being used is known as a **Capacitor Discharge** System. This system differs radically from conventional units in that a relatively high voltage current is fed into a capacitor which discharges through a pulse transformer (ignition coil) to generate the ignition spark. The secondary current is generated by the rapid build-up rather than by collapse of the primary current. The result is a high-energy ignition spark ideally suited to high-speed, two-stroke engine operation.

One development which made the new systems possible was the introduction of semi-conductors suitable for ignition system control. While solid state technology and the capacitor discharge system are not interdependent they are uniquely compatible and each has features which are desirable from the standpoint of reliability and performance.

A flywheel magneto is most generally used as the primary current source in engines of the size and type found on personal water vehicles, because of the relatively high voltage obtainable and compact, light-weight parts available. If battery current is used as the power source, it must be amplified or converted to obtain the necessary voltage.

The introduction of the new ignition systems is bringing unfamiliar words into use which might be defined in the following non-technical terms:

CAPACITOR. A Condenser; temporary storage point for the high-energy electrical force which generates the spark.

DIODE. A device which will allow electrical current to flow in one direction but will block a reverse flow.

GATE CONTROLLED SWITCH. A semi-conductor which will pass the flow of electrical current in one direction only when a second, small "TRIGGER CURRENT" opens the "GATE." Current will not flow in the reverse direction at any time. Properly called "GATE CONTROLLED SILICON RECTIFIER." Sometimes called "SCR."

PULSE TRANSFORMER. Similar in purpose, and sometimes in appearance, to the ignition coil of a conventional ignition system. Contains the primary and secondary ignition coils and converts the primary pulse current into the secondary ignition current which fires the plug. Cannot generally be interchanged with regular ignition coil.

RECTIFIER. Any device which allows the flow of current in one direction only, or converts Alternating Current to Direct Current. Diodes are sometimes used in combination to form a BRIDGE RECTIFIER.

SCR. See GATE CONTROLLED SWITCH.

SEMI-CONDUCTOR. Any of several materials which permit partial or controlled flow of electrical current. Used in the manufacture of Diodes, Rectifiers, SCR's, Thermistors, Thyristors, etc.

SILICON SWITCH. See GATE CONTROLLED SILICON SWITCH.

SOLID STATE. That branch of electronic technology which deals with the use of semi-conductors as control devices. See SEMI-CONDUCTOR.

Fig. 1-24—As flywheel rotates, an alternating current is generated in ignition primary wire.

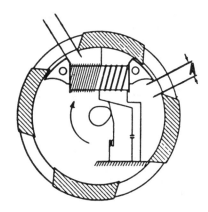

Fig. 1-25—The distance (A) between trailing edge of magnet and leading edge of pole shoe when primary voltage is highest is known as EDGE GAP.

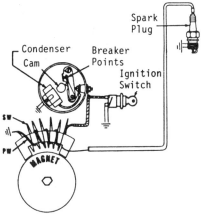

Fig. 1-26—Schematic view of typical magneto ignition system. Coil primary winding is shown at (PW) and secondary winding at (SW). Ignition switch grounds the primary winding to stop the engine.

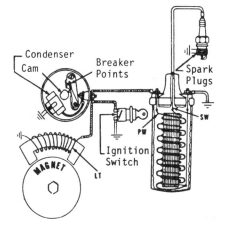

Fig. 1-27—Schematic view of energy transfer type magneto. Low tension generator coil is shown at (LT). When breaker points are closed, current completes circuit through the points. When breaker points open, current rushes into high-tension coil primary winding (PW) and induces voltage in secondary (SW). Ignition switch grounds the low tension circuit to stop engine.

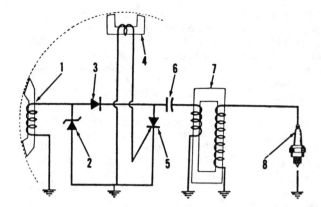

Fig. 1-28—Schematic diagram of a typical Capacitor Discharge "Solid State" ignition system.
1. Generating coil
2. Zener diode
3. Diode
4. Trigger coil
5. Gate Controlled Switch (SCR)
6. Capacitor
7. Pulse transformer (coil)
8. Spark Plug

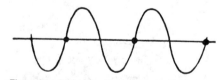

Fig. 1-32—Drawing showing the simplicity of typical modern rectifier construction. Type shown is selenium.

THERMISTOR. A solid state regulating device which decreases in resistance as its temperature rises. Used for "Temperature Compensating" a control circuit.

THYRISTOR. A "Safety Valve" placed in the circuit which will not pass the regular current in either direction but is used to provide surge protection for the other elements.

TRIGGER. The timed, small current which controls, or opens, the "Gate", thus initiating the spark.

ZENER DIODE. A Zener Diode will permit free flow of current in one direction, and will also permit current to flow in the opposite direction when the voltage reaches a pre-determined level.

Fig. 1-28 shows a circuit diagram of a typical single cylinder, capacitor discharge, breakerless ignition system using permanent flywheel magnets as the energy source. The magnets pass by the input generating coil (1) to charge the capacitor (6), then by the trigger coil (4) to open the gate and permit the discharge pulse to enter the pulse transformer (7) and generate the spark which fires the plug. Only half of the generated current passes through diode (3) to charge the capacitor. Reverse current is blocked by diode (3) but passes through diode (2) to complete the reverse circuit. Diode (2) may be a Zener Diode to limit the maximum voltage of the forward current. When the flywheel magnet passes by the trigger coil (4) a small electrical current is generated which opens the gate of the SCR (5) allowing the capacitor to discharge through the pulse transformer (7). The rapid voltage rise in the transformer primary coil induces a high-voltage secondary current which forms the ignition spark when it jumps the spark plug gap.

CHARGING SYSTEM

FLYWHEEL ALTERNATORS. Alternating current is readily available on engines using a flywheel magneto or energy transfer ignition system by installing an additional armature core (battery charge coil) in a position similar to the ignition coil. The principle of this type of system is similar to the flywheel magneto, however only one winding is necessary. The voltage and amperage can be limited by the resistance (length, diameter, etc.) of the wire used in the battery charge coil windings and the alternating current (AC) generated is satisfactory for lighting requirements. However, if a battery is used, the generated Alternating current must be changed to Direct Current (DC) usually via a rectifier.

RECTIFIER. Repair of rectifier is limited to renewal of the unit, however certain precautions and inspections may be more easily accomplished after a brief description of its operation.

Direct current (DC), like the type available from a battery, has an established negative terminal and a positive terminal. Alternating current such as generated by a magneto or alternator changes polarity as the magnetic field of force is broken by the armature core (lighting coil). This simply means that one end of the coil wire is first negative than as the flywheel (magnets) move on, the current reverses direction and the same end becomes positive. If the AC current were connected to a battery (DC), the current would first flow into the battery, then as the AC changed polarity (direction) it would withdraw the same amount.

Electricity in a wire is similar to liquid in a pipe. In a pipe, a check valve can be installed to allow a liquid to flow only in one direction as shown in Fig. 1-30. A rectifier is a similar valve for an elec-

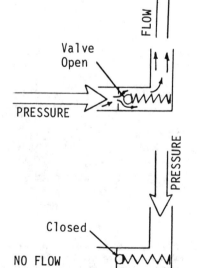

Fig. 1-30—A check valve can be installed in a pipe to allow a liquid to flow only in one direction. A rectifier serves a similar function in an electrical system.

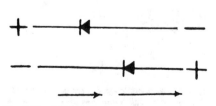

Fig. 1-31—A rectifier serves a similar function to the check valve in Fig. 1-30 allowing current to pass only in one direction.

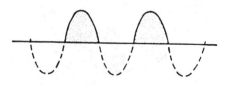

Fig. 1-33—Elaborate testing equipment shows alternating current as a wave. The curved "S" line between the dots is called a cycle.

Fig. 1-34—Alternating current shown by dotted lines is unused when using only one rectifier.

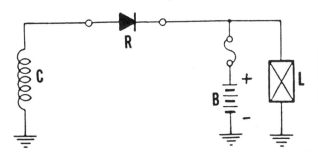

Fig. 1-35—Drawing of a simple electrical system which has only one rectifier. Alternator generator coils are shown at (C). Battery at (B), Rectifier at (R) and Load is at (L).

trical system Fig. 1-31. The simplicity of modern rectifier construction is shown in Fig. 1-32. The changing of AC polarity can be shown on elaborate testing equipment similar to drawing Fig. 1-33. Where the curved line crosses the center line is the exact time that the current reverses polarity. Installation of a rectifier stops current flow in one direction so the current flow can be pictured as shown by the solid line in Fig. 1-34. Half of the current generated (shown by the broken lines) is lost. A typical, simple, complete system is shown in Fig. 1-35.

In order to use the current which is normally lost in the previously described simple system, a combination of rectifiers can be used. Normally they are constructed as one rectifying unit. Fig. 1-36 shows a typical complete system.

Rectifiers must be installed to allow current flow from the alternator into the battery. If the rectifier terminals are reversed, current from the battery will be fed into the battery charge coil and coil and/or rectifier will be damaged by the resulting short circuit. The rectifier may be damaged if the system is operated without the battery connected or if battery terminals are reversed. Direction of current flow through the rectifier can be easily checked with a battery, light and wire (or ohmmeter) as shown in Fig. 1-37.

If the rectifier will not pass current in either direction using the simple test shown in Fig. 1-37, or if light continues to burn with connections reversed, rectifier may be considered faulty. Paint should not be scraped from rectifier plates and plates should not be discolored (from heat) or bent. The center bolt torque is pre-set and should NOT be disturbed.

RECTIFIER/REGULATOR. Some charging systems are equipped with a

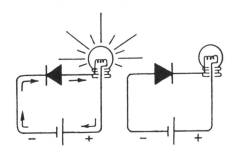

Fig. 1-37—A simple test can be made as shown on a rectifier to show which direction current can flow. Wires should be connected to rectifier so current is allowed to pass as shown by arrows in wiring diagrams.

rectifier/regulator assembly. The rectifier assembly changes AC current to DC current as previously outlined under RECTIFIER and the regulator assembly prevents overcharging of the battery.

SPARK PLUG

In any spark ignition engine, the spark plug provides the means for igniting the compressed fuel:air mixture in the cylinder. Before an electric charge can move across an air gap, the intervening air must be charged with electricity, or ionized. The spark plug gap becomes more easily ionized if the spark plug ground is of negative polarity. If the spark plug is properly gapped and the system is not shorted, not more than 7,000 volts may be required to initiate a spark. Higher voltage is required as the spark plug warms up, or if compression pressures or the distance of the air gap is increased. Compression pressures are highest at full throttle and relatively slow engine speeds, therefore, high voltage requirements or a lack of available secondary voltage most often shows up as a miss during maximum acceleration from a slow engine speed. There are many different types and sizes of spark plugs which are designed for a number of specific requirements.

THREAD SIZE. The threaded, shell portion of the spark plug and the attaching holes in the cylinder are manufactured to meet certain industry established standards. The diameter is referred to as "Thread Size." Those commonly used are: 10 mm, 14 mm, 18 mm, 7/8 inch and ½ inch pipe.

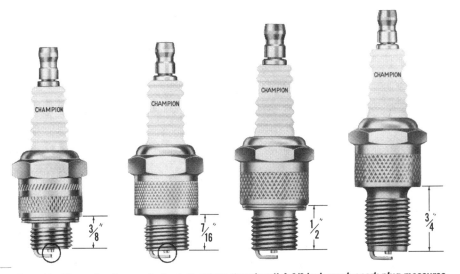

Fig. 1-36—Wiring diagram of full wave rectifier system. The four diodes shown are usually constructed as one unit.

Fig. 1-39—Views showing spark plugs of various "reaches." A 3/8 inch reach spark plug measures 3/8 inch from firing end of shell to gasket surface of shell. The two plugs at left side illustrate the difference in plugs normally used in two-stroke cycle and four-stroke cycle engines; refer to the circle electrodes. Spark plug at left has a shortened ground electrode. The short ground electrode will operate cooler than longer ground electrode.

REACH. The length of thread, and the thread depth in cylinder head or wall are also standardized throughout the industry. This dimension is measured from gasket seat of plug to cylinder end of thread.

HEAT RANGE. During engine operation, part of the heat generated during combustion is transferred to the spark plug, and from the plug to the cooling medium through the shell threads and gasket. The operating temperature of the spark plug plays an important part in engine operation. If too much heat is retained by the plug, the fuel:air mixture may be ignited by contact with the heated surface before the ignition spark occurs. If not enough heat is retained, partially burned combustion products (soot, carbon and oil) may build up on the plug tip resulting in "fouling" or shorting out of the plug. If this happens, the secondary current is dissipated uselessly as it is generated instead of bridging the plug gap as a useful spark, and the engine will misfire.

The operating temperature of the plug tip can be controlled, within limits, by altering the length of the path the heat must follow to reach the threads and gasket of the plug. Thus, a plug with a short, stubby insulator around the center electrode will run cooler than one with a long slim insulator. Most plugs in the more popular sizes are available in a number of heat ranges which are interchangeable within the group. The proper heat range is determined by engine design and the type of service. Like most other elements of design, the plug type installed as original equipment is usually a compromise and is either the most suitable plug for average conditions; or the best plug to meet the two extremes of service expected. No one spark plug, however, can be ideally suited for long periods of slow-speed operation and still be the best possible type for high-speed operation.

COOLING SYSTEM

Much of the heat of combustion enters the working parts of the engine rather than performing useful work, and must be controlled to prevent internal engine damage. In any internal combustion engine, the commonly used term "Cooling System" is somewhat misleading; a more scientifically accurate term would be "Temperature Control System."

Energy expended as heat through the cooling medium or out the exhaust pipe is wasted energy, and amounts to more than two-thirds of the thermal (chemical) energy produced in the combustion process. It is the role of the design engineer to extract the largest part of the energy generated and convert it to useful work. If he is to do this, he must carefully CONTROL engine operating temperature which, if too high will destroy the working parts of the engine and interfere with the combustion process. If the engine is overcooled, however, a greater amount of the potential energy is expended in attempting to equalize engine and combustion temperatures.

AIR COOLED. Air cooling is the simplest and easiest to build into a lightweight two-stroke engine. The amount of cooling realized is a product of surface (fin) area, air flow and air temperature.

WATER-COOLED. Water cooling provides excellent temperature stability along with inherent ability for noise suppression.

Water is picked up through an intake and is directed to the jet pump impeller. A portion of the thrust of water produced by the jet pump impeller is directed through a cooling system opening and carried to the engine through a supply hose or routed to the engine through passages. After circulating through the engine, the water is directed to the exhaust where it is used to cool the outgoing exhaust and to silence exhaust noise.

JET PUMP

The jet pump impeller is driven by the engine via a drive shaft on some models. The rotating impeller draws water into intake area of jet pump housing. The rotating impeller accelerates the flow of water and forces the water out rear of jet pump through an outlet nozzle or a steering nozzle creating a propulsive thrust to propel the vehicle forward. Two types of jet pumps are used, an axial and a centrifugal.

On an axial type jet pump (Fig. 1-42), the impeller is mounted within a tube. Water must pass through the impeller to be expelled out the rear of the jet pump. An axial type pump is basically a high volume/low pressure water pump.

On a centrifugal type jet pump (Fig. 1-43), water is drawn into the jet pump housing where the rotating impeller slings the incoming water against the side of the impeller housing. The water is looped around the impeller housing then expelled out the rear of the jet pump. A centrifugal type jet pump is basically a low volume/high pressure water pump.

Fig. 1-42—Cross-sectional view of a typical axial jet pump assembly. Arrows indicate direction of water flow.

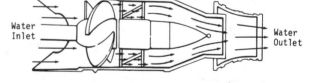

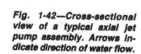

Water Inlet

Water Outlet

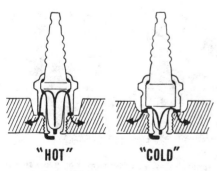

"HOT"   "COLD"

Fig. 1-40—Spark plug tip temperature is controlled by the length of the path heat must travel to reach cooling surface of the engine cylinder head.

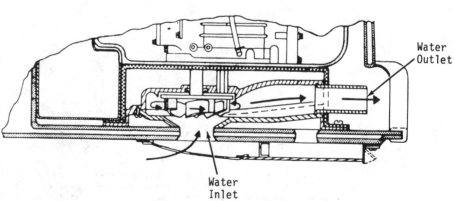

Water Outlet

Water Inlet

Fig. 1-43—Cross-sectional view of a typical centrifugal jet pump assembly. Arrows indicate direction of water flow.

SERVICE FUNDAMENTALS

TROUBLE-SHOOTING

Most performance problems such as failure to start, failure to run properly or missing out are caused by malfunction of the ignition system or fuel system. The experienced serviceman generally develops and follows a logical sequence in trouble-shooting which will most likely lead him quickly to the source of trouble. One such sequence might be as follows:

FAILS TO START

1. Remove and examine spark plugs. If fuel is reaching the cylinder in proper amount, there should be an odor of gasoline on the plugs if they are cold. Too much fuel can foul the plugs causing engine not to start. Fouled plugs are wet in appearance and easily detected. The presence of fouled plugs is not a sure indication that the trouble has been located; however, the engine might have started before fouling occurred if ignition system has been in good shape.

2. With spark plug removed, use an insulated tool and hold wire about $1/8$ to $1/4$ inch (3.17-6.35 mm) away from an unpainted part of the cylinder head or cylinder and crank the engine sharply. The resulting spark may not be visible in bright daylight but a distinct snap should be heard as the spark jumps the gap.

If carburetor and ignition were both apparently in good condition when tested in (1) and (2) above, check other elements of the engine such as crossed spark plug wires, improper timing, etc. A systematic search will usually pinpoint the cause of trouble with minimum delay or confusion.

DIAGNOSIS. If the presence of fuel was not apparent when checked as in (1) above; and the spark seemed satisfactory when checked as in (2), systematically check the fuel system for the cause of trouble. The following are some of the probable causes:
 a. No fuel in tank
 b. Fuel shut off valve closed
 c. Fuel tank vent closed or plugged
 d. Fuel pump bad
 e. Choke or starting valve incorrectly used or malfunctioning
 f. Water or dirt in the fuel
 g. Fuel line pinched or kinked
 h. Clogged fuel shut off, fuel line or filter
 i. Carburetor dirty or incorrectly adjusted
 j. Reed valves not seating or stuck shut

If ignition trouble was indicated when checked as outlined in (2) above, check the electrical system for causes of trouble. Some probable causes are as follows:
 a. Battery voltage low (Electric start models)
 b. Ignition breaker points improperly adjusted
 c. Shorted wire or stop switch
 d. Open (broken) wire
 e. Loose or corroded connections
 f. Condenser shorted
 g. Incorrect gap between primary coil and flywheel magnets (magneto and energy transfer ignition)
 h. Flywheel loose
 i. Electronic ignition component malfunction
 j. Ignition breaker points stuck open
 k. High tension coil not properly grounded (energy transfer ignition)
 l. Ignition breaker point contacts pitted, burned or dirty
(New ignition points are sometimes coated with protective oil.)

FAULTY RUNNING ENGINE

The diagnosis of trouble in a running engine depends on experience, knowledge and acute observation. A continuous miss on one cylinder of a two cylinder engine can usually be isolated by observing the items listed in the previous paragraphs FAILS TO START.

Faults such as not enough power (or speed) can usually be traced to improper tuning. Make sure that flame arrestor is clean, in good condition and the exhaust pipe and muffler is open (not clogged). Ignition timing and carburetor(s) must be correctly adjusted. The carburetor jet sizes, clip position in valve needle and idle mixture needle settings listed in the individual service sections in this manual are "normal" settings. Altitude above sea level, riders weight, driving habits etc. may require different sizes and settings than those listed. On engines with two carburetors, make certain that the throttles are syn-

chronized to open exactly the same amount. Ignition timing on two cylinder engines must be the same for each cylinder. In addition to normal engine tuning procedures, check the following: Impeller or jet pump damage. Damaged pistons, rings and/or cylinders. Loose cylinder head nuts or leaking head gasket. Leaking crankcase seals.

SPECIAL NOTES ON TROUBLE-SHOOTING

ENGINE OVERHEATS. The following lists some probable causes of engine overheating.
1. Check for dirt or debris accumulated on or between cooling fins on cylinder and head (air-cooled models).
2. Too lean fuel:air adjustment of carburetor.
3. Improper ignition timing. Check breaker point gap or magneto base plate setting.
4. Two-stroke engines being operated with an improper fuel-lubricating oil mixture may overheat due to lack of lubrication; refer to appropriate engine service section in this manual for recommended lubrication requirements.
5. Missing or bent shields or blower housing. (On models with cooling blower, never attempt to operate without all shields and blower housing in place).
6. Engines being operated under loads in excess of rated engine horsepower or at extremely high ambient (surrounding) air temperatures may overheat.
7. Cooling system malfunction on water-cooled models.
8. Fuel requirements not met.

TWO-STROKE CYCLE ENGINE EXHAUST PORTS. Two-stroke engines, and especially those being operated on an overly rich fuel:air mixture or with too much lubricating oil mixed with the fuel, will tend to build up carbon in the cylinder exhaust ports.

On two-stroke cycle engines that are hard to start, or where complaint is loss of power, it is wise to remove the exhaust components as needed to inspect the exhaust ports for carbon build up.

TWO-STROKE CYCLE ENGINES WITH REED VALVES. On two-stroke cycle engine, the incoming fuel:air mixture must be compressed in engine crankcase in order for the mixture to properly reach the engine cylinder. On engines utilizing reed type carburetor or crankcase intake valve, a bent or broken reed will not allow compression build up in the crankcase. Thus, if such an engine seems otherwise OK, remove and inspect the reed valve unit. Refer to appropriate vehicle service section for information on individual two-stroke cycle engine.

SPARK PLUG. The appearance of the spark plug will be altered by use and careful examination of the plug tip can contribute useful information. It must be remembered that contributing factors differ in two-stroke cycle and four-stroke engine operation and although the appearance of two spark plugs may be similar, the corrective measures may depend on whether the engine is of two stroke or four stroke design. The accompanying pictures (Figs. 2-1 through 2-8) are provided by Champion Spark Plug Company to illustrate typical conditions. Listed also are the probable causes and suggested corrective measures.

MAINTENANCE

SPARK PLUG

The recommended type of spark plug, heat range and electrode gap is listed in the Tune-Up table under appropriate vehicle section. Under light loads or low speed, a spark plug of the same size with a higher (hotter) heat range may be installed. If subjected to heavy loads or high speed, a colder plug may be necessary.

The spark plug electrode gap should be adjusted on most plugs by bending the ground electrode. Refer to Fig. 2-7. Some spark plugs have an electrode gap which is not adjustable.

Before a plug is cleaned with abrasive, it should be thoroughly degreased with a nonoily solvent and air-dried to prevent a build up of abrasive in recess of plug.

After plug is cleaned by abrasive, and before gap is set, the electrode surfaces between the grounded and insulated electrodes should be cleaned and returned as nearly as possible to original shape by filing with a point file. Failure to properly dress the points can result in high secondary voltage requirements, and misfire of the plugs.

Spark plugs are usually cleaned by abrasive action commonly referred to as "sand blasting." Actually, ordinary sand is not used, but a special abrasive which is nonconductive to electricity even when melted, thus the abrasive cannot short out the plug current. Extreme care should be used in cleaning the plugs after sand blasting, because any particles of abrasive left on the plug may cause damage to piston rings, piston or cylinder walls.

Fig. 2-1—Two-stroke cycle engine plug of correct heat range. Insulators light tan to gray with few deposits. Electrodes not burned.

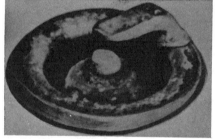

Fig. 2-3—Electrodes badly eroded, deposits white or light gray and gritty, insulator has "blistered" appearance. Could be caused by lean carburetor mixture, fast timing, overloading, or improperly operating cooling system. Could also be caused by incorrect heat range (too hot) for operating conditions. Check timing, carburetor adjustment and cooling system. If timing, carburetor adjustment, cooling system and engine speed are correct, install a colder plug.

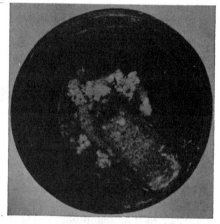

Fig. 2-5—Core bridging from center electrode to shell. Fused deposits sometimes have the appearance of tiny beads or glasslike bubbles. Caused by excessive combustion chamber deposits which in turn could be the result of; excessive carbon from prolonged usage; use of improper oil or incorrect fuel:oil ratio; high speed operation immediately following prolonged trolling.

Fig. 2-2—Damp or wet black carbon coating over entire firing end of plug. Could be caused by prolonged trolling, rich carburetor mixture, too much oil in fuel, crankcase bleed passage plugged, or low ignition voltage. Could also be caused by incorrect heat range (too cold) for operating conditions. Correct the defects or install a hotter plug.

Fig. 2-4—Gray, metallic aluminum deposits on plug. This condition is caused by internal engine damage. Engine should be overhauled and cause of damage corrected.

Fig. 2-6—Gap bridging. Usually results from the same causes outlined in Fig. 2-5.

CARBURETOR

The bulk of carburetor service consists of cleaning, inspection and adjustment. After considerable service it may become necessary to overhaul the car-

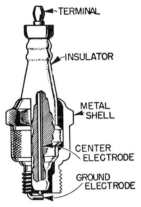

Fig. 2-7—Cross-sectional view of spark plug showing typical construction and nomenclature. Recommended gap between center electrode and ground electrode is listed in appropriate section for each vehicle.

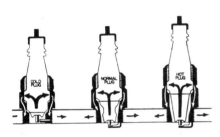

Fig. 2-8—A principle characteristic of "COLD" plug is that it has a shorter path for heat to travel from the insulator tip to the metal shell than the "HOT" plug shown at the right.

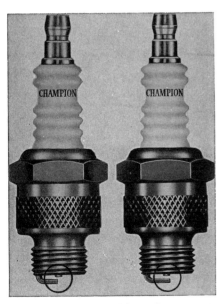

Fig. 2-9—The two-stroke spark plug is shown on left. Note the shorter ground electrode.

buretor and renew worn parts to restore original operating efficiency. Although carburetor condition affects engine operating economy and power, ignition and engine compression must also be considered to determine and correct causes of poor performance.

Before dismantling carburetor for cleaning or overhaul, clean all external surfaces and remove accumulated dirt and grease. If fuel starvation is suspected, all filters in fuel delivery system should be inspected. Under no circumstances should any filters be left off. Filter plugging is most often caused by inadequate fuel handling methods; if filters are removed the plugging will most likely occur in the carburetor, the need for cleaning will be more frequent and the work more difficult. Refer to appropriate vehicle service section for specific carburetor information. Dismantle carburetor and note any discrepancies to assure correction during overhaul. Thoroughly clean all

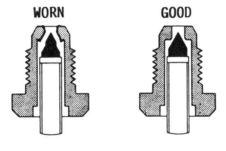

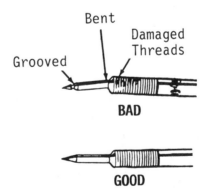

Fig. 2-11—Mixture adjustment needles should be renewed if damaged as shown at top. Never attempt to straighten a bent needle.

parts and inspect for damage or wear. Wash jets and passages and blow clear with clean, dry compressed air. Do not use a drill or wire to clean jets as the possible enlargement of calibrated holes will disturb operating balance.

Low speed and high speed mixture adjustment needles (Fig. 2-11) must not be bent, worn or grooved.

IGNITION AND CHARGING SYSTEMS

The fundamentals of the ignition and charging systems are outlined under DESIGN FUNDAMENTALS section. Refer to the appropriate vehicle section for specific service information.

LUBRICATION

MIXING GASOLINE AND OIL. Most two-stroke engines are lubricated by oil mixed with the gasoline. The manufacturers carefully determine which type of oil and how much oil should be mixed with the gasoline to provide the most desirable operation, then list these mixing instructions. Often two or more gasoline to oil ratios will be listed depending upon type of oil or severity of service. You should always follow the manufacturer's recommended mixing instructions, because mixing the wrong amount of oil or using the wrong type of oil can cause extensive engine damage. Too much oil can cause lower power, spark plug fouling and excessive carbon buildup. Not enough oil will cause inadequate lubrication and will probably result in scuffing, seizure or other forms of engine damage. Only use gasoline type and octane rating recommended by manufacturer. Never use gasoline which has been stored for a long period of time.

Accurate measurement of gasoline and oil is necessary to assure correct lubrication. Proper quantities of gasoline and oil for some of the more common mixture ratios are shown in Fig. 2-12.

When mixing, use a separate approved safety container which is large enough to hold the desired amount of fuel with additional space for mixing. Pour about one-half of the required amount of

Fig. 2-12—Refer to adjacent table for proper quantities of gasoline and oil for some of the more common fuel mixture ratios.

Ratio	Gasoline	Oil
16:1	1 Gallon	.50 Pint (237 mL)
20:1	1 Gallon	.40 Pint (189 mL)
30:1	1 Gallon	.27 Pint (126 mL)
32:1	1 Gallon	.25 Pint (118 mL)
40:1	1 Gallon	.20 Pint (95 mL)
50:1	1 Gallon	.16 Pint (76 mL)
100:1	1 Gallon	.08 Pint (38 mL)

gasoline into container, add the required amount of oil, then shake vigorously until completely mixed. Pour remaining amount of gasoline into container, then complete mixing by shaking. Serious engine damage can be caused by incomplete mixing. Never attempt to mix gasoline and oil in the unit's fuel tank.

Always observe safe handling practices when working with gasoline. Gasoline is extremely flammable. Do not smoke or allow sparks or open flame around fuel or in the presence of fuel vapors. Be sure area is well ventilated. Observe fire prevention rules.

REPAIRS

Because of the close tolerance of the internal parts, cleanliness is of utmost importance. It is suggested that the exterior of the engine and all nearby areas be absolutely clean before any repair is started. The manufacturer's recommended torque values for tightening screw fasteners should be followed closely. The soft threads in aluminum castings are often damaged by carelessness in over-tightening fasteners or in attempting to loosen or remove seized parts.

A given amount of heat applied to aluminum will cause it to expand a greater amount than will steel under similar conditions. Because of the different expansion characteristics, heat is usually recommended for easy installation of bearings, pins, etc., in aluminum castings. Sometimes, heat can be used to free parts that are seized or where an interference fit is used. Various heating devices can be used. Thermal crayons are available which can be used to

determine the temperature of a heated part. These crayons melt when the part reaches specified temperature, and a number of crayons for different temperatures are available. Temperature indicating crayons are usually available at welding equipment supply houses.

On two-stroke engines, the crankcase and combustion chambers must be sealed against pressure and vacuum leakage. To ensure a perfect seal, nicks, scratches and warpage are to be avoided, especially where no gasket is used. Slight imperfections can be removed by using a fine-grit sandpaper. Flat surfaces can be lapped by using a surface plate or a smooth piece of plate glass, and a sheet of fine sandpaper or lapping compound. Use a figure-eight motion with minimum pressure, and remove only enough metal to eliminate the imperfection. Bearing clearance must not be lessened by removing metal from the joint.

Use only the specified gaskets when reassembling, and use an approved gasket cement or sealing compound unless otherwise stated. All friction surfaces, including bearings and seals, should be coated with oil before assembling.

It is desirable to lock some threaded parts when assembling using a product recommended by the manufacturer or a suitable thread locking solution.

REPAIRING DAMAGED THREADS

Damaged threads in castings can be renewed by use of thread repair kits which are recommended by a number of manufacturers. Use of thread repair

kits is not difficult, but instructions must be carefully followed. Refer to Figs. 2-13 through 2-15 which illustrate the use of Heli-Coil thread repair kits that are manufactured by the Heli-Coil Corporation, Danbury, Connecticut.

Heli-Coil or similar thread repair kits are available through the parts departments of most engine and equipment manufacturers; the thread inserts are available in most common thread sizes and types.

PISTON, PIN, RINGS AND CYLINDER

Two-stroke engines do not have a complex valve mechanism and the piston rings have no oil control function. On the other hand, carbon build up is more likely to occur, and where oil consumption is the most common service problem on four-stroke engines, carbonization is the two-stroke counterpart.

The simple construction of two-stroke engines and the benefits to be gained from periodic carbon removal make decarbonization a part of the recommended maintenance procedure of most two-stroke experts. Because the piston rings have no oil control function, ring renewal is not required at carbon removal except to correct for wear or other damage.

Excessive carbon build up can be harmful in two ways. First, it insulates to keep the heat from escaping normally. Second, it raises the compression ratio to create more heat. This places an additional heat load on that portion of the cylinder which is scraped clean of carbon by the piston rings.

Fig. 2-13—First step in repairing damaged threads is to drill out old threads using exact size drill recommended in instructions provided with thread repair kit. Drill all the way through an open hole or all the way to bottom of blind hole, making sure hole is straight and that centerline of hole is not moved in drilling process. (Series of photos provided by Heli-Coil Corp., Danbury, Conn.)

Fig. 2-14—Special drill taps are provided in thread repair kit for threading drilled hole to correct size for outside of thread insert. A standard tap cannot be used.

Fig. 2-15—A thread insert and a complete repair are shown above. Special tools are provided in thread repair kit for installation of thread insert.

The need for carbon removal is often first indicated by inability to properly adjust the carburetor. If performance is erratic and improper carburetion is indicated, but attempts to adjust the carburetor fail, check first for excessive carbon build-up. No cleaning or adjustment of the carburetor can materially improve performance if exhaust passages are partially carbon blocked.

No problems will be encountered in removing cylinder head and/or cylinder for carbon removal provided normal standards of care and cleanliness are observed.

Examine the parts as engine is disassembled for clues to engine condition, to correct possible future trouble, or identify the cause or existing trouble. As an example, refer to Fig. 2-17. On this particular piston, the skirt is not scored and the first glance will show melted aluminum which has covered the ring on one side. The melted spot (D) on top and below piston crown is conclusive proof of detonation damage and the cause must be corrected during overhaul or the same failure can be expected to reoccur.

If pistons are scuffed or scored, look for metal transfer to cylinder walls. Metal transfer and score marks must be removed from cylinder walls with a hone. Chrome plated cylinder bores should not be honed.

Full strength muriatic acid can be used to remove aluminum deposits from a cast iron cylinder bore. Use acid carefully, it can cause painful burns if spilled on the skin and the fumes are toxic. It is most easily used by carefully transferring a small amount in a plastic squeeze bottle, or to another small container and applying with a cotton swab.

DO NOT allow the acid to spill or run onto aluminum portions of the cylinder, it will rapidly attack and dissolve the metal. Do not use the acid on a chrome bore. When applied to aluminum deposits, the acid will immediately start to boil and foam. When the action stops the aluminum has been dissolved or the acid is diluted; wipe the area with an old rag or towel which can be discarded. If deposits remain, repeat the process. Flush the area with water when aluminum is removed. Water will dilute the acid and can be used to stop the action if desired, or if acid runs off onto aluminum portion of cylinder, is accidentally spilled, etc. Immediately coat treated portion of cylinder with oil, as the acid makes the cast iron especially susceptible to rust.

A rule of thumb says scuffing or scoring of piston above the piston pin is due to overheating. Damage below the pin is more likely due to insufficient lubrication or improper fit. Overheating may be caused by a lean mixture, overloading, a damaged cooling system, air leaks in carburetor mounting gasket or manifold, blow-by (stuck or broken rings) as well as carbon buildup.

Fig. 2-18—Ring side clearance in groove should be measured with feeler gage as shown. Clearance should be within recommended limits and the same all the way around piston.

The greatest cylinder wear of a two-stroke engine generally occurs in port area of cylinder wall instead of at top of ring travel. Cast iron or aluminum bores should be measured using ring gap as an indicator or an inside micrometer. Check for spots on chromed bores which are different in appearance. Spots may be metal deposits from overheated pistons or may be where the thin chrome plating is worn through. Deposited metal can be scraped or carefully hand sanded from the chrome. If plating is worn through, cylinder must be renewed. Aluminum will be easily scratched by a sharp object but chrome will not.

On models with cast iron cylinder, the bore should be honed when engine is overhauled, to true the bore, remove the glaze and remove the ridge at top and bottom of ring travel area. If ridge is not removed, new unworn rings may strike the ridge and bend ring lands in piston as shown at (F—Fig. 2-20). The finished cylinder should have a light cross-hatch pattern (Fig. 2-21). After honing, wash cylinder assembly with soap and water, then swab with new oil on a clean rag until all tendency of rag to discolor is gone. Washing in solvent will not remove the abrasive from finished cylinder walls.

Some manufacturers have oversize piston and ring sets available. If care and approved procedures are used, installation of oversize units should result in a highly satisfactory overhaul.

The cylinder bore may be oversized by using either a boring bar or hone; however, if a boring bar is used, finish sizing should be done with a hone.

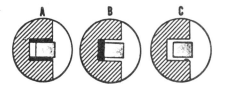

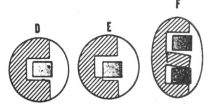

Fig. 2-20—Examine piston for damage before removing old rings. Shown are some common faults.

A. Carbon buildup, sides of groove
B. Carbon buildup behind ring
C. Incomplete carbon removal, loose carbon
D. Nicks in groove
E. Stepped wear
F. Broken or bent land

Fig. 2-17—Top and bottom view of piston severely damaged by detonation. Spot (D) on top and bottom of crown show where metal has started to melt. Absence of scoring on skirt rules out seizure, overheating or lack of lubrication as a contributing cause.

Fig. 2-19—Gap between ends of ring should be within recommended limits.

Fig. 2-21—A cross-hatch pattern as shown should be obtained by moving hone up and down cylinder bore as it is being turned by slow speed electric drill.

Before attempting to rebore, first check to be sure that new standard units cannot be fitted within the recommended clearances and that the correct oversize is available.

Some manufacturers recommend that after boring a cylinder to an oversize, the top and bottom edges of cylinder wall ports be rounded to prevent rings from catching.

When assembling piston on connecting rod, observe special precautions outlined in the individual service sections.

Lubricate piston pin bearing, piston, rings and cylinder as engine is assembled. Run engine with slightly rich carburetor setting during break-in period and do not overload, to prevent overheating until the parts wear in. It is sometimes advisable to install a hotter heat range spark plug in an attempt to prevent oil fouling in a newly started engine. Plug fouling during this period is not uncommon and it is advisable to have spare plugs along when running in a newly overhauled engine.

CONNECTING ROD, CRANKSHAFT AND BEARINGS

A built-up type crankshaft assembly should only be disassembled if the necessary tools and experience are available to service this type of crankshaft. Manufacturer's recommended crankshaft specifications are listed in each individual service section.

FAZER

WERKS MARINE, INC.
3552 St. Johns Industrial Park
Jacksonville, FL 32216

FAZER (Late 1986) AND FAZE II

NOTE: Metric fasteners are used throughout the engine.

General

Engine Make............................Cuyuna
Engine Type......................Two-Stroke;
Water-Cooled
HP/Rated Rpm..........................40/6250
Number of Cylinders.......................2
Bore.................................2.658 in.
(67.5 mm)
Stroke...............................2.362 in.
(60.0 mm)
Displacement.....................26.1 cu. in.
(428 cc)
Compression Ratio.....................7.2:1
Engine Lubrication....................Pre-Mix
Fuel:Oil Ratio 40:1
Engine Oil Recommendation ....Two-Stroke;
BIA Certified TC-W

Tune-Up

Spark Plug:
NGK B8ES
Champion N3C
Electrode Gap.............0.035-0.040 in.
(0.9-1.0 mm)
Ignition:
Type ....Nippondenso CDI
Timing ....28° BTDC or 0.17 in.
(4.4 mm) @ 1800 rpm
Carburetor:
Make................................Mikuni
Model..................BN38 Diaphragm
Bore Size...........................1.3 in.
(34 mm)
Low Speed Needle Setting............3/4 Turn
High Speed Needle Setting...........3/4 Turn

Sizes—Clearances

Cylinder Wear Limit...................2.660 in.
(67.55 mm)
Piston-to-Cylinder Wall
Clearance....................0.005-0.010 in.
(0.13-0.25 mm)
Piston Pin Diameter..............0.6298-0.6299 in.
(15.996-16.000 mm)

Sizes—Clearances (Cont.)

Piston Pin Bore Diameter..........0.6301-0.6311 in.
(16.004-16.030 mm)
Connecting Rod Small End
Diameter......................0.8661-0.8667 in.
(22.000-22.013 mm)
Piston Ring End Gap—Top and
Second...........................0.007-0.031 in.
(0.18-0.79 mm)
Maximum Crankshaft Runout.............0.003 in.*
(0.08 mm)

*Refer to text for measuring procedures.

Capacities

Fuel Tank.............................3.5 gal.
(13.2 L)

Tightening Torques

Cylinder Head Cap Screws..............16-18 ft.-lbs.
(22-24 N·m)
Crankcase Base Nuts...................16-18 ft.-lbs.
(22-24 N·m)
Intake Manifold.......................20-22 ft.-lbs.
(27-30 N·m)
Exhaust Manifold Cap Screws...........30 ft.-lbs.
(41 N·m)
Spark Plug............................20-22 ft.-lbs.
(27-30 N·m)
Flywheel Nut..........................46-50 ft.-lbs.
(63-68 N·m)
Drive Flange-to-Crankshaft
Cap Screw ....55 ft.-lbs.
(75 N·m)
Drive Flange-to-Jet Pump
Cap Screw ....30 ft.-lbs.
(41 N·m)
Standard Screws:
5 mm..............................40-50 in.-lbs.
(4.5-5.6 N·m)
6 mm..............................6-8 ft.-lbs.
(8-11 N·m)

LUBRICATION

All Models

The engine is lubricated by oil mixed with the fuel. Fuel:oil ratios should be 20:1 during break-in (first three gallons) of a new or rebuilt engine and 40:1 for normal service when using a BIA certified two-stroke TC-W engine oil. Manufacturer recommends regular or no-lead automotive gasoline having a minimum octane rating of 88. Gasoline and oil should be thoroughly mixed.

A Brut type jet pump is used. After every 12 hours of operation in fresh water or after each operation in salt water, grease jet pump front bearing and rear bushing with white lithium grease. Inject grease into grease fitting at rear of jet pump outlet body to grease rear bushing. Raise passenger seat and remove storage compartment, then inject grease into grease fitting at front of jet pump intake housing to grease front ball bearing. Reinstall storage compartment.

FUEL SYSTEM

All Models

CARBURETOR. Refer to Fig. F-1 for an exploded view of Mikuni type BN38 diaphragm carburetor used on all models. For cold engine starts, choke plate (21—Fig. F-1) is actuated by a choke knob on control panel via a cable and linkage.

Initial setting of low speed mixture needle (22) and high speed mixture needle (30—Fig. F-4) is ¾ turn out from a lightly seated position. Final carburetor adjustments must be made with engine at normal operating temperature and running. Depress throttle lever to slightly accelerate engine.

NOTE: Engine must stop when throttle lever is released to complete closed position.

Clockwise rotation of either needle leans the mixture. Adjust low speed mixture needle (22—Fig. F-1) until smooth acceleration from the idle position is noted. To adjust high speed fuel:air mixture, the engine spark plugs must be removed and their insulator tip color noted.

NOTE: Make sure that fuel tank contains a 40:1 fuel mixture.

Make sure cooling system will receive an adequate supply of water, then operate and sustain engine at wide-open throttle for a suitable test period. Stop the engine with throttle in wide-open position. Remove spark plugs and note insulator tip color. Normal insulator tip color is brown to light tan. If insulator tip appears to be light tan to white in color, then mixture is too lean and high speed mixture needle (30) should be rotated outward (counterclockwise) ¼ turn to richen mixture. If insulator tip appears to be dark brown to black in color, then mixture is too rich and high speed mixture needle (30) should be rotated inward (clockwise) ¼ turn to lean mixture. Clean, regap and reinstall spark plugs and continue test procedures until spark plug insulator tips are a normal color.

The fuel pump and regulating diaphragm (12) can be removed after removing the six through-bolts. Note that alignment tabs on components (3 through 12) are provided to assist in proper alignment during reassembly.

Do not remove choke plate, throttle plate or shafts unless necessary. The choke and throttle plate retaining screws are either staked or retained with a thread locking solution to prevent loosening. If screws are removed, properly stake or apply a suitable thread locking solution on threads prior to assembly. Inlet needle valve lever (17) must be flush with floor of housing

recess when needle valve is seated. Refer to Fig. F-5. If lever must be adjusted, push down on lever immediately above spring to collapse the spring, then bend the end which contacts needle valve.

FUEL PUMP. The fuel pump is an integral part of the carburetor. The fuel pump assembly can be overhauled without overhauling the complete carburetor.

With reference to Fig. F-1, disassemble the fuel pump assembly. Inspect all components for excessive wear or any other damage and renew if needed. Clean components as needed with a suitable cleaning solution. Blow dry with clean compressed air. If compressed air is not available, use only lint-free cloths to wipe dry. Make sure all passages are clear of any obstructions.

With reference to Fig. F-1, reassemble the fuel pump assembly with new gaskets. Securely tighten the six through-bolts.

FUEL FILTER. An inline fuel filter is located between fuel tank and fuel pump. Periodically remove inline fuel filter and blow through inlet side of filter with low air pressure to check for blockage. Very little restriction should be noted. Renew fuel filter if excessive restriction or contamination is noted.

FLAME ARRESTOR. Periodically remove flame arrestor (F—Fig. F-7) and

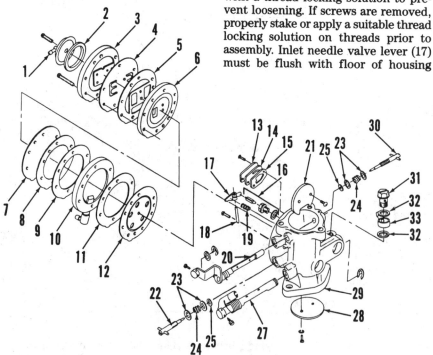

Fig. F-1—Exploded view of Mikuni type BN38 diaphragm carburetor used on all models.

1. Fuel inlet cover		
2. Gasket	10. Diaphragm cover	18. Pivot shaft
3. Inlet body	11. Gasket	19. Spring
4. Check valve	12. Regulating	20. Choke shaft
diaphragm	diaphragm	21. Choke plate
5. Gasket	13. Plate	22. Low speed mixture
6. Pump body	14. Diaphragm	needle
7. Diaphragm	15. Gasket	23. Washers
8. Gasket	16. Inlet valve assy.	24. Springs
9. Gasket	17. Valve lever	25. "O" rings

27. Throttle shaft	
28. Throttle plate	
29. Body	
30. High speed mixture	
needle	
31. Banjo bolt	
32. Gaskets	
33. Return line fitting	

Fig. F-4—View identifies location of high speed mixture needle (30).

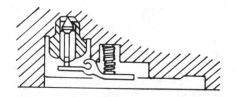

Fig. F-5—Inlet needle valve lever should be flush with floor of housing recess as shown.

clean assembly with a suitable cleaning solution. Blow dry with clean compressed air. Inspect assembly for any damage and renew if needed. Install flame arrestor and make sure assembly fits tightly around neck of carburetor. Securely tighten three through-bolts (B).

IGNITION

All Models

All models are equipped with a simultaneous capacitor discharge ignition system. The ignition timing is electronically advanced as the magneto base plate is fixed. Ignition timing should not require adjustment, after first being correctly set, unless magneto base plate is moved or and ignition component is renewed.

IGNITION TIMING. Ignition timing should be 28 degrees BTDC or 0.174 inch (4.4 mm) at 1800 rpm. Ignition timing can be checked using a suitable power timing light.

Timing marks must be placed on flywheel (9—Fig. F-9) and ignition housing (1). Remove both spark plugs and ground spark plug leads to engine. Position a suitable dial indicator assembly so indicator needle projects through spark plug hole into number two cylinder head (cylinder towards front of vehicle). Remove ignition housing cover (13) and gasket (12). Position a suitable tool on nut (11) and rotate crankshaft clockwise (viewed from front of engine) until piston in number two cylinder is at top dead center (TDC). Zero dial indicator, then rotate crankshaft counterclockwise until dial indicator reads 0.174 inch (4.4 mm) before top dead center (BTDC). Use a suitable marking device and place marks on ignition housing and flywheel so marks are aligned. Remove dial indicator assembly and install spark plugs.

Tighten spark plugs to 20-22 ft.-lbs. (27-30 N·m) and attach spark plug leads.

NOTE: Some models are equipped with access plug (14) in ignition housing cover (13). On these models, the plug can be removed and the flywheel and ignition housing marked without removing ignition housing cover. If this procedure is used, the power take-off end of the crankshaft must be used to rotate crankshaft. When reinstalling access plug, make sure a suitable sealant is used around access plug to prevent water from seeping into ignition housing.

Immerse vehicle in water so jet pump pickup is properly submerged or connect a supplemental water supply to cooling system supply hose after removing hose from jet pump outlet fitting (F—Fig. F-10) and using a suitable adapter.

To check ignition timing, start engine and accelerate to 1800 rpm. Note flywheel timing mark in relation to mark on ignition housing. If ignition timing is incorrect, magneto base plate (6—Fig. F-9) must be repositioned. Stop engine, then rotate flywheel until openings are aligned with the two magneto base plate retaining screws. Use a suitable tool and reach through flywheel openings. Loosen magneto base plate screws. Rotate magneto base plate clockwise to retard ignition timing and counterclockwise to advance ignition timing. Tighten magneto base plate screws, then recheck ignition timing. Continue procedure until correct ignition timing is obtained.

Install a new ignition housing gasket (12). Install ignition housing (13) and securely tighten retaining cap screws.

TROUBLE-SHOOTING. If ignition malfunction occurs, use only approved procedures to prevent damage to the components. The fuel systems should be checked first to make certain that faulty running is not caused by incorrect mixture or contaminated fuel. Make sure malfunction is not due to spark plug, wiring or wiring connection failure. Trouble-shoot ignition circuit using a suitable ohmmeter as follows:

Fig. F-10—Water for engine cooling system is supplied through jet pump outlet fitting (F).

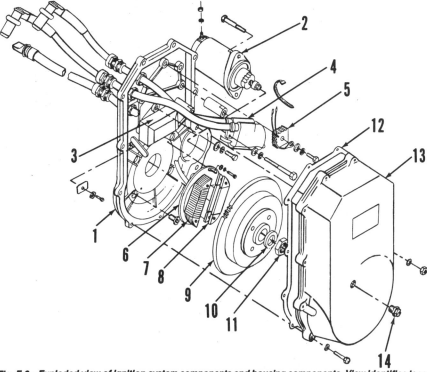

Fig. F-9—Exploded view of ignition system components and housing components. View identifies location of lighting coil, rectifier/regulator assembly and electric starter.

1. Ignition housing	8. Charge & trigger coil	12. Gasket
2. Electric starter	9. Flywheel	13. Ignition housing
3. CDI module	5. Rectifier/regulator	10. Lockwasher	cover
4. Ignition coil	6. Magneto base plate	11. Nut	14. Access plug
	7. Lighting coil		

Fig. F-7—Remove three through-bolts (B) to withdraw flame arrestor (F).

Separate the three-wire and two-wire connector between magneto components and CDI module. Refer to Fig. F-11. Check condition of charge coil by attaching one tester lead to red/black wire leading to magneto assembly and attaching other tester lead to black/red wire leading to magneto assembly. Charge coil can be considered satisfactory if resistance reading is within the limits of 16,200-19,800 ohms. Check condition of trigger coil by attaching one tester lead to black/red wire leading to magneto assembly and attaching other tester lead to black/white wire leading to magneto assembly. Trigger coil can be considered satisfactory if resistance reading is within the limits of 2.0-2.4 ohms.

To check condition of ignition coil, separate the white/blue wire and black wire at connector and remove high tension wires from spark plugs. Attach one tester lead to terminal end of white/blue wire leading to coil and other tester lead to terminal end of black wire leading to coil. Primary coil resistance reading should be within the limits of 0.28-0.38 ohms. Attach a tester lead to each high tension wire. Secondary coil resistance reading should be within the limits of 3120-4680 ohms.

If no components are found defective in the previous tests and ignition malfunction is still suspected, then install a known good CDI module and recheck engine operation.

CHARGING SYSTEM

All Models

All models are equipped with a lighting coil, rectifier/regulator, battery and ignition switch. The lighting coil should produce 32 ac volts at 6000 rpm.

The battery electrolyte level should be checked periodically and filled to maximum level with distilled water if required. The battery should be removed from the vehicle and the battery caps removed when charging. Do not exceed maximum charging rate of two amperes.

NOTE: Make sure battery charging area is well ventilated.

The lighting coil can be statically tested using a suitable ohmmeter. Refer to Fig. F-11. Separate two yellow wires leading from lighting coil to rectifier/regulator assembly at connector block. Measure resistance between the two yellow wires leading to lighting coil. Resistance reading should be 0.16-0.20 ohms. Check for continuity between each of the lighting coil wires and ground. Tester should show infinite resistance at each wire. To check rectifier/regulator assembly, first make sure battery is fully charged, lighting coil test good and all wiring is in good condition and all connectors fit tightly or are securely fastened. Attach a suitable voltmeter directly on battery terminals. Immerse vehicle in water so jet pump pickup is properly submerged or connect a supplemental water supply to cooling system supply hose after removing hose from jet pump outlet fitting (F—Fig. F-10) and using a suitable adapter. Start and run engine while observing voltmeter. The voltmeter should show approximately 13.5 dc volts.

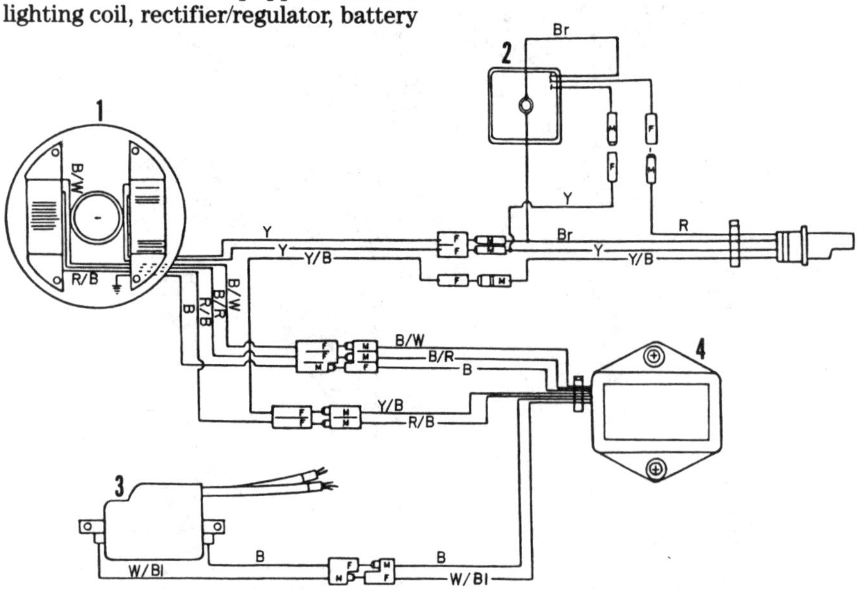

COOLING SYSTEM

All Models

All models are water-cooled. Forced water is supplied to the engine through jet pump outlet fitting (F—Fig. F-10). As jet pump impeller rpm increases, so does water circulation through cooling system.

Make sure jet pump water intake grill on bottom of hull is kept clean. Inspect all hoses periodically for cracks, kinks or any other damage. The cooling system should be flushed out after each operating period when vehicle is used in contaminated or salt water. The cooling system should be flushed out prior to extended periods of storage and prior to usage after extended periods of storage.

To flush the cooling system, connect a supplemental water supply to cooling system supply hose after removing hose from jet pump outlet fitting (F—Fig. F-10) and using a suitable adapter. Use only clean, fresh water.

NOTE: Do not turn on water until engine is ready to be started as exhaust flooding could occur.

Start engine and retain throttle lever in idle position. Allow water to circulate through system for approximately five minutes. Make sure supplemental water supply is turned off at approximately same time engine is stopped. Disconnect supplemental water supply and reattach cooling system supply hose to jet pump outlet fitting (F). If vehicle is to be stored for an extended period, start the engine and allow to run for a maximum of 5 to 10 seconds. All water remaining in exhaust system will be forced out, preventing damage from developing contaminates or freezing.

NOTE: Make sure engine is not operated without a supply of water longer than 5 to 10 seconds or damage to engine or downstream exhaust components could result.

To drain water from engine, remove plug (P—Fig. F-15) at rear of exhaust manifold. Use clean compressed air and blow through cooling system supply hose to force water out through plug (P) opening. Tilt vehicle to the starboard side to completely drain cooling system. Reinstall manifold plug (P) and securely tighten.

ENGINE

All Models

REMOVE AND REINSTALL. Raise passenger seat and disconnect battery

Fig. F-11—View showing ignition system and charging system wiring schematic.

1. Magneto assy.			
2. Rectifier/regulator	B. Black	Br. Brown	R/B. Red/black
3. Ignition coil	R. Red	B/R. Black/red	W/Bl. White/blue
4. CDI module	Y. Yellow	B/W. Black/white	Y/B. Yellow/black

cables from battery, then remove battery from vehicle. Remove storage compartment. Detach engine wiring harness from control panel harness at connector. Disconnect fuel supply line and return line from fuel pump and plug fuel lines. Remove fuel tank and plug fuel lines and fittings. Disconnect throttle control cable and choke cable from carburetor and remove cables from mounting bracket. Remove exhaust components, as needed, to allow removal of engine assembly. Remove cooling system supply hose from engine inlet fitting. Remove electric starter power supply cable from starter solenoid or starter motor. Remove carburetor assembly with flame arrestor and cover intake manifold passage to prevent entrance of foreign debris. Remove any other component that will restrict removal of engine assembly. Remove fasteners retaining the engine mounting plate to the vehicle hull. Use a suitable lifting device to hoist engine assembly from vehicle. Place engine assembly on a clean work bench.

To reinstall engine assembly, use a suitable lifting device to hoist engine assembly into vehicle. Install fasteners retaining engine mounting plate to vehicle hull, then securely tighten. Complete reassembly in reverse order of disassembly.

DISASSEMBLY. Remove the fasteners retaining the engine mounting plate to the engine assembly. Use a suitable lifting device to hoist engine assembly from engine mounting plate. Set engine assembly on a clean work area for complete disassembly.

Remove any downstream exhaust components and exhaust manifold. Disconnect pulse line from fitting (23—Fig. F-20). Remove intake manifold (27) and water manifold (24). Detach spark plug leads from spark plugs, then remove spark plugs. Remove electric starter (2—Fig. F-9). Remove ignition housing cover (13) and gasket (12). Remove flywheel retaining nut (11) and lockwasher (10), then use a suitable puller and withdraw flywheel (9). Withdraw key (18—Fig. F-20) from slot

in crankshaft end. Remove the two magneto base plate (6—Fig. F-9) mounting screws, then position magneto base plate assembly to the side to allow access to ignition housing (1) mounting screws. Remove the four ignition housing mounting screws, then withdraw ignition housing with ignition system and charging system components. Remove cylinder heads (1—Fig. F-20). Lift "O" rings (2 and 3) from grooves in top of cylinder. Invert engine assembly so base of crankcase is facing upward. Remove crankcase base nuts and washers. Securely hold assembled components together, then invert assembly so top of cylinders are facing upward. Identify

pistons and cylinders for correct reassembly. Use a soft-faced mallet and lightly tap on side of cylinders to break cylinders loose from crankcase. Lift cylinders off pistons while supporting each piston as cylinder slides clear of piston. Separate pistons from connecting rods. Make sure piston components for each cylinder are kept together.

NOTE: Piston pin puller 11-48-307 or a suitable equivalent must be used to remove piston pin (7) from piston (6). Damage to connecting rod may result if correct tools are not used.

Use a soft-faced mallet and lightly tap upper crankcase half (10) to break crankcase halves apart. Lift upper crankcase half (10) off lower crankcase half (22). Crankshaft and piston assembly can now be removed from lower crankcase half (22).

Engine components are now ready for overhaul as outlined in the appropriate following paragraphs. Refer to the following section for assembly procedure.

ASSEMBLY. Refer to specific service sections when assembling the

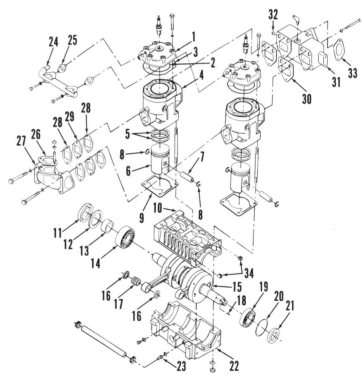

Fig. F-20—Exploded view of engine assembly. All models are equipped with thrust ring (12). A center thrust ring is used on Cuyuna Engine Model 21330 and later. Seal (11) and collar (13) on Cuyuna Engine Model 22037 and earlier differs in collar outside diameter and seal opening diameter from later models.

1. Cylinder head	10. Upper crankcase half	18. Key	26. Gasket
2. "O" ring	11. Seal	19. Ball bearing	27. Intake manifold
3. "O" ring	12. Thrust ring	20. "O" ring	28. Gasket
4. Cylinder	13. Collar	21. Seal	29. Insulator plate
5. Piston rings	14. Ball bearing	22. Lower crankcase half	30. Gasket
6. Piston	15. Crankshaft assy.	23. Pulse fitting	31. Exhaust manifold
7. Piston pin	16. Stop plates	24. Water manifold	32. Drain plug
8. Retaining clips	17. Needle bearing	25. Gasket	33. Gasket
9. Cylinder base gasket			34. Grommets

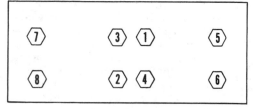

Magneto
End

Fig. F-21—Crankcase base nuts should be tightened in the sequence shown. Refer to text for tightening torque specifications.

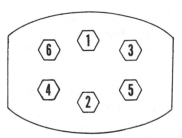

Fig. F-22—Cylinder head cap screws should be tightened in the sequence shown. Refer to text for tightening torque specifications.

crankshaft, connecting rod and piston. Make sure all joint and gasket surfaces are clean, free from nicks and burrs and hardened cement or carbon.

Whenever the engine is disassembled, it is recommended that all gasket surfaces and mating surfaces without gaskets be carefully checked for nicks, burrs and warped surfaces which might interfere with a tight seal. Cylinder head, head end of cylinder and mating surfaces of crankcase should be checked on a surface plate and lapped, if necessary, to provide a smooth surface. Do not remove any more metal than is necessary.

When assembling power head, first lubricate all friction surfaces and bearings with engine oil. Place collar (13—Fig. F-20) and thrust ring (12) onto pto end of crankshaft. Lubricate lip of seal (11) with a suitable high-temperature grease, then install seal (11) onto pto end of crankshaft. Make certain seal (11) is installed with open side (spring side) towards bearing (14). Install crankshaft assembly (15) into lower crankcase half (22). Rotate center seal on crankshaft until outer pinch line is aligned with crankcase halves mating surface on either side of lower crankcase half. Apply a coat of a form-in-place gasket compound on mating surfaces of lower crankcase half and upper crankcase half, then position upper crankcase half on lower crankcase half.

Position stop plates (16) on outside of connecting rods and lubricate needle bearing (17) with engine oil. Position piston assemblies over connecting rods, then install piston pins (7). Retain piston pins with new retaining clips (8). Position open end of clip (8) to face 12

o'clock or 6 o'clock position. Lubricate pistons and piston rings with engine oil. Install new cylinder base gaskets (9), then use suitable tools to install cylinders (4). Securely hold assembled components together, then invert assembly so base of crankcase is facing upward. Mount intake manifold (27) on cylinders (4) with new gaskets (28) and insulator plates (29). Tighten intake manifold cap screws to 20-22 ft.-lbs. (27-30 N·m) using a crisscross pattern. Using tightening sequence shown in Fig F-21, tighten the crankcase base nuts in 5 ft.-lbs. (7 N·m) increments until a final torque of 16-18 ft.-lbs. (22-24 N·m) is obtained. Invert assembly so top of cylinders are facing upward. Install "O" rings (2 and 3—Fig. F-20) into grooves on top of cylinders (4). Position cylinder heads (1) on cylinders. Using tightening

sequence shown in Fig. F-22, tighten the cylinder head cap screws in 5 ft.-lbs. (7 N·m) increments until a final torque of 16-18 ft.-lbs. (22-24 N·m) is obtained. Mount exhaust manifold (31—Fig. F-20) with gaskets (30) on cylinders. Tighten exhaust manifold cap screws to 30 ft.-lbs. (41 N·m) using a crisscross pattern.

Install seal (21) into ignition housing (1—Fig. F-9). Make certain seal (21—Fig. F-20) is installed with open side (spring side) towards bearing (19). Install "O" ring (20) onto outside of ignition housing neck. Lubricate lip of seal (21) with a suitable high-temperature grease. Lubricate "O" ring (20) with a thin coating of a water-resistant grease. Install grommets (34) into upper crankcase half (10) slots. Reassemble ignition housing to crankcase assembly. Tighten the four ignition housing mounting screws to 16-18 ft.-lbs. (22-24 N·m) using a crisscross pattern. Align mark at base of magneto base plate (6—Fig. F-9) with long mark at bottom of ignition housing (1) and install magneto base plate. Apply Loctite 222 or a suitable equivalent thread locking solution on threads of magneto base plate retaining screws, then install screws with flat washers and lockwashers and securely tighten.

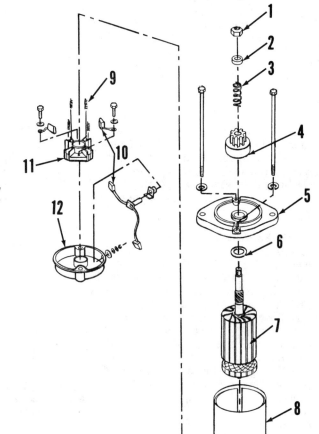

Fig. F-24—Exploded view of electric starter assembly used on all models.

1. Nut
2. Spring seat
3. Spring
4. Starter drive
5. Frame head
6. Thrust washer
7. Armature
8. Frame
9. Spring
10. Brushes
11. Brush holder
12. End cap

Install flywheel key (18—Fig. F-20) in slot of crankshaft, then install flywheel (9—Fig. F-9). Apply a few drops of Loctite 242 or a suitable equivalent thread locking solution to threads on crankshaft end, then install lockwasher (10) and flywheel retaining nut (11). Tighten nut (11) to 46-50 ft.-lbs. (63-68 N·m).

RINGS, PISTONS, CYLINDERS AND CYLINDER HEADS. The pistons are fitted with two piston rings. Piston rings are interchangeable in grooves but must be installed with manufacturer's marking facing towards closed end (top) of piston. Piston ring end gap should be 0.007-0.031 inch (0.18-0.79 mm). Piston-to-cylinder wall clearance should be 0.005-0.010 inch (0.13-0.25 mm). Pistons and rings are available in standard size as well as 0.020 inch (0.5 mm) oversize. Cylinder should be bored to an oversize if cylinder is out-of-round or taper exceeds 0.002 inch (0.05 mm). Install piston on connecting rod so arrow on piston crown will point towards exhaust port when piston is in cylinder.

When installing cylinders, lubricate piston rings and cylinders and refer to ASSEMBLY section.

CONNECTING RODS, BEARINGS AND CRANKSHAFT. Connecting rods, bearings and crankshaft are a pressed together unit. Crankshaft should be disassembled ONLY by experienced service personnel and with proper service equipment.

Caged needle bearings are used at piston end of connecting rod. Maximum allowable limit of crankshaft runout is 0.003 inch (0.08 mm). Measure magneto end of crankshaft 0.7 inch (17.78 mm) from crankshaft end and pto end of crankshaft 1.0 inch (25.4 mm) from crankshaft end.

When installing crankshaft, lubricate bearings with engine oil and refer to ASSEMBLY section.

ELECTRIC STARTER

All Models

All models are equipped with electric starter shown in Fig. F-24. Disassembly is evident after inspection of unit and reference to exploded view. When servicing starter motor, scribe reference marks across motor frame to aid in reassembly. Inspect all components for excessive wear or any other damage and renew if needed.

During reassembly, apply a light coat of a form-in-place gasket compound on frame head (5—Fig. F-24) and end cap (12) where caps mate with frame (8).

After reassembly, bench test starter motor before installing on engine. Prior to installation, apply a light coat of a form-in-place gasket compound around outside of frame head (5) where frame head mates with ignition housing.

BILGE PUMP

All Models

When the vehicle is operated, the jet pump forces water past siphon tube (T—Fig. F26). The passing force of water creates a vacuum effect, thus drawing (siphoning) any water out of vehicle bilge. Make sure all hoses, strainer in vehicle bilge and one-way check valve are kept clean of all foreign debris. Disassemble and clean or renew components if needed. Check operation of one-way check valve as follows. Remove one-way check valve from hoses. Use low air pressure and blow through one-way check valve openings. Air should flow freely through one-way check valve in the direction indicated by arrow on outside of valve. Air should not pass through valve when applied to opposite end. Make sure one-way check valve is installed with outside arrow pointing towards jet pump. Make sure all hose connections are tight or vacuum loss will result in siphoning system malfunction.

DRIVE SHAFT

All Models

REMOVE AND REINSTALL. Raise passenger seat and disconnect battery cables from battery, then remove battery from vehicle. Remove storage compartment. Remove exhaust components, as needed to allow engine assembly to be slid forward. Remove any other components that will restrict engine assembly from being slid forward. Remove fasteners retaining the engine mounting plate to the vehicle hull. Slide engine assembly forward 3-4 inches (76-101 mm).

NOTE: If care is exercised, engine wiring harness, fuel supply line, fuel return line, throttle control cable, choke cable and cooling system supply hose need not be disconnected.

Lift drive shaft from vehicle.

Install drive shaft with soft (black) coupler in jet pump drive flange and hard (white) coupler in crankshaft drive flange. Install fasteners retaining engine mounting plate to vehicle hull, then securely tighten. Complete reassembly in reverse order of disassembly.

INSPECTION. Inspect crankshaft drive flange, hard (white) coupler, jet pump drive flange, soft (black) coupler and drive shaft for excessive wear or any other damage and renew if needed. Tighten drive flange-to-crankshaft cap screw to 55 ft.-lbs. (75 N·m) and drive flange-to-jet pump cap screw to 30 ft.-lbs. (41 N·m).

JET PUMP

All Models

DISASSEMBLY AND INSPECTION. Remove jet pump guard and disconnect steering cable end from outlet nozzle (1—Fig. F-31). Remove cooling system supply hose from fitting on top of outlet body (4). Disconnect clear bilge siphon hose from side of outlet body (4). Loosen band clamp (5), then withdraw outlet body (4) and band clamp (5). Withdraw impeller (9), pin (10), shims (11) and nose cone (12) out rear of jet pump.

Raise passenger seat and disconnect battery cables from battery, then remove battery from vehicle. Remove storage compartment. Remove exhaust components, as needed, to allow engine assembly to be slid forward. Remove any other components that will restrict engine assembly from being slid forward. Remove fasteners retaining the engine mounting plate to the vehicle hull. Slide engine assembly forward 3-4 inches (76-101 mm).

NOTE: If care is exercised, engine wiring harness, fuel supply line, fuel return line, throttle control cable, choke cable and cooling system supply hose need not be disconnected.

Lift drive shaft from vehicle. Remove hex head screw retaining jet pump drive flange. Reinstall pin (10) into impeller shaft. Install tool 11-40-303 over impeller shaft and position tool slots to engage pin. Place a chain wrench on jet pump drive flange, then rotate drive flange counterclockwise while pre-

Fig. F-26—View identifies location of siphon tube (T) in rear of jet pump.

venting impeller shaft rotation with tool 11-40-303. Completely unscrew propeller shaft from threaded adapter (23) and withdraw out rear of jet pump. Withdraw jet pump drive flange with adapter (23). Use a suitable tool and pry out seal (22). Remove snap ring (21). Use a suitable punch and hammer and drive bearing (20) out front of intake housing. Pry out seal (19). Remove fasteners to withdraw intake housing (16) with grill (25) and anode (26).

Inspect impeller shaft for wear on friction surfaces of bearings and oil seals. Inspect impeller (9) and wear ring (14) for excessive wear or any other damage. Inspect all bearings for freedom of rotation and damaged components. Inspect outlet body (4) and intake housing (16) for damage. Renew all gaskets, "O" rings and seals during reassembly. Renew any other components that are excessively worn or are diagnosed with any other damage.

ASSEMBLY. Apply a 3/16 inch (4.7 mm) bead of RTV silicone sealer around gasket (24—Fig. F31) where gasket mates with hull. Apply a 1/4 inch (6.35 mm) bead of RTV silicone sealer at base and back side of "O" ring (15). Install intake housing (16) with grill (25) and anode (26) into vehicle and evenly tighten fasteners. Wipe all excess RTV silicone sealer from outside of hull. Ap-

ply additional RTV silicone sealer, if needed, around mating area of intake housing (16) and hull to ensure no water leakage will result. Apply a white lithium grease on seals (19 and 22) and install seal (19), bearing (20), snap ring (21) and seal (22) into front of intake housing (16). Install threaded adapter (23) and jet pump drive flange into front of intake housing (16). Apply a suitable thread seizure preventing solution to threads on end of impeller shaft (13). Reach impeller shaft through intake housing (16) and thread into adapter (23). Hold jet pump drive flange and hand tighten impeller shaft using tool 11-40-303 to secure impeller shaft against bearing (20). Install hex head retaining screw in jet pump drive flange. Place a chain wrench on drive flange and use the correct sized hex head socket and tool to tighten retaining screw to 30 ft.-lbs. (41 N·m).

Install drive shaft with soft (black) coupler in jet pump drive flange and hard (white) coupler in crankshaft drive flange. Install fasteners retaining engine mounting plate to vehicle hull, then securely tighten. Complete reassembly in reverse order of disassembly.

Remove pin (10). Install nose cone (12), shims (11), pin (10) and impeller (9). Align and seat impeller (9) on pin (10). Hold pressure against impeller and measure clearance between impeller

blades and wear ring (14). Clearance should be 0.012-0.018 inch (0.30-0.46 mm). If clearance is too low, then add one shim (11). If clearance is too high, then remove one shim (11). Adjust shim (11) thickness until correct clearance is obtained. Grease bushing (6) with white lithium grease. Install outlet body (4) on impeller shaft (13). Align tab at front of outlet body (4) with notch in intake housing (16) and assemble components. Install band clamp (5) with adjusting nut on top and tighten nut until ¾ inch (19.05 mm) of stud protrudes through nut. Install clear bilge siphon hose, cooling system supply hose and connect steering cable end on outlet nozzle ball fitting (2). Install jet pump guard. Inject white lithium grease into grease fitting (3) at rear of outlet body (4) and grease fitting (17) at front of jet pump intake housing (16).

STEERING

All Models

ADJUSTMENT. With handlebar in straight ahead position, jet pump outlet nozzle (1—Fig. F-31) should be centered or at a 90 degree angle to stern of vehicle. If not, secure handlebar in a straight ahead position. Remove jet pump guard and detach cable end from outlet nozzle ball fitting (2). Loosen locknut securing cable end and rotate cable end in direction required to center outlet nozzle. Reattach cable end and check outlet nozzle setting. Tighten locknut securing cable end after correct adjustment is obtained. Reinstall jet pump guard.

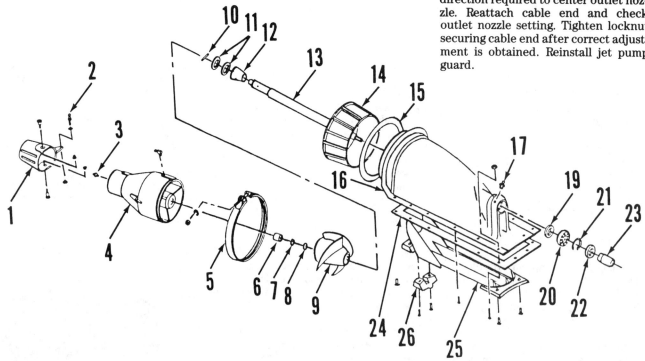

Fig. F-31—Exploded view of jet pump assembly.

1. Outlet nozzle	6. Bushing	10. Pin	14. Wear ring	19. Seal	23. Threaded adapter
2. Ball fitting	7. Seal	11. Shims	15. "O" ring	20. Bearing	24. Gasket
3. Grease fitting	8. Seal	12. Nose cone	16. Intake housing	21. Snap ring	25. Grill
4. Outlet body	9. Impeller	13. Impeller shaft	17. Grease fitting	22. Seal	26. Anode
5. Band clamp					

FUNJET BOATS

D&D MARINE MANUFACTURING INC.
8900 Kirby Drive, Suite 190
Houston, TX 77054

FUNJET (1984-1987)

NOTE: Metric fasteners are used throughout engine and jet pump.

General

Engine Make	Suzuki
Engine Type	Two-Stroke; Water-Cooled
HP/Rated Rpm:	
Prior to 1985	50/5300
After 1984	60/5300
Number of Cylinders	2
Bore:	
50 HP Models	80 mm
	(3.15 in.)
60 HP Models	84 mm
	(3.31 in.)
Stroke	72 mm
	(2.83 in.)
Displacement:	
50 HP Models	723 cc
	(44.12 cu. in.)
60 HP Models	798 cc
	(48.7 cu. in.)
Compression Ratio:	
50 HP Models	7.0:1
60 HP Models	6.5:1
Engine Lubrication	Pre-Mix
Fuel:Oil Ratio	50:1
Engine Oil Recommendation	Two-Stroke; BIA Certified TC-W

Tune-Up

Engine Idle Speed	650-700 rpm
Spark Plug:	
NGK	BR8HS
Champion	RL78C
Electrode Gap	0.6-0.7 mm
	(0.024-0.028 in.)
Ignition:	
Type	CDI
Timing	8° BTDC @ 1000 rpm
	25° BTDC @ 5000 rpm
Carburetor:	
Make	Mikuni
Model	B40-32
Bore Size	40 mm
	(1.57 in.)
Main Jet	155
Air Jet	1.2
Pilot Jet	70
Idle Mixture Setting	1¾ Turns
Float Height:	
50 HP Models	15.4-17.5 mm
	(0.60-0.68 in.)
60 HP Models	16.5-18.5 mm
	(0.65-0.73 in.)

Sizes—Clearances

Cylinder Wear Limit:	
50 HP Models	80.1 mm
	(3.153 in.)
60 HP Models	84.1 mm
	(3.314 in.)
Piston-to-Cylinder Wall Clearance:	
50 HP Models	0.078-0.092 mm
	(0.0031-0.0036 in.)
60 HP Models	0.112-0.127 mm
	(0.0044-0.0050 in.)
Piston Pin Diameter	19.995-20.000 mm
	(0.7872-0.7874 in.)
Piston Pin Bore Diameter	19.998-20.006 mm
	(0.7873-0.7876 in.)
Piston Ring End Gap:	
Top and Second	0.2-0.4 mm
	(0.008-0.016 in.)
Service Limit	0.8 mm
	(0.031 in.)
Maximum Connecting Rod Small End Side Shake	5.0 mm
	(0.20 in.)
Maximum Crankshaft Runout at Main Bearing Journal	0.05 mm
	(0.002 in.)
Maximum Reed Stopper Opening:	
50 HP Models	8.8 mm
	(0.346 in.)
60 HP Models	7.95 mm
	(0.313 in.)
Maximum Reed Valve Stand Open	0.2 mm
	(0.008 in.)

Capacities

Fuel Tank	22.7 L
	(6 gal.)

Tightening Torques

Carburetor Mounting Nuts	10-13 N·m
	(7-10 ft.-lbs.)
Cylinder Head Cap Screws—	
50 HP Models:	
6 mm	7-9 N·m
	(5-7 ft.-lbs.)
8 mm	34-39 N·m
	(25-29 ft.-lbs.)
60 HP Models:	
6 mm	7-9 N·m
	(5-7 ft.-lbs.)
8 mm	34-39 N·m
	(25-29 ft.-lbs.)

Tightening Torques (Cont.)

10 mm	39-58 N·m (29-43 ft.-lbs.)
Crankcase Cap Screws	36-39 N·m (26-29 ft.-lbs.)
Engine Exhaust Cover Cap Screws	8-11 N·m (6-8 ft.-lbs.)
Reed Plate Cap Screws	4-7 N·m (3-5 ft.-lbs.)
Spark Plug	25-27 N·m (18-20 ft.-lbs.)
Flywheel Nut	196 N·m (144 ft.-lbs.)
Exhaust Chamber Base	19-24 N·m (14-18 ft.-lbs.)

Tightening Torques (Cont.)

Engine Mounting Nuts	21-24 N·m (15-18 ft.-lbs.)
Pinion Gear Nut	22-26 N·m (16-19 ft.-lbs.)
Pinion Shaft Cover	19-23 N·m (14-17 ft.-lbs.)
Impeller Shaft Nut	68 N·m (50 ft.-lbs.)
Jet Pump Front Cover Cap Screws	19-23 N·m (14-17 ft.-lbs.)
Jet Pump Nozzle Nuts	30-39 N·m (22-29 ft.-lbs.)
Jet Pump Mounting Cap Screws	34-39 N·m (25-29 ft.-lbs.)

LUBRICATION

All Models

The engine is lubricated by oil mixed with the fuel. Fuel:oil ratios should be 25:1 during break-in of a new or rebuilt engine and 50:1 for normal service when using a BIA certified two-stroke TC-W engine oil. When using any other type of two-stroke engine oil, fuel:oil ratios should be 20:1 during break-in and 30:1 for normal service. Manufacturer recommends regular or no-lead automotive gasoline having an 85-95 octane rating. Gasoline and oil should be thoroughly mixed.

The jet pump gears and bearings are lubricated by oil contained in the gearcase. SAE 90 hypoid marine gear oil should be used. The gearcase is drained and filled through the same plug port (D—Fig. FJ-1). To drain the oil, place the vehicle so gearcase is parallel to a flat, level surface. Remove "OIL FILL" plug (D) and "OIL CHECK" plug (V). Allow lubricant to drain into a suitable container. To fill gearcase, add oil through "OIL FILL" plug (D) opening until oil begins to flow from "OIL CHECK" plug (V). Reinstall "OIL CHECK" plug (V) with a new gasket, if needed, and tighten plug. Reinstall "OIL FILL" plug (D) with a new gasket, if needed, and tighten plug.

Whenever the engine and jet pump assembly is removed from vehicle, grease jet pump output nozzle bushing by injecting a water-resistant grease into grease fitting at rear of jet pump output nozzle.

FUEL SYSTEM

All Models

CARBURETOR. Mikuni type B40-32 carburetors are used on all models. Refer to Fig. FJ-3 for an exploded view of carburetor assemblies. Initial setting of idle mixture screw (7—Fig. FJ-3) from a lightly seated position should be 1¾ turns. Final carburetor adjustment should be made with engine at normal operating temperature and running. Make sure cooling system will receive an adequate supply of water prior to operating engine. Adjust idle mixture screw (7) so engine idles smoothly and will accelerate cleanly without hesitation. If necessary, readjust throttle stop screw (2) so engine idle speed is at recommended 650-700 rpm.

Main fuel metering is controlled by main jet (10). Standard main jet size for normal operation is number 155.

To check float height, remove float bowl and invert carburetor. Distance (A—Fig. FJ-4) between main jet (10) and bottom of float (13) should be 15.4-17.5 mm (0.60-0.68 in.) on 50 hp models and 16.5-18.5 mm (0.65-0.73 in.) on 60 hp models. Adjust float height by bending float tang (T).

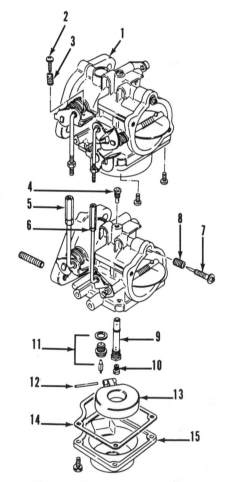

Fig. FJ-3—Exploded view of Mikuni type B40-32 carburetors.

1. Body
2. Throttle stop screw
3. Spring
4. Pilot jet
5. Throttle shaft connector
6. Choke shaft connector
7. Idle mixture screw
8. Spring
9. Main nozzle
10. Main jet
11. Inlet valve assy.
12. Float pin
13. Float
14. Gasket
15. Float bowl

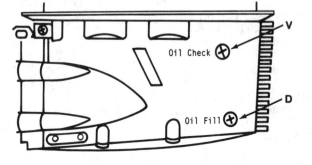

Fig. FJ-1—View identifying jet pump gearcase "OIL FILL" plug (D) and "OIL CHECK" plug (V).

To synchronize throttle plate opening of top carburetor with bottom carburetor, use Suzuki carburetor balancer tool 09913-13121 or equivalent and make adjustment at throttle shaft connector (5—Fig. FJ-3).

Synchronize upper and lower carburetor choke plates, then adjust choke solenoid actuating arm so that choke plates fully close when solenoid plunger is fully retracted.

REED VALVES. The inlet reed valves (Fig. FJ-6) are located on a reed plate between inlet manifold and crankcase. Models prior to 1985 are equipped with steel reed valves. Models after 1984 are equipped with fiberglass reed valves. The reed petals should seat very lightly against the reed plate throughout

their entire length with the least possible tension. Tip of reed petal must not stand open more than 0.2 mm (0.008 in.) from contact surface. Reed stopper opening should not exceed 8.8 mm (0.346 in.) on 50 hp models and 7.95 mm (0.313 in.) on 60 hp models.

Renew reeds if petals are broken, cracked, warped, rusted or bent. Never attempt to bend a reed petal or to straighten a damaged reed. Never install a bent or damaged reed. Seating surface of reed plate should be smooth and flat. When installing reeds or reed stopper, make sure that petals are centered over the inlet holes in reed plate and that the reed stoppers are centered over reed petals. Apply a suitable thread locking solution on reed stopper mounting screws and securely tighten. Apply a thin coating of a form-in-place gasket compound on both sides of reed plate prior to assembling reed plate and intake manifold to crankcase.

FUEL PUMP. A diaphragm type fuel pump is mounted on the side of engine cylinder block and is actuated by pressure and vacuum pulsations from the engine crankcases. Refer to Fig. FJ-8 for exploded view of fuel pump assembly used on models prior to 1985.

Refer to Fig. FJ-9 for exploded view of fuel pump used on models after 1984.

When servicing pump, scribe reference marks across pump body to aid in reassembly. Defective or questionable parts should be renewed. Diaphragm should be renewed if air leaks or cracks are found, or if deterioration is evident.

FUEL TANK AND FUEL FILTER. A carry-on type fuel tank is used. If an inline fuel filter is used, periodically remove inline fuel filter and blow through inlet side of filter with low air pressure to check for blockage. Very little restriction should be noted. Renew inline fuel filter if excessive restriction is noted. If a fuel strainer is attached on the bottom of the fuel tank pickup line, remove and clean strainer if contamination is suspected.

IGNITION

All Models

All models are equipped with a simultaneous capacitor discharge ignition system. The ignition timing is electronically advanced as the magneto base plate is fixed. Ignition timing should not

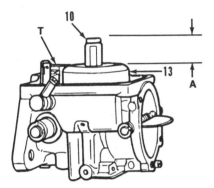

Fig. FJ-4—Float height (A) should be 15.4-17.5 mm (0.60-0.68 in.) on 50 hp models and 16.5-18.5 mm (0.65-0.73 in.) on 60 hp models measured between main jet (10) and bottom of float (13). Bend float tang (T) to adjust.

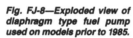

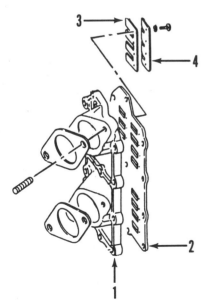

Fig. FJ-6—Exploded view of intake manifold and reed valve assembly.

1. Intake manifold   3. Reed petals
2. Reed plate   4. Reed stopper

Fig. FJ-8—Exploded view of diaphragm type fuel pump used on models prior to 1985.

1. Cover
2. Diaphragm
5. Body
6. Spring
8. Diaphragm
10. Base
11. "O" rings
12. Insulator block

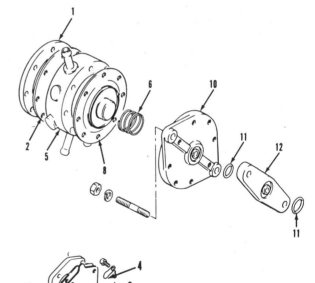

Fig. FJ-9—Exploded view of diaphragm type fuel pump used on models after 1984.

1. Cover
2. Diaphragm
3. Gasket
4. Check valves
5. Body
6. Spring
7. Spring seat
8. Diaphragm
9. Gasket
10. Base

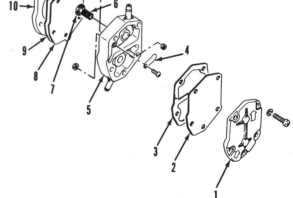

require adjustment, after first being correctly set, unless magneto base plate is moved or an ignition component is renewed.

Ignition timing should be 8 degrees BTDC at 1000 rpm and 25 degrees BTDC at 5000 rpm. Ignition timing can be checked using a suitable power timing light. Immerse vehicle in water so jet pump is submerged or connect a supplemental water supply to flush inlet after removing plug (P—Fig. FJ-14) and using adapter 0510-503.

NOTE: When using a supplemental water supply, do not turn on water until engine is ready to be started as exhaust flooding could occur. Manufacturer recommends using only medium water pressure. Operate engine only at low rpm and for short periods of time.

To check ignition timing, start engine and accelerate to 1000 rpm. Note flywheel timing marks (M—Fig. FJ-15) in relation to index mark (I) on flywheel housing. If ignition timing is incorrect, stop engine and reposition magneto base plate. Make sure supplemental water supply is turned off at approximately same time engine is stopped.

50 HP Models

TROUBLE-SHOOTING. If ignition malfunction occurs, use only approved procedures to prevent damage to the components. The fuel system should be checked first to make certain that faulty running is not caused by incorrect mixture or contaminated fuel. Make sure malfunction is not due to spark plug, wiring or wiring connection failure. Trouble-shoot ignition circuit using Suzuki pocket tester number 09900-25002 or a suitable ohmmeter as follows:

Check condition of low-speed capacitor charge coil by separating the red/black wire connector at magneto base plate and attach a tester lead. Attach the other tester lead to engine ground. Low-speed charge coil can be considered satisfactory if resistance reading is within the limits of 112-149 ohms. Check condition of high-speed charge coil by separating the red/black wire connector and blue/red wire connector at magneto base plate and attach a tester lead to each wire. High-speed charge coil can be considered satisfactory if resistance reading is within the limits of 1.62-1.98 ohms.

To check condition of ignition coil, separate the white/black wire connector at coil and remove high tension wires from spark plugs. Attach one tester lead to white/black wire and other tester lead to coil ground. Primary coil resistance should be within the limits of 0.28-0.38 ohm. Attach a tester lead to each high tension wire. Secondary coil resistance reading should be within the limits of 2980-4030 ohms.

To check condition of CDI module, use tester or ohmmeter in conjunction with test chart shown in Fig. FJ-17. Renew CDI module if required.

60 HP Models

TROUBLE-SHOOTING. If ignition malfunction occurs, use only approved procedures to prevent damage to the components. The fuel system should be checked first to make certain that faulty running is not caused by incorrect mixture or contaminated fuel. Make sure malfunction is not due to spark plug, wiring or wiring connection failure. Trouble-shoot ignition circuit using Suzuki pocket tester number 09900-25002 or a suitable ohmmeter as follows:

Check condition of low-speed capacitor charge coil by separating the blue/red wire connector and black wire connector at magneto base plate and attach a tester lead to each wire. Low-speed charge coil can be considered satisfactory if resistance reading is within the limits of 135-165 ohms. Check condition of high-speed charge coil (pulser coil) by separating the white/red wire connector and black wire connector at magneto base plate and attach a tester lead to each wire. High-speed charge coil can be considered satisfactory if resistance reading is within the limits of 7.29-8.91 ohms.

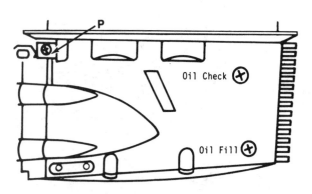

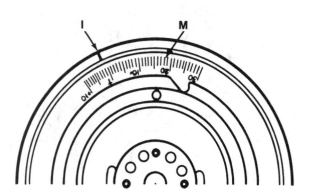

Fig. FJ-14—Remove jet pump plug (P) and use adapter 0510-503 to attach a supplemental water supply.

Fig. FJ-15—Recommended flywheel timing mark (M) should align with index mark (I) on flywheel housing when engine is operated at recommended speed for correct ignition timing.

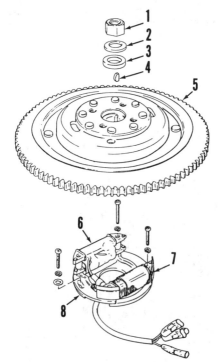

Fig. FJ-16—Exploded view of magneto and case components used on models prior to 1985.

1. Nut
2. Lockwasher
3. Flat washer
4. Key
5. Flywheel
6. High/low-speed coil assy.
7. Lighting coil
8. Magneto baseplate

+ Tester Lead / − Tester Lead	Blue /Red	Red /Black	Black	White /Black
Blue /Red		A	A	A
Red /Black	B		B	B
Black	C	C		A
White /Black	C	C	C	

Fig. FJ-17—Use adjacent chart and values listed below to test condition of CDI module on 50 hp models.

A. Tester needle should show deflection then return toward infinite resistance.*
B. Infinite
C. Continuity
*Momentarily touch blue/red and white/black wires together prior to performing test.

To check condition of ignition coil, separate the black/white wire connector at coil and remove high tension wires from spark plugs. Attach one tester lead to black/white wire and other tester lead to coil ground. Primary coil resistance reading should be within the limits of 0.076-0.104 ohm. Attach a tester lead to each high tension wire. Secondary coil resistance reading should be within the limits of 2980-4030 ohms.

To check condition of CDI module, use tester or ohmmeter in conjunction with test chart shown in Fig. FJ-20. Renew CDI module if required.

CHARGING SYSTEM

All Models

All models are equipped with a lighting coil, rectifier, 20 ampere fuse and battery. The lighting coil should produce 6 amperes at 5000 rpm.

On nonmaintenance-free batteries, the battery electrolyte level should be checked periodically and filled to maximum level with distilled water if required. The battery should be removed from the vehicle and the battery caps removed when charging.

NOTE: Remove 20 ampere fuse prior to removing battery to prevent possible damage to CDI module. Make sure battery charging area is well ventilated.

The lighting coil can be statically tested using a suitable ohmmeter. Refer to Fig. FJ-22. Separate yellow wire and red wire leading from lighting coil to rectifier assembly at connectors. Measure resistance between the two wires leading to lighting coil. Resistance reading should be 0.41-0.50 ohms on 50 hp models and 0.33-0.41 ohms on 60 hp models. Check for continuity between

each of the lighting coil wires and ground. Tester should show infinite resistance at each wire. To check rectifier assembly, first make sure battery is fully charged, lighting coil and in-line 20 ampere fuse test good, all wiring is in good condition and all connectors fit tightly or are securely fastened. Connect a supplemental water supply to flush inlet after removing plug (P—Fig. FJ-14) and using adapter 0510-503.

NOTE: Do not turn on water until engine is ready to be started as exhaust flooding could occur. Manufacturer recommends using only medium water pressure.

Start and run engine. Attach a suitable ammeter between terminal end of fuse and positive battery lead.

NOTE: If a center function type ammeter is NOT being used, make sure ammeter is connected after engine is started or damage to ammeter could result.

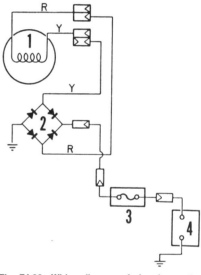

Fig. FJ-22—Wiring diagram of charging system used on all models.

1. Lighting coil
2. Rectifier
3. Fuse (20 ampere)
4. Battery
R. Red
Y. Yellow

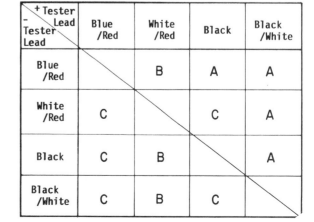

To check condition of ignition coil separate the black/white wire connector...

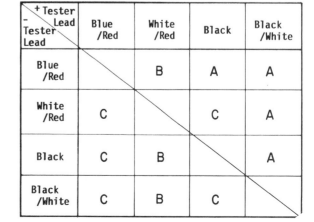

Fig. FJ-19—Exploded view of magneto and case components used on models after 1984.

1. Nut
4. Key
5. Flywheel
7. Lighting coil
8. Magneto base plate
9. Cover
10. Spacer
11. Low-speed coil
12. High-speed coil
13. Magneto case
14. Gasket

Fig. FJ-20—Use chart shown above and values listed below to test condition of CDI module on 60 hp models.

A. Tester needle should show deflection then return toward infinite resistance.
B. Infinite
C. Continuity

+ Tester Lead / − Tester Lead	Blue /Red	White /Red	Black	Black /White
Blue /Red		B	A	A
White /Red	C		C	A
Black	C	B		A
Black /White	C	B	C	

Funjet Boats

Accelerate engine to 5000 rpm while observing ammeter.

NOTE: Do not hold engine speed at 5000 rpm for longer than 10 seconds. Allow engine to return to idle and stabilize before repeating test.

The ammeter should show approximately 6 amperes. Make sure supplemental water supply is turned off at approximately same time engine is stopped.

COOLING SYSTEM

All Models

All models are water-cooled. Forced water is supplied to the engine through holes at the top, rear of jet pump wear ring. As jet pump impeller rpm increases, so does water circulation through cooling system.

Make sure jet pump water intake is kept clean. Inspect all hoses periodically for cracks, kinks or any other damage.

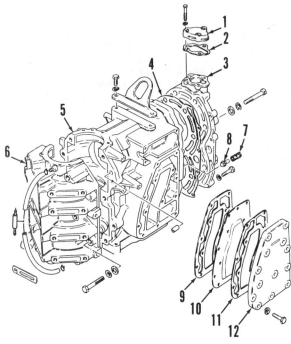

Fig. FJ-24—Exploded view of cylinder block and related components used on 50 hp models.

1. Cover
2. Gasket
3. Cylinder head
4. Gasket
5. Cylinder block
6. Crankcase
7. Spring
8. Valve
9. Gasket
10. Inner exhaust cover
11. Gasket
12. Outer exhaust cover

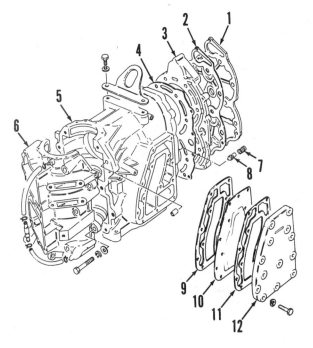

Fig. FJ-25—Exploded view of cylinder block and related components used on 60 hp models.

1. Cylinder head cover
2. Gasket
3. Cylinder head
4. Gasket
5. Cylinder block
6. Crankcase
7. Spring
8. Valve
9. Gasket
10. Inner exhaust cover
11. Gasket
12. Outer exhaust cover

PERSONAL WATER VEHICLE

The cooling system should be flushed out after each operating period when vehicle is used in contaminated or salt water. The cooling system should be flushed out prior to extended periods of storage and prior to usage after extended periods of storage.

To flush the cooling system, connect a supplemental water supply to flush inlet after removing plug (P—Fig. FJ-14) and using adapter 0510-503. Use only clean, fresh water.

NOTE: Do not turn on water until engine is ready to be started as exhaust flooding could occur. Manufacturer recommends using only medium water pressure.

Operate engine at low rpm and for a short period of time to flush system. Make sure supplemental water supply is turned off at approximately same time engine is stopped.

ENGINE

All Models

REMOVE AND REINSTALL. Disconnect battery cables from battery and remove battery from vehicle. Detach engine wiring harness from control panel harness at connector. Disconnect carry-on fuel tank supply line from fuel pump feed line at connector. Disconnect throttle control cable from upper carburetor. Remove the fasteners retaining jet pump outlet nozzle to thrust gate nozzle and fasteners retaining engine and jet pump assembly to vehicle. Use a suitable lifting device to hoist engine and jet pump assembly from vehicle. Place engine and jet pump assembly on a clean work area.

Use a suitable lifting device to hoist engine and jet pump assembly into vehicle. Secure engine and jet pump assembly to vehicle by securely tightening fasteners. Securely tighten fasteners retaining jet pump outlet nozzle to thrust gate nozzle. Complete reinstallation in reverse order of removal.

DISASSEMBLY. Remove the nine nuts, flat washers and lockwashers retaining the engine mounting plate to the engine assembly. Use a suitable lifting device to hoist engine assembly from engine mounting plate. Remove engine base gasket, then set engine assembly on a clean work area for complete disassembly.

Remove the air intake silencer. Disconnect the fuel lines and choke solenoid actuator from the carburetors. Remove the nuts and lockwashers retaining the carburetors. Slide carburetors and gaskets off intake manifold studs. Remove starter motor, ignition components, fuel pump, rectifier, flywheel and magneto base plate assembly. Remove magneto case with base gasket and upper crankshaft seal (11—Fig. FJ-26 or Fig. FJ-27). Remove outer exhaust cover (12—Fig. FJ-24 or Fig. FJ-25), gasket (11) inner exhaust cover (10) and gasket (9). Remove intake manifold (1—Fig. FJ-6) and reed plate (2) with reed valve assemblies. Remove cylinder head cover (1—Fig. FJ-24 or Fig. FJ-25), gasket (2), cylinder head (3) and gasket (4). Clean carbon from combustion chamber and any foreign material accumulation in water passages. Withdraw spring (7) and valve (8) from cylinder block. Remove crankcase retaining cap screws and separate crankcase (6) from cylinder block (5). Remove drive shaft seal housing (22—Fig. FJ-26 or FJ-27). Crankshaft and piston assembly can now be removed from cylinder block.

Engine components are now ready for overhaul as outlined in the appropriate following paragraphs. Refer to the following section for assembly procedure.

ASSEMBLY. Refer to specific service sections when assembling the crankshaft, connecting rod, piston and reed valves. Make sure all joint and gasket surfaces are clean, free from nicks and burrs and hardened cement or carbon.

Whenever the engine is disassembled, it is recommended that all gasket surfaces and mating surfaces without gaskets be carefully checked for nicks, burrs and warped surfaces which might interfere with a tight seal. Cylinder head, head end of cylinder block and some mating surfaces of manifold and crankcase should be checked on a surface plate and lapped, if necessary, to provide a smooth surface. Do not remove any more metal than is necessary.

When assembling engine, first lubricate all friction surfaces and bearings with engine oil. Place thrust rings (15—Fig. FJ-26 or Fig. FJ-27) in cylinder block, then install crankshaft assembly. Make certain main bearing locating pins engage notches (N—Fig. FJ-28) in cylinder block. Apply a suitable high temperature grease to lip portion of crankshaft and drive shaft seals, then install lower crankshaft seal (20—Fig. FJ-26 or Fig. FJ-27) ensuring seal flange properly engages groove in cylinder block. Install drive shaft seal or seals (21) into seal housing (22). Apply a sufficient amount of water-resistant grease on seal housing (22) to fill area between lower crankshaft seal and drive shaft

seal, then install seal housing to cylinder block. Apply a coat of a form-in-place gasket compound on mating surfaces of crankcase and cylinder block and position crankcase on cylinder block. Using tightening sequence shown in Fig. FJ-29, tighten the crankcase screws in 11 N·m (8 ft.-lbs.) increments until a final torque of 36-39 N·m (26-29 ft.-lbs.) is obtained. Install upper crankshaft seal (11—Fig. FJ-26 or Fig. FJ-27) into magneto case with open side towards cylinder block, then install magneto case with gasket on cylinder block assembly.

Cylinder head gasket should be installed with a light coating of a form-in-place gasket compound applied on both sides. With valve (8—Fig. FJ-24 or Fig. FJ-25) and spring (7) installed in cylinder block, position cylinder head, cylinder head cover and related gaskets on cylinder block. Use tightening sequence shown in Fig. FJ-30 and tighten cylinder head cap screws to the following torque values. On 50 hp models, tighten 6 mm cap screws to 8-12 N·m (6-9 ft.-lbs.) and 10 mm cap screws to 40-60 N·m (29-44 ft.-lbs.). On 60 hp models, tighten 6 mm cap screws to 7-9 N·m (5-7 ft.-lbs.), 8 mm cap screws to 34-39 N·m (25-29 ft.-lbs.) and 10 mm cap screws to 39-58 N·m (29-43 ft.-lbs.).

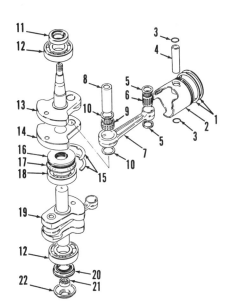

Fig. FJ-26—Exploded view of crankshaft assembly used on 50 hp models.

1. Piston rings	13. Upper crank half
2. Piston	14. Upper crank half
3. Piston pin clips	15. Thrust rings
4. Piston pin	16. Labyrinth seal
5. Thrust washers	17. "O" ring
6. Needle bearing	18. Ball bearing
7. Connecting rod	19. Lower crank assy.
8. Crankpin	20. Lower crankshaft seal
9. Needle bearing	
10. Thrust washers	21. Drive shaft seal
11. Upper crankshaft seal	22. Drive shaft seal housing
12. Ball bearings	

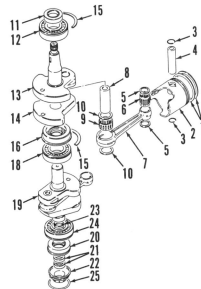

Fig. FJ-27—Exploded view of crankshaft assembly used on 60 hp models.

1. Piston rings	14. Upper crank half
2. Piston	15. Thrust rings
3. Piston pin clips	16. Labyrinth seal
4. Piston pin	18. Ball bearing
5. Thrust washers	19. Lower crank assy.
6. Needle bearing	20. Lower crankshaft seal
7. Connecting rod	
8. Crankpin	21. Drive shaft seals
9. Needle bearing	22. Drive shaft seal housing
10. Thrust washers	
11. Upper crankshaft seal	23. Seal
12. Ball bearing	24. Ball bearing
13. Upper crank half	25. "O" ring

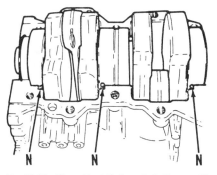

Fig. FJ-28—View of installed crankshaft assembly showing main bearing locating notches.

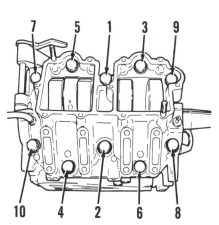

Fig. FJ-29—Crankcase cap screws should be tightened in the sequence shown above.

Funjet Boats

RINGS, PISTONS AND CYLINDERS. The pistons are fitted with two piston rings. Piston rings are interchangeable in grooves but must be installed with manufacturer's marking facing towards closed end (top) of piston. Piston ring end gap should be 0.2-0.4 mm 0.008-0.016 in.) with a maximum allowable ring end gap of 0.8 mm (0.031 in.). Piston-to-cylinder wall clearance should be 0.097-0.112 mm (0.0038-0.0044 in.) on 50 hp models and 0.112-0.127 mm (0.0044-0.0050 in.) on 60 hp models. Pistons and rings are available in standard size as well as 0.25 mm (0.010 in.) and 0.50 mm (0.020 in.) oversizes. Cylinder should be bored to an oversize if cylinder is out-of-round or taper exceeds 0.10 mm (0.004 in.). Install piston on connecting rod so arrow on piston crown will point towards exhaust port when piston is in cylinder.

CONNECTING RODS, BEARINGS AND CRANKSHAFT. Connecting rods, bearings and crankshaft are a pressed together unit. Crankshaft should be disassembled ONLY by experienced service personnel and with proper service equipment.

Caged needle bearings are used at both large and small ends of the connecting rod. Determine rod bearing wear by measuring connecting rod small end side-to-side movement as shown at (A—Fig. FJ-31). Normal side-to-side movement is 5 mm (0.20 in.) or less. Maximum allowable limit of crankshaft runout is 0.05 mm (0.002 in.) measured at bearing surfaces with crankshaft ends supported.

When installing crankshaft, lubricate pistons, rings, cylinders and bearings with engine oil and refer to ASSEMBLY section.

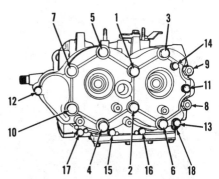

Fig. FJ-30—Cylinder head cap screws should be tightened in the sequence shown. Refer to text for tightening torque specifications.

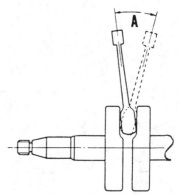

Fig. FJ-31—Maximum side-to-side shake (A) at small end of connecting rod should be 5 mm (0.20 in.) or less.

ENGINE MOUNTING PLATE AND MUFFLER

All Models

R&R AND OVERHAUL. Disconnect battery cables from battery and remove battery from vehicle. Detach engine wiring harness from control panel harness at connector. Disconnect carry-on fuel tank supply line from fuel pump feed line at connector. Disconnect throttle control cable from upper carburetor.

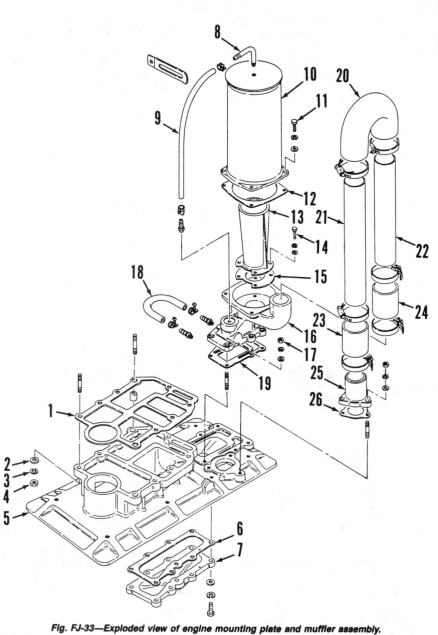

Fig. FJ-33—Exploded view of engine mounting plate and muffler assembly.

1. Gasket
2. Flat washers
3. Lockwashers
4. Nuts
5. Engine mounting plate
6. Gasket
7. Plate
8. Fitting
9. Hose
10. Cooling chamber
11. Screws
12. Gasket
13. Exhaust diffuser
14. Screws
15. Gasket
16. Exhaust chamber base
17. Nuts
18. Hose
19. Gasket
20. Hose
21. Exhaust tube
22. Exhaust tube
23. Hose
24. Hose
25. Exhaust neck
26. Gasket

Remove the fasteners retaining jet pump outlet nozzle to thrust gate nozzle and fasteners retaining engine and jet pump assembly to vehicle. Use a suitable lifting device to hoist engine and jet pump assembly from vehicle. Place engine and jet pump assembly on a clean work area.

Remove the eight nuts and lockwashers retaining the engine mounting plate to the jet pump housing. Use a suitable lifting device to hoist engine assembly from jet pump assembly. Place engine assembly on a clean work bench. Remove the nine nuts, flat washers and lockwashers retaining the engine mounting plate to the engine assembly. Use a suitable lifting device to hoist engine assembly from engine mounting plate.

Refer to Fig. FJ-33 for an exploded view of engine mounting plate and muffler components. Disassemble components after reference to exploded view. Clean any foreign material accumulation in water passages and blow clear with clean compressed air. Check all gasket suffaces for nicks, burrs and warped surfaces which might interfere with a tight seal. Inspect all hoses for cracks, swollen areas or any other signs of damage or deterioration. Renew all gaskets and any other components diagnosed with damage. Apply a form-in-place gasket compound on both sides of gaskets (6, 12, 15, 19 and 26) prior to assembly. Tighten exhaust chamber base (16) retaining nuts (17) to 19-24 N·m (14-18 ft.-lbs.). Tighten exhaust diffuser (13) retaining screws (14) to 16-19 N·m (12-14 ft.-lbs.). Tighten cooling chamber (10) retaining screws (11) to 19-24 N·m (14-18 ft.-lbs.). Securely tighten nuts retaining exhaust neck (25) and screws retaining plate (7). Make sure all hose clamps are securely tightened.

Apply a form-in-place gasket compound on both sides of gasket (1). Use a suitable lifting device to hoist engine assembly onto engine mounting plate. Install the nine flat washers (2), lockwashers (3) and nuts (4) retaining the engine mounting plate to the engine assembly and tighten to 20-24 N·m (15-18 ft.-lbs.). Apply a form-in-place gasket compound on both sides of gasket located between engine mounting plate and jet pump housing. Apply a light coating of a water-resistant grease on drive shaft splines. Use a suitable lifting device to hoist engine assembly onto jet pump assembly. Align eight engine mounting plate studs with holes in jet pump housing.

NOTE: Rotate drive shaft, if needed, to align drive shaft and crankshaft splines.

Install the eight lockwashers and nuts and tighten to 34-39 N·m (25-29 ft.-lbs.).

Use a suitable lifting device to hoist engine and jet pump assembly into vehicle. Secure engine and jet pump assembly to vehicle by securely tightening fasteners. Securely tighten fasteners retaining jet pump outlet nozzle to thrust gate nozzle. Complete reinstallation in reverse order of removal.

ELECTRIC STARTER

All Models

All models are equipped with electric starter shown in Fig. FJ-35. Disassembly is evident after inspection of unit and reference to exploded view. When servicing starter motor, scribe reference marks across motor frame to aid in reassembly. Starter brushes have a standard length of 16 mm (0.63 in.) and should be renewed if worn to 12 mm (0.47 in.). Commutator has a standard diameter of 33 mm (1.30 in.) and should be renewed if worn to a diameter of 31 mm (1.22 in.). Commutator undercut should be 0.5-0.8 mm (0.02-0.03 in.). If undercut is 0.2 mm (0.007 in.) or less, then use a suitable tool to remove the mica between commutator sections until undercut between each section is within the recommended range. After

reassembly, bench test starter motor before installing on engine.

BILGE PUMP

All Models

All models are equipped with an electric bilge pump located at stern of vehicle. A toggle switch located on vehicle control panel is used to supply electrical power to bilge pump. Make sure pickup area at base of bilge pump is kept clean of all foreign debris. Inspect bilge pump discharge hose for cracks or any other signs of damage or deterioration and renew if needed. Make sure hose fits tightly on bilge pump outlet and on fitting in side of hull.

If bilge pump malfunctions, first make sure toggle switch, wiring and inline fuse are in good condition and properly operate prior to renewing bilge pump.

JET PUMP

All Models

REMOVE AND REINSTALL. Disconnect battery cables from battery and remove battery from vehicle. Detach engine wiring harness from control panel harness at connector. Disconnect carry-on fuel tank supply line from fuel

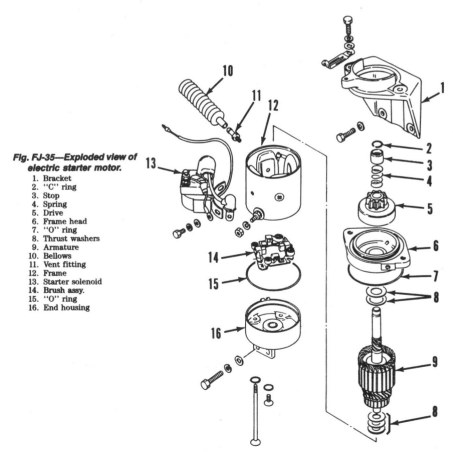

Fig. FJ-35—Exploded view of electric starter motor.
1. Bracket
2. "C" ring
3. Stop
4. Spring
5. Drive
6. Frame head
7. "O" ring
8. Thrust washers
9. Armature
10. Bellows
11. Vent fitting
12. Frame
13. Starter solenoid
14. Brush assy.
15. "O" ring
16. End housing

pump feed line at connector. Disconnect throttle control cable from upper carburetor. Remove the fasteners retaining jet pump outlet nozzle to thrust gate nozzle and fasteners retaining engine and jet pump assembly to vehicle. Use a suitable lifting device to hoist engine and jet pump assembly from vehicle. Place engine and jet pump assembly on a clean work area.

Remove the eight nuts and lockwashers retaining the engine mounting plate to the jet pump housing. Use a

suitable lifting device to hoist engine assembly from jet pump assembly. Place engine assembly on a clean work bench.

Apply a form-in-place gasket compound on both sides of gasket located between engine mounting plate and jet pump housing. Apply a light coating of a water-resistant grease on drive shaft splines. Use a suitable lifting device to hoist engine assembly onto jet pump assembly. Align eight engine mounting plate studs with holes in jet pump housing.

NOTE: Rotate drive shaft, if needed, to align drive shaft and crankshaft splines.

Install the eight lockwashers and nuts and tighten to 34-39 N·m (25-29 ft.-lbs.).

Use a suitable lifting device to hoist engine and jet pump assembly into vehicle. Secure engine and jet pump assembly to vehicle by securely tightening fasteners. Securely tighten fasteners retaining jet pump outlet nozzle to thrust gate nozzle. Complete reinstallation in reverse order of removal.

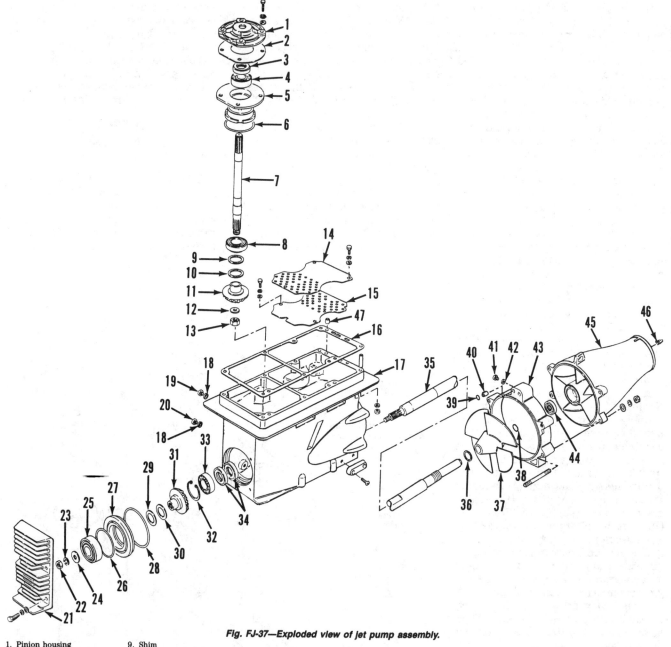

Fig. FJ-37—Exploded view of jet pump assembly.

1. Pinion housing	9. Shim	16. Gasket	24. Flat washer	32. Snap ring	40. Dowel pin
2. Gasket	10. Thrust washer	17. Housing	25. Roller bearing	33. Ball bearing	41. Flush plug
3. Seal	11. Pinion gear	18. Gasket	26. "O" ring	34. Seals	42. Gasket
4. Ball bearing	12. Thrust washer	19. Check plug	27. Bearing carrier	35. Impeller shaft	43. Wear ring
5. Bearing carrier	13. Nut	20. Fill plug	28. "O" ring	36. Thrust washer	44. Seal
6. "O" ring	14. Upper exhaust	21. Front cover	29. Shim	37. Impeller	45. Outlet nozzle
7. Pinion shaft	plate	22. Nut	30. Thrust washer	38. "O" ring	46. Grease fitting
8. Tapered roller	15. Lower exhaust	23. Lockwasher	31. Drive gear	39. "O" ring	47. Dowel pin
bearing	plate				

OVERHAUL. Remove the four countersunk screws retaining rear ski to jet pump housing, then lift jet pump assembly free from rear ski. Remove fill plug (20—Fig. FJ-37) and check plug (19) and allow lubricant to drain into a suitable container.

Remove outlet nozzle (45) and wear ring (43). Prevent impeller shaft rotation, then use a suitable spanner wrench and rotate impeller (37) clockwise to remove. Note thrust washer (36) located in front of impeller (37). Remove front cover (21) and "O" ring (26). Prevent impeller shaft rotation, then use a suitable tool to remove nut (22) and withdraw lockwasher (23) and flat washer (24). Slide impeller shaft (35) out rear of jet pump housing (17). Scribe a reference mark on the forward portion of pinion housing (1). Mark should face forward when reassembling pinion housing (1) to jet pump housing (17). Remove the four cap screws, lockwashers and flat washers securing pinion housing (1), then carefully withdraw pinion housing (1) and gasket (2). Grasp pinion shaft (7) and lift upward to withdraw components (3 through 13) from housing (17). Separate components (3 through 13), if needed, with reference to Fig. FJ-37. Remove components (25 and 27 through 31) by inserting impeller shaft (35) into housing (17) and driving components outward from housing. Use a soft-faced mallet to tap on impeller shaft end. Remove snap ring (32). Remove bearing (33) and seals (34) by using suitable tools and driving components out front of housing or by using a suitable slide-hammer puller assembly.

Inspect gears for excessive wear or any other damage on teeth and splines. Inspect shafts for wear on splined and friction surfaces of bearings and oil seals. Inspect impeller (37) and wear ring (43) for excessive wear or any other damage. Inspect all bearings for freedom of rotation and damaged components. Inspect bearing carrier (5), bearing carrier (27), jet pump housing (17), front cover (21) and outlet nozzle (45) for damage. Make sure water inlet holes at rear of housing (17) are clean of any foreign matter. Use clean compressed air to check for obstruction. Renew all gaskets, "O" rings and seals during reassembly. Renew any other components that are excessively worn or are diagnosed with any other damage.

Reassemble components (1 through 13) and (21 through 34) with the exception of "O" rings (6 and 26).

NOTE: Apply an industrial blueing on drive gear teeth (31) prior to installation. The blueing is used to check gear tooth contact pattern.

Install components into housing (17). Tighten pinion gear nut (13) to 22-26 N·m (16-19 ft.-lbs.). Tighten impeller shaft nut (22) to 68 N·m (50 ft.-lbs.). Tighten pinion housing (1) cap screws to 22-26 N·m (16-19 ft.-lbs.). Tighten front cover (21) cap screws to 19-23 N·m (14-17 ft.-lbs.).

Position a suitable dial indicator and related tools on pinion shaft so backlash between pinion gear (11) and drive gear (31) can be measured. Push impeller shaft (35) inward, then grasp pinion shaft (7) and pull upward. Check backlash between teeth of gears. Backlash should be between 0.15-0.30 mm (0.006-0.012 in.). If not, remove and separate components (1 through 13) and adjust thickness of shim (9) to obtain recommended backlash. Reassemble and install components, then verify recommended backlash has been obtained. Push impeller shaft (35) inward, then grasp pinion shaft (7) and pull upward. Maintain pressure on impeller shaft and rotate pinion shaft a few turns clockwise while maintaining upward pressure. Remove front cover (21) and components (22 through 31). Check drive gear tooth contact pattern on drive side of gear. If pattern is in center of tooth, then no shim adjustment is required. If pattern is towards toe of tooth (center of gear), then shim (9) must be decreased and shim (29) must be increased in equal amounts to maintain correct backlash. If pattern is towards heel of tooth (outside of gear), then shim (9) must be increased and shim (29) must be decreased in equal amounts to maintain correct backlash. Continue procedure until pattern is in center of tooth and backlash is correct.

Remove front cover (21) and install "O" ring (26). Remove pinion components (1 through 13) and install "O" ring (6). Complete reassembly in reverse order of disassembly. Make sure pinion housing (1) is installed with reference mark facing towards front of housing. Apply a water-resistant grease on impeller shaft (35) threads, then install and rotate impeller (37) counterclockwise to thread onto impeller shaft. Use spanner wrench and securely tighten impeller on impeller shaft. Apply a water-resistant grease on lip portion of seal (44) and outlet nozzle bushing. Refer to LUBRICATION section for procedure to fill jet pump gearcase with oil. Refer to previous REMOVE AND REINSTALL section for procedure to reinstall jet pump assembly.

DIRECTIONAL CONTROL

All Models

ADJUSTMENT. The vehicle operational direction is controlled by thrust gate (G—Fig. FJ-39) via cable (C) and lever (L—Fig. FJ-40). When lever (L) is placed in full forward "'F'" position, thrust gate (G—Fig. FJ-39) should completely uncover deflector nozzle (N) opening. When lever (L—Fig. FJ-40) is placed in full reverse "R" position, thrust gate (G—Fig. FJ-39) should completely close-off deflector nozzle (N) opening. Neutral position is located midway between complete forward and complete reverse position. To adjust position of thrust gate (G), remove linkage joint (J) from ball joint on thrust gate (G) bracket. Rotate linkage joint, as needed, in direction required. Reconnect linkage joint (J) to thrust gate ball joint and check directional control operation in the water with the engine at idle position.

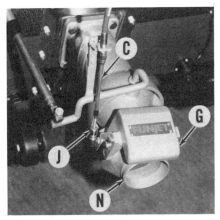

Fig. FJ-39—Cable (C) is attached to thrust gate (G) by linkage joint (J) and thrust gate ball joint. Thrust gate (G) controls vehicle operational direction by position over deflector nozzle (N) opening.

Fig. FJ-40—Lever (L) controls movement of thrust gate (G—Fig. FJ-39) via cable (C—Fig. FJ-39).

STEERING

All Models

ADJUSTMENT. With steering wheel in straight ahead position, deflector nozzle (N—Fig. FJ-39) should be centered or at a 90 degree angle to stern of vehicle. If not, secure steering wheel in a straight ahead position. Remove two nuts (N—Fig. FJ-41) and withdraw steering cable (S) from deflector nozzle bracket (B). Loosen fastener securing tube (T) and rotate tube, as needed, in direction required to center deflector nozzle (N—Fig. FJ-39). Secure steering tube (T—Fig. FJ-41) position, then reinstall steering cable (S) on deflector nozzle bracket (B) and retain with two

Fig. FJ-41—Steering cable (S) is retained to deflector nozzle bracket (B) by two nuts (N). Adjust centering of deflector nozzle (N—Fig. FJ-39) by rotating tube (T) as outlined in text.

nuts (N). Check steering operation and repeat adjustment procedures to reposi-tion deflector nozzle (N—Fig. FJ-39) if required.

JET SKI

KAWASAKI MOTORS CORP., U.S.A.
9950 Jeronimo Road
Irvine, CA 92718-2016

JS300 AND JS300SX

NOTE: Metric fasteners are used throughout vehicle.

General

Engine Make	Own
Engine Type	Two-Stroke; Water-Cooled
Number of Cylinders	1
Bore	76 mm (2.99 in.)
Stroke	64.9 mm (2.55 in.)
Displacement	294 cc (17.94 cu. in.)
Compression Ratio	7.2:1
Engine Lubrication	Oil Injection
Engine Oil Recommendation	Kawasaki Jet Ski or Two-Stroke; BIA Certified TC-W

Tune-Up

Engine Idle Speed	1700-1900 rpm
Spark Plug:	
NGK	B7ES
Champion	N4G
Electrode Gap	0.7-0.8 mm (0.027-0.031 in.)
Ignition:	
Type	CDI
Timing	18° BTDC @ 6000 rpm
Carburetor:	
Make	Mikuni
Model	BN34 Diaphragm
Bore Size	28 mm (1.1 in.)

Sizes—Clearances

Cylinder Bore	76.050-76.065 mm (2.9940-2.9947 in.)
Service Limit	76.10 mm (2.996 in.)
Piston Diameter Measured 18 mm (0.71 in.) from Skirt Bottom and 90° to Pin Bore	75.961-75.976 mm (2.990-2.991 in.)
Service Limit	75.81 mm (2.985 in.)
Piston-to-Cylinder Wall Clearance	0.074-0.084 mm (0.0030-0.0033 in.)
Piston Ring End Gap	0.2-0.4 mm (0.008-0.016 in.)
Service Limit	0.7 mm (0.027 in.)
Maximum Cylinder Head Warp	0.025 mm (0.001 in.)
Connecting Rod Radial Clearance	0.037-0.049 mm (0.0015-0.0019 in.)

Sizes—Clearances (Cont.)

Service Limit	0.10 mm (0.004 in.)
Connecting Rod Side Clearance	0.45-0.55 mm (0.018-0.022 in.)
Service Limit	0.8 mm (0.03 in.)
Maximum Connecting Rod Bend or Twist Measured Over a 100 mm (3.9 in.) Length	0.2 mm (0.008 in.)
Maximum Crankshaft Runout at Main Bearing Journal	0.08 mm (0.003 in.)

Capacities

Fuel Tank:	
Model JS300	13 L (3.5 gal)
Model JS300SX	19 L (5 gal.)
Engine Oil Tank:	
Model JS300	1.7 L (0.45 gal.)
Model JS300SX	2.2 L (0.58 gal.)
Starter Gear Housing	0.2 L (0.42 pt.)

Tightening Torques

Carburetor Mounting Nuts	19 N·m (14 ft.-lbs.)
Cylinder Head Nuts	25 N·m (18 ft.-lbs.)
Cylinder Base Nuts	34 N·m (25 ft.-lbs.)
Engine Mounting Cap Screws	37 N·m (27 ft.-lbs.)
Engine Drive Flange	98 N·m (72 ft.-lbs.)
Drive Shaft Drive Flange	98 N·m (72 ft.-lbs.)
Intermediate Housing Mounting Cap Screws	16 N·m (12 ft.-lbs.)
Intermediate Housing Front Cover Cap Screws	16 N·m (12 ft.-lbs.)
Jet Pump Mounting Cap Screws	22 N·m (16 ft.-lbs.)
Flywheel Screw	39 N·m (29 ft.-lbs.)
Spark Plug	27 N·m (20 ft.-lbs.)

Tightening Torques (Cont.)
Standard Fasteners:

5 mm	3.4-4.9 N·m
	(30-43 in.-lbs.)
6 mm	5.9-7.8 N·m
	(52-69 in.-lbs.)
8 mm	14-19 N·m
	(10-14 ft.-lbs.)
10 mm	25-39 N·m
	(18-29 ft.-lbs.)
12 mm	44-61 N·m
	(32-45 ft.-lbs.)
14 mm	73-98 N·m
	(54-72 ft.-lbs.)
16 mm	115-155 N·m
	(85-114 ft.-lbs.)
18 mm	165-225 N·m
	(121-165 ft.-lbs.)
20 mm	225-325 N·m
	(165-239 ft.-lbs.)

LUBRICATION

All Models

The engine is lubricated by oil mixed with the fuel. All models are equipped with oil injection. The manufacturer recommends using Kawasaki Jet Ski Oil or a BIA certified two-stroke TC-W engine oil. During break-in (first five hours or three tankfuls) of a new or rebuilt engine, mix fuel with oil in fuel tank at a ratio of 50:1. Switch to straight fuel in fuel tank at the completion of the break-in period. Manufacturer recommends regular or no-lead automotive gasoline having a minimum octane rating of 87. Gasoline and oil should be thoroughly mixed in fuel tank when used during break-in period.

Grease intermediate housing through grease fitting (F—Fig. JS1-1) with Shell MP or Alvania EP1 grease every 25 hours or more frequent if needed. Inject Shell MP or Alvania EP1 grease into grease fitting (G—Fig. JS1-2) at rear of jet pump housing every 25 hours or more frequent if needed to grease rear bushing.

Starter gear housing (H—Fig. JS1-3) should contain 0.2 L (0.42 pt.) of a good quality SAE 10W-40, 10W-50, 20W-40 or 20W-50 automotive oil with an API classification of SE or SF. Starter gear housing oil should be renewed every 100 hours or more frequent if needed.

Remove plug at base of housing and fill cap (C) to drain oil. Install drain plug and pour 0.2 L (0.42 pt.) of recommended oil into fill cap (C) opening to fill starter gear housing.

Lubricate all cables, linkage and pivots with WD-40 or Bel-Ray 6 in 1 every 25 hours or more frequent if needed.

FUEL SYSTEM

All Models

CARBURETOR. Refer to Fig. JS1-5 for an exploded view of Mikuni type BN34 diaphragm carburetor used on all models. (On JS300 models, choke plate (21—Fig. JS1-5) is actuated by choke knob (K—Fig. JS1-6) on control panel via a cable and linkage. On JS300SX models, choke plate (21—Fig. JS1-5) is actuated by choke knob (K—Fig. JS1-7) on left side of riding platform via a cable and linkage.

Initial setting of low speed mixture needle (22—Fig. JS1-5) is 5/8 turn out from a lightly seated position on JS300 models and 1-9/16 turns out from a lightly seated position on JS300SX models. Initial setting of high speed mixture needle (29) is 1 turn out from a lightly seated position on JS300 models and 1-1/4 turns out from a lightly seated position on JS300SX models. Final carburetor adjustments must be made with

engine at normal operating temperature and running. Clockwise rotation of either needle leans the mixture. Adjust low speed mixture needle (22) until smooth acceleration from the idle position is noted. After adjusting low speed mixture needle, adjust idle speed screw (37—Fig. JS1-8) until engine idle speed is approximately 1700-1900 rpm with throttle lever completely released. To adjust high speed fuel:air mixture, the engine spark plug must be removed and insulator tip color noted.

NOTE: Make sure that fuel tank contains straight fuel.

Make sure cooling system will receive an adequate supply of water, then operate and sustain engine at wide-open throttle for a suitable test period. Stop the engine with throttle in wide-open position. Remove spark plug and note insulator tip color. Normal insulator tip color is brown to light tan. If insulator tip appears to be light tan to white in color, then mixture is too lean and high speed mixture needle (29—Fig. JS1-5) should be rotated outward (counterclockwise) ¼ turn to richen mixture. If insulator tip appears to be dark brown to black in color, then mixture is too rich and high speed mixture needle (29) should be rotated inward (clockwise) ¼ turn to lean mixture. Clean, regap and reinstall spark

Fig. JS1-1—Intermediate housing is greased through grease fitting (F).

Fig. JS1-2—Jet pump drive shaft rear bushing is greased through grease fitting (G) at rear of jet pump housing.

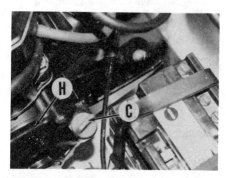

Fig. JS1-3—Refer to text for starter gear housing (H) recommended lubricant and lubricant quantity. Add lubricant through fill cap (C) opening.

plug and continue test procedure until spark plug insulator tip is normal color.

The fuel pump and regulating diaphragm (12) can be removed after removing the six through-bolts. Note that alignment tabs on components (3 through 12) are provided to assist in proper alignment during reassembly.

Do not remove choke plate, throttle plate or shafts unless necessary. The choke and throttle plate retaining screws are either staked or retained with a thread locking solution to prevent loosening. If screws are removed, properly stake or apply a suitable thread locking solution on threads prior to assembly. Inlet needle valve lever (17) must be flush with floor of housing recess when needle valve is seated. Refer to Fig. JS1-9. If lever must be adjusted, push down on lever immediately above spring to collapse the spring, then bend the end which contacts needle valve.

REED VALVES. A vee type reed valve assembly is located between the intake manifold and crankcase. Remove intake manifold for access to reed valve assembly.

Renew reeds if petals are broken, cracked, warped or bent. Do not at-

Fig. JS1-8—View identifies location of idle speed screw (37).

Fig. JS1-5—Exploded view of Mikuni type BN34 diaphragm carburetor used on all models.

1. Fuel inlet cover	11. Gasket	20. Choke shaft
2. Gasket	12. Regulating diaphragm	21. Choke plate
3. Inlet body	13. Plate	22. Low speed mixture needle
4. Check valve diaphragm	14. Diaphragm	23. Washers
5. Gasket	15. Gasket	24. Springs
6. Pump body	16. Inlet valve assy.	25. "O" rings
7. Diaphragm	17. Valve lever	26. Throttle shaft
8. Gasket	18. Pivot shaft	27. Throttle plate
9. Gasket	19. Spring	28. Body
10. Diaphragm cover		

29. High speed mixture needle	33. Spacers
30. Banjo bolt	34. Bracket
31. Gaskets	35. Cable lever
32. Return line fitting	36. Spring
	37. Idle screw

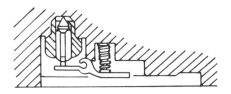

Fig. JS1-9—Inlet needle valve lever should be flush with floor of housing recess as shown.

Fig. JS1-6—View identifies location of choke knob (K) and fuel selector valve (V) on JS300 models.

Fig. JS1-7—On JS300SX models, choke knob (K) is located on left side of riding platform and is rotated to control choke plate position.

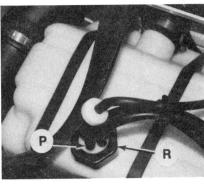

Fig. JS1-10—Ring nut (R) secures pickup assembly (P) in fuel tank.

tempt to bend or straighten reeds. Reed seating surface on reed blocks should be smooth and flat. Maximum allowable reed petal stand open is 0.2 mm (0.008 in.).

FUEL PUMP. The fuel pump is an integral part of the carburetor. The fuel pump assembly can be overhauled without overhauling the complete carburetor.

With reference to Fig. JS1-5, disassemble the fuel pump assembly. Inspect all components for excessive wear or any other damage and renew if needed. Clean components as needed with a suitable cleaning solution. Blow dry with clean compressed air. If compressed air is not available, use only lint-free cloths to wipe dry. Make sure all passages are clear of any obstructions.

With reference to Fig. JS1-5, reassemble the fuel pump assembly with new gaskets. Securely tighten the six through-bolts.

FUEL TANK AND FUEL FILTER. A fuel strainer is attached on the bottom of the "ON" fuel tank pickup line and on the bottom of the "RES" fuel tank pickup line. The pickup lines are contained within fuel tank pickup assembly (P—Fig. JS1-10). On JS300 models, an inline sediment bowl (I—Fig. JS1-11) is located between fuel selector valve (V—Fig. JS1-6) and carburetor fuel pump intake. After every 25 hours of

operation or more frequent if needed, unscrew ring nut (N—Fig. JS1-11) and withdraw cup (C) with sealing ring from base. Clean cup with a suitable cleaning solution. Renew sealing ring and securely tighten nut (N) during installation of cup (C). After every 25 hours of operation or more frequent if needed, fuel tank strainers (S—Fig. JS1-12) should be cleaned. Unscrew ring nut (R—Fig. JS1-10) and withdraw pickup assembly (P). Clean strainers (S—JS1-12) with a suitable cleaning solution and a soft-bristled brush if needed. Renew sealing ring and securely tighten nut (R—Fig. JS1-10) during installation of pickup assembly (P).

THROTTLE LEVER FREE PLAY. Throttle lever should have a small amount of free play prior to activating carburetor throttle shaft when throttle lever is in released position. To adjust, rotate locknuts (N—Fig. JS1-13) up or down cable housing end as needed until a small amount of free play is noted. Tighten locknuts (N) to retain adjustment.

FLAME ARRESTOR. A flame arrestor is located beneath cover (C—Fig. JS1-14). Every 25 hours or more frequent if needed, remove two cap screws (S) on each side of cover and withdraw cover and flame arrestor. Inspect flame arrestor for contamination and use clean compressed air to blow clean.

Renew flame arrestor if damage is noted. Install flame arrestor with curved side facing down. Apply Loctite Lock N' Seal or a suitable equivalent on threads of the four cap screws (S) retaining cover (C) and securely tighten.

OIL INJECTION

All Models

BLEEDING PUMP. To bleed trapped air from oil supply line or pump, first make sure vehicle is level and oil tank is full.

Use a short piece of a suitable sized hose and an adapter and connect a supplemental water supply to fitting on exhaust manifold after removing cooling system supply hose (H—Fig. JS1-18) routed from jet pump.

NOTE: When using a supplemental water supply, do not turn on water until engine is ready to be started as exhaust flooding could occur. Operate engine only at low rpm or during a test, do not exceed recommended high rpm and only operate for a short period of time.

Fig. JS1-14—Remove two cap screws (S) on each side of cover (C) to withdraw cover (C) and flame arrestor.

Fig. JS1-11—On JS300 models, a sediment bowl assembly (I) is used. Unscrew ring nut (N) to withdraw cup (C) with sealing ring.

Fig. JS1-13—Rotate locknuts (N) up or down cable housing end as needed to adjust throttle lever free play.

Fig. JS1-12—View identifies fuel tank strainers (S). Reserve "RES" is longest pickup line.

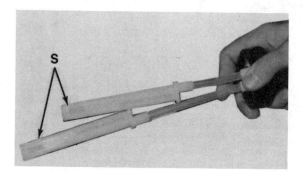

Fig. JS1-16—View identifies oil injection pump assembly (P), air bleed screw (B) and transparent outlet hose (T).

Place a container under oil pump (P—Fig. JS1-16). Open oil pump air bleed screw (B) two or three turns to allow oil to seep out around screw threads. After no air bubbles are noticed, close air bleed screw (B).

Start engine, then turn on supplemental water supply. Adjust water pressure to where a small amount of water is being discharged out bypass outlet on side of hull. Note transparent outlet hose (T). Allow engine to idle until no air bubbles are noted in transparent outlet hose (T).

Turn off supplemental water supply and stop engine.

NOTE: Make sure engine is not operated without a supply of water longer than 10-15 seconds or damage to engine and/or exhaust components could result.

OIL PUMP OUTPUT. Connect a supplemental water supply as previously outlined under BLEEDING PUMP.

NOTE: A fuel:oil mixture of 50:1 must be supplied to engine during test.

Disconnect transparent outlet hose (T—Fig. JS1-16) from engine inlet fitting. Route end of transparent outlet hose (T) into a suitable measuring container. Connect a tachometer to engine. Start engine, then turn on supplemental water supply. Adjust water pressure to where a small amount of water is being discharged out bypass outlet on side of hull. Accelerate engine to 6000 rpm and maintain for one minute. After one minute, note amount of oil in measuring container. Allow engine to return to idle position, then turn off supplemental water supply and stop engine.

NOTE: If oil pump output test must be reperformed, allow engine to idle for a short period with supplemental water supply circulating through cooling system. Do not sustain engine at a high rpm for an extend-ed period when not operated under a load and do not exceed the recommended testing rpm of 6000.

Oil pump can be considered satisfactory if measured oil is within the range of 3.3-4.1 mL (0.11-0.14 oz.). If oil pump output is not within the recommended range, then oil pump must be renewed.

IGNITION

All Models

All models are equipped with a capacitor discharge ignition system. The ignition timing is electronically advanced as the magneto base plate is fixed. Ignition timing should not require adjustment, after first being correctly set, unless magneto base plate is moved or an ignition component is renewed.

IGNITION TIMING. Ignition timing should be 18 degrees or 1.99 mm (0.08 in.) BTDC at 6000 rpm. Ignition timing can be checked using a suitable power timing light. Remove oil injection pump assembly (P—Fig. JS1-16) and flywheel cover (F—Fig. JS1-18).

NOTE: A fuel:oil mixture of 50:1 must be supplied to engine during test.

Note flywheel timing mark (M—Fig. JS1-19) and crankcase timing mark (T).

Use a short piece of a suitable sized hose and an adapter and connect a supplemental water supply to fitting on exhaust manifold after removing cooling system supply hose (H—Fig. JS1-18) routed from jet pump.

NOTE: When using a supplemental water supply, do not turn on water until engine is ready to be started as exhaust flooding could occur. Operate engine only at low rpm or during a test, do not exceed recommended high rpm and only operate for a short period of time.

Connect a tachometer to engine. Start engine, then turn on supplemental water supply. Adjust water pressure to where a small amount of water is being discharged out bypass outlet on side of hull. Accelerate engine to 6000 rpm. Use power timing light and check alignment of flywheel timing mark (M—Fig. JS1-19) with crankcase timing mark (T). Allow engine to return to idle position, then turn off supplemental water supply and stop engine.

NOTE: Make sure engine is not operated without a supply of water longer than 10-15 seconds or damage to engine and/or exhaust components could result.

NOTE: If ignition timing test must be reperformed, allow engine to idle for a short period with supplemental water supply circulating through cooling system. Do not sustain engine at a high rpm for an extended period when not operated under a load and do not exceed the recommended testing rpm of 6000.

If ignition timing is incorrect, remove flywheel retaining screw, then use a suitable puller and withdraw flywheel. Loosen magneto base plate screws and rotate base plate as needed. Tighten magneto base plate screws, then reinstall flywheel and tighten retaining screw to 39 N·m (29 ft.-lbs.).

Recheck ignition timing. Continue procedure until correct ignition timing is obtained. Apply a water-resistant grease on flywheel cover (F—Fig. JS1-18) "O" ring. Apply a suitable thread locking solution on threads of flywheel cover retaining screws, then install flywheel cover (F) and securely tighten screws.

Fig. JS1-18—A supplemental water supply can be connected to fitting on exhaust manifold after removing cooling system supply hose (H) routed from jet pump. Engine flywheel is located behind flywheel cover (F). Unscrew cap (C) and withdraw wiring harness leading to electric box to expose terminal ends of wires leading to ignition exciter coil and charging system charge coil.

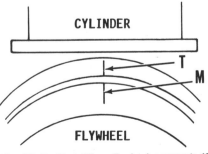

Fig. JS1-19—Mark (M) on flywheel represents 18 degrees BTDC. When engine is operated at 6000 rpm, flywheel mark (M) should align with crankcase mark (T).

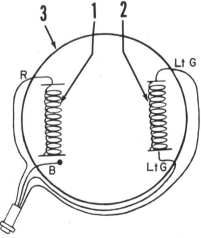

Fig. JS1-20—View identifying magneto components and color of leads.

1. Exciter coil
2. Charge coil
3. Magneto base plate

B. Black
R. Red
Lt G. Light green

TROUBLE-SHOOTING. If ignition malfunction occurs, use only approved procedures to prevent damage to the components. The fuel system should be checked first to make certain that faulty running is not caused by contaminated fuel. Make sure malfunction is not due to spark plug, wiring or wiring connection failure. Trouble-shoot ignition circuit using a suitable ohmmeter as follows:

Unscrew cap (C—Fig. JS1-18) and withdraw wiring harness leading to electric box to expose terminal ends of wires leading to exciter coil. Refer to Fig. JS1-20. Check condition of exciter coil (1) by attaching one tester lead to terminal end of red wire (R) and attaching other tester lead to terminal end of black wire (B) leading to magneto assembly. Exciter coil can be considered satisfactory if resistance reading is within the limits of 168-252 ohms. Exciter coil is serviceable after removing flywheel cover and flywheel. Make sure a suitable puller is used to withdraw flywheel. Tighten flywheel retaining screw to 39 N·m (29 ft.-lbs.). Recheck ignition timing as previously outlined

under IGNITION TIMING. Apply a water-resistant grease on flywheel cover "O" ring. Apply a suitable thread locking solution on threads of flywheel cover retaining screws, then install flywheel cover (F—Fig. JS1-18) and securely tighten screws.

Ignition coil secondary winding resistance should be 5000-7500 ohms. If no components are found faulty, then renew CDI module/ignition coil assembly with a known good assembly and recheck engine operation.

CHARGING SYSTEM

All Models

All models are equipped with a charge coil, rectifier/regulator and battery. Standard battery has a 19 ampere hour, 12 volt rating. The charge coil should produce 12-15 ac volts when engine is operated throughout rpm range. Rectifier/regulator assembly should prevent regulated voltage from exceeding 15 dc volts.

The battery electrolyte level should be checked periodically and filled to max-

imum level with distilled water if required. The battery should be removed from the vehicle and the battery caps removed when charging. The manufacturer recommends charging the battery at a rate of 1.9 amperes for a period of 10 hours. Do not exceed recommended charging rate.

NOTE: Make sure battery charging area is well ventilated.

The charge coil can be statically tested using a suitable ohmmeter. Unscrew cap (C—Fig. JS1-18) and withdraw wiring harness leading to electric box to expose terminal ends of wires leading to charge coil. Refer to Fig. JS1-20. Check condition of charge coil (2) by attaching one tester lead to terminal end of one light green wire (Lt G) and attaching other tester lead to terminal end of remaining light green wire (Lt G). Resistance reading should be 2.4-3.6 ohms. Check resistance between each charge coil wire and black wire. Tester should show 1.2-1.8 ohms resistance at each wire. To check rectifier/regulator assembly, refer to chart shown in Fig. JS1-21. To check rectifier/regulator during operation, first make sure battery is fully charged, charge coil test good and all wiring is in good condition and all connectors fit tightly or are securely fastened. Attach test leads of a suitable voltmeter directly on battery terminals.

Use a short piece of a suitable sized hose and an adapter and connect a supplemental water supply to fitting on exhaust manifold after removing cooling system supply hose (H—Fig. JS1-18) routed from jet pump.

NOTE: Do not turn on water until engine is ready to be started as exhaust flooding could occur.

Start engine, then turn on supplemental water supply. Adjust water pressure to where a small amount of water is being discharged out bypass outlet on side of hull. Accelerate engine while observing voltmeter. The voltmeter should

+Tester Lead / −Tester Lead	Orange	Ground	Light Green	Light Green
Orange		A	A	A
Ground	A		A	A
Light Green	B	B		A
Light Green	B	B	A	

Fig. JS1-21—Use adjacent chart and values listed below to test condition of rectifier/regulator assembly.
 A. Infinite resistance
 B. Continuity

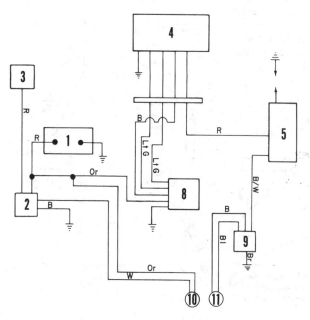

Fig. JS1-22—Wiring diagram typical of all JS300 and JS300SX models. On JS300SX models, a controller is connected in black/white (B/W) wire between CDI module/ignition coil (5) and stop switch relay (9). Components (2, 5, 8 and 9) are contained within electric box.

 1. Battery
 2. Starter solenoid
 3. Starter motor
 4. Magneto assy.
 5. CDI module/ignition coil
 8. Rectifier/regulator
 9. Stop switch relay
 10. Start switch
 11. Stop switch
 B. Black
 R. Red
 W. White
 Bl. Blue
 Br. Brown
 Or. Orange
 B/W. Black/white
 Lt. G. Light green

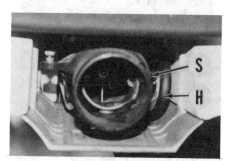

Fig. JS1-23—View identifies jet pump cooling system supply hose (H) and bilge siphon hose (S). Bilge siphon hose fitting is located on top jet pump steering nozzle on Model JS300SX.

show approximately 15 dc volts. Allow engine to return to idle position then turn off supplemental water supply and stop engine.

NOTE: Make sure engine is not operated without a supply of water longer than 10-15 seconds or damage to engine and/or exhaust components could result.

COOLING SYSTEM

All Models

All models are water-cooled. Forced water is supplied to the engine through jet pump outlet fitting and directed through hose (H—Fig. JS1-23) to fitting on exhaust manifold. As jet pump impeller rpm increases, so does water circulation through cooling system.

Make sure jet pump water intake grill (W—Fig. JS1-24) is kept clean. Inspect all hoses periodically for cracks, kinks or any other damage and renew if needed. The cooling system should be flushed out after each operating period when vehicle is used in contaminated or salt water. The cooling system should be flushed out prior to extended periods of storage and prior to usage after extended periods of storage.

To flush the cooling system, use a short piece of suitable sized hose and an adapter and connect a supplemental water supply to fitting on exhaust manifold after removing cooling system supply hose (H—Fig.JS1-18) routed from jet pump. Use only clean, fresh water.

NOTE: Do not turn on water until engine is ready to be started as exhaust flooding could occur. Operate engine only at low rpm.

Start engine then turn on supplemental water supply. Adjust water pressure to where a small amount of water is being discharged out bypass outlet on side of hull. Allow water to circulate through system for several minutes. Turn off supplemental water supply. If vehicle is to be stored for an extended period, raise rear of vehicle and quickly accelerate engine between idle and one-quarter throttle a couple of times. This is to force out all water within exhaust system, thus preventing damage from developing contaminates or freezing.

NOTE: Make sure engine is not operated without a supply of water longer than 10-15 seconds or damage to engine and/or exhaust components could result.

ENGINE

All Models

REMOVE AND REINSTALL. Disconnect battery cables from battery and remove battery from vehicle. Remove throttle cable and choke cable from carburetor. Remove hoses from carburetor, label if needed and plug openings. Remove flame arrestor and carburetor fasteners, then withdraw components. Cover intake manifold passage to prevent entrance of foreign debris. Remove oil supply hose from oil injection pump and plug openings. Disconnect all electrical wiring that will interfere with engine removal and label for reassembly. Remove cooling system hoses from exhaust pipe and elbow. Remove exhaust pipe and elbows. Remove drive coupler shield (S—Fig. JS1-34). Remove four cap screws (C—Fig. JS1-26) and washers retaining engine to vehicle hull. Note shims located under engine mounts and identify each shim for installation in original location. Remove any other components that will interfere with engine removal. Use a suitable lifting device to hoist engine assembly from vehicle. Place engine assembly on a clean work bench.

Use a suitable lifting device to hoist engine assembly into vehicle. Make sure

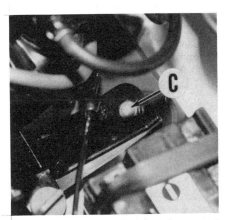

Fig. JS1-26—Cap screw (C) and washer on each side of front and rear engine crankcase mounts retains engine assembly to engine bases.

Fig. JS1-24—Jet pump water intake grill (W) must be kept clean of all foreign debris.

coupler is located between engine drive flange and drive shaft drive flange. Install shims into original locations under engine mounts. Lay a straightedge (S—Fig. JS1-27) across top of engine drive flange and drive shaft drive flange. Engine drive flange should be 0-0.3 mm (0-0.012 in.) higher than drive shaft drive flange. Measure distance (A—Fig. JS1-28) and distance (B). Distance (B) should not exceed distance (A) by more than 0.6 mm (0.024 in.). Measure clearance between engine drive flange and coupler and drive shaft drive flange and coupler. Total of the two clearance measurements should not exceed 0.5 mm (0.020 in.). If recommended settings are not measured, then adjust thickness of shims located under engine mounts until recommended settings are obtained. Apply Loctite Lock N' Seal or a suitable equivalent on threads of four cap screws (C—Fig. JS1-26) and tighten cap screws to 37 N·m (27 ft.-lbs.). Remeasure as previously outlined to verify engine drive flange to drive shaft flange settings are as recommended. Adjust shim thickness if needed.

Complete reassembly in reverse order of disassembly.

DISASSEMBLY. Remove cylinder head nuts, then pry cylinder head off cylinder. Remove cylinder base nuts, then withdraw cylinder. Remove oil injection pump and flywheel cover. Hold flywheel with a suitable tool and rotate engine drive flange off crankshaft using Kawasaki tool 57001-1025. Remove electric starter motor. Drain oil from starter gear housing. Remove starter gear housing, crankshaft collar and "O"

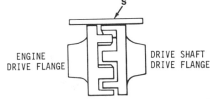

Fig. JS1-27—Engine drive flange should be 0-0.3 mm (0-0.012 in.) higher than drive shaft drive flange. Lay straightedge (S) across components and use a feeler gage to measure.

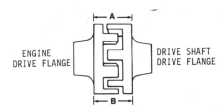

Fig. JS1-28—Distance (B) should not exceed distance (A) by more than 0.6 mm (0.024 in.).

ring. Use a suitable puller and withdraw starter clutch and idle gear. Remove screw retaining flywheel, then use a suitable puller and withdraw flywheel. Remove magneto base plate with ignition components. Remove eight cap screws securing crankcase halves together. Three crankcase screws outside starter gear housing are stainless steel. Identify cap screws for installation in original locations. Use Kawasaki tool 57001-1098, 156 or a suitable puller assembly and separate starter gear housing crankcase half from crankshaft assembly and flywheel side crankcase half. Press crankshaft assembly from flywheel side crankcase.

Engine components are now ready for overhaul as outlined in the appropriate following paragraphs. Refer to the following section for assembly procedure.

ASSEMBLY. Refer to specific service sections when assembling the crankshaft, connecting rod and piston. Make sure all joint and gasket surfaces are clean, free from nicks and burrs and hardened cement or carbon.

Whenever the engine is disassembled, it is recommended that all gasket surfaces and mating surfaces without gaskets be carefully checked for nicks, burrs and warped surfaces which might interfere with a tight seal. Cylinder head and mating surfaces of crankcase halves should be checked on a surface plate and lapped, if necessary, to provide a smooth surface. Do not remove any more metal than is necessary.

When assembling engine, first lubricate all friction surfaces and bearings with engine oil. Press oil seal into flywheel side crankcase half with

manufacturer's marks toward flywheel. Press oil seal into starter gear housing crankcase half with manufacturer's marks toward inside of crankcase. Apply a high temperature grease on lip of each oil seal. Press crankshaft main bearings into crankcase halves. Position Kawasaki tool 57001-1174 or a suitable equivalent over connecting rod and adjust tool to fit tightly between crankshaft halves.

NOTE: The tool is used to protect crankshaft alignment during installation of crankshaft assembly into crankcase halves.

Press crankshaft assembly into flywheel side crankcase half. Wipe mating surfaces of crankcase halves clean and make sure surfaces are dry. Apply a coating of Kawasaki Bond or a suitable form-in-place gasket compound on crankcase mating surface of flywheel side crankcase half. Press starter gear housing crankcase half onto flywheel side crankcase half. Remove special tool from connecting rod. Install eight crankcase securing cap screws into original locations. Apply Loctite Lock N' Seal or a suitable equivalent on threads of three stainless steel screws prior to installation. Tighten all screws in small increments using a crisscross pattern until securely tightened.

NOTE: Make sure crankshaft assembly rotates freely. If not, split crankcase halves and repair as needed.

Reassemble flywheel side and starter gear side of crankcase in reverse order of disassembly while noting the following: Align mark on magneto base plate with projection on crankcase and securely tighten two retaining screws. Tighten flywheel screw to 39 N·m (29 ft.-lbs.). The manufacturer recommends applying a molybdenum disulfide grease

on starter gear holder where starter gear bushing rides and on starter gear bushing. One-way clutch assembly should rotate freely when rotated in counterclockwise direction and lock when rotated in clockwise direction. Install a new "O" ring into starter gear housing cover and flywheel cover. Install starter gear housing cover and apply Loctite Lock N' Seal or a suitable equivalent on threads of retaining screws and securely tighten. Install engine drive flange and tighten to 98 N·m (72 ft.-lbs.) using Kawasaki tool 57001-1025. Refill starter gear housing as outlined in LUBRICATION section. Install flywheel cover and apply Loctite Lock N' Seal or a suitable equivalent on threads of retaining screws and securely tighten.

Tighten cylinder base nuts to 34 N·m (25 ft.-lbs.). Apply a thin coating of a RTV silicone sealer on both sides of cylinder head gasket. Install cylinder head gasket with arrow facing up and pointing toward exhaust side of cylinder. Install cylinder head so tab on cylinder head aligns with tab on cylinder head gasket. Use a crisscross pattern and tighten cylinder head nuts to 25 N·m (18 ft.-lbs.).

PISTON, PIN, RINGS AND CYLINDER. Recommended piston skirt-to-cylinder clearance is 0.074-0.084 mm (0.0030-0.0033 in.). Bore cylinder to 0.50 mm (0.020 in.) or 1.0 mm (0.040 in.) oversize if measured piston skirt-to-cylinder clearance is beyond limit. Piston and piston rings are available in 0.50 mm (0.020 in.) and 1.0 mm (0.040 in.) oversizes. Inspect cylinder wall for scoring. If minor scoring is noted, cylinder should be honed to smooth out cylinder wall.

Recommended piston ring end gap for top and second ring is 0.2-0.4 mm (0.008-0.016 in.) with a service limit of 0.7 mm (0.027 in.). The top and second piston ring is semi-keystone shaped. Install piston rings on piston with manufacturer's mark facing top of piston. Make sure piston rings properly align with locating pins in ring grooves.

When reassembling, install piston on connecting rod so arrow on top of piston faces toward exhaust side of cylinder after assembly. Install new piston pin retaining clips (1—Fig. JS1-30); openings of retaining clips must face top or bottom of piston. Coat bearing, piston, rings and cylinder bore with engine oil during assembly.

CONNECTING ROD, CRANKSHAFT AND BEARINGS. The crankshaft assembly should only be disassembled if the necessary tools and experience are available to service this type of

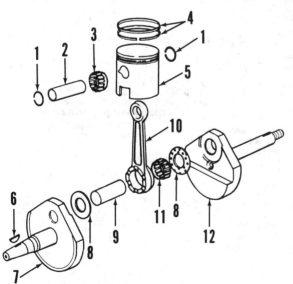

Fig. JS1-30—Exploded view of crankshaft assembly.
1. Clips
2. Piston pin
3. Needle bearing
4. Piston rings
5. Piston
6. Key
7. Crank half
8. Thrust washers
9. Crankpin
10. Connecting rod
11. Needle bearing
12. Crank half

crankshaft. Crankshaft components are available individually.

Maximum crankshaft runout measured at main bearing journals with crankshaft ends supported in lathe centers is 0.08 mm (0.003 in.). Connecting rod radial clearance should be 0.037-0.049 mm (0.0015-0.0019 in.) with a service limit of 0.10 mm (0.004 in.). Connecting rod side clearance should be 0.45-0.55 mm (0.018-0.022 in.) with a service limit of 0.8 mm (0.03 in.). Maximum allowable connecting rod bend or twist measured over a 100 mm (3.9 in.) length is 0.2 mm (0.008 in.).

Lubricate bearings, piston, rings and cylinder with engine oil prior to installation. Tighten crankcase and cylinder head screws as outlined in ASSEMBLY section.

ELECTRIC STARTER

All Models

All models are equipped with electric starter shown in Fig. JS1-32. Disassembly is evident after inspection of unit and reference to exploded view. When servicing starter motor, scribe reference marks across motor frame to aid in reassembly.

Starter brushes have a standard length of 12 mm (0.47 in.) and should be renewed if worn to 8.5 mm (0.33 in.). Commutator has a standard diameter of 28 mm (1.10 in.) and should be renewed

if worn to a diameter of 27 mm (1.06 in.). During reassembly, apply Loctite Superflex or a suitable RTV silicone sealer around frame opening for terminal end of positive brush assembly and on sealing surfaces of frame, frame head and end housing where components mate.

BILGE PUMP

All Models

When the vehicle is operated, the jet pump forces water past siphon hose (S—Fig. JS1-23) opening. The passing force of water creates a vacuum effect, thus drawing (siphoning) any water out of vehicle bilge. Make sure all hoses and strainer (R—Fig. JS1-34) are kept clean of all foreign debris. Disassemble and clean or renew components if needed. Make sure all hose connections are tight or vacuum loss will result in siphoning system malfunction. An antisiphon loop is positioned at top, rear of engine compartment to prevent water from being drawn into hull when engine is not being operated. Make sure small breather

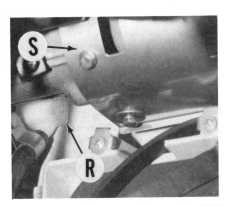
Fig. JS1-34—View identifies drive coupler shield (S) and location of bilge strainer (R).

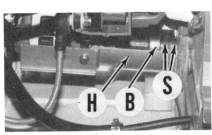
Fig. JS1-36—Cutaway view showing a typical intermediate housing setup. After removing intermediate housing assembly as outlined in text, remove drive shaft drive flange and front cover. Tap intermediate housing (H) off rear of drive shaft using a soft-faced mallet. Bearing (B) is located on drive shaft at front and rear of intermediate housing. Two seals (S) are located in rear of intermediate housing and two seals are located in front cover. An "O" ring is used around outside of front cover. A shim may be used between front cover and front drive shaft bearing.

hole in plastic fitting of antisiphon loop is clear. If hole is plugged, water could be drawn into engine compartment when engine is stopped or idling. Clean hole only with compressed air. Using a tool to clean hole could enlarge hole size, thus causing a vacuum loss at bilge strainer during operation. The lower vacuum will result in a decrease in bilge siphoning efficiency.

INTERMEDIATE HOUSING AND DRIVE FLANGE

All Models

R&R AND OVERHAUL. Disconnect battery cables from battery and remove battery from vehicle. Remove throttle cable and choke cable from carburetor. Remove hoses from carburetor, label if needed and plug openings. Remove flame arrestor and carburetor fasteners, then withdraw components. Cover intake manifold passage to prevent entrance of foreign debris. Remove oil supply hose from oil injection pump and plug openings. Disconnect all electrical wiring that will interfere with engine removal and label for reassembly. Remove cooling system hoses from exhaust pipe and elbow. Remove exhaust pipe and elbows. Remove drive coupler shield (S—Fig. JS1-34). Remove four cap screws (C—Fig. JS1-26) and washers retaining engine to vehicle hull. Note shims located under engine mounts and identify each shim for installation in original location. Remove any other components that will interfere with engine removal. Use a suitable lifting device to hoist engine assembly from vehicle. Place engine assembly on a clean work bench.

Remove jet pump water intake grill (W—Fig. JS1-38) and cover (R). Detach steering linkage joint (J) at ball joint on steering nozzle (N). Remove bilge siphon hose and cooling system supply hose from fittings on jet pump housing. Remove four jet pump mounting cap screws (two at front and two at rear).

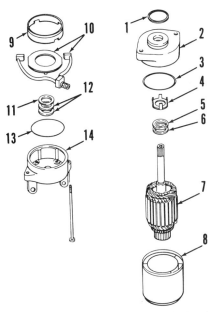
Fig. JS1-32—Exploded view of typical electric starter assembly.

1. "O" ring	9. Brush plate holder
2. Frame head	10. Brush assy.
3. Seal ring	11. Thick thrust washer
4. Tab washer	12. Thinner thrust washers
5. Insulator	13. Seal ring
6. Thrust washer	14. End housing
7. Armature	
8. Frame	

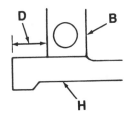
Fig. JS1-37—Refer to text after reassembling intermediate housing. Measure distance (D) between surface of intermediate housing (H) and surface of drive shaft front bearing (B) to determine if a shim is needed between front cover and bearing.

Jet Ski (JS300 & JS300SX)

PERSONAL WATER VEHICLE

Be careful and use a suitable sharp tool and cut silicone sealer between jet pump mounting flanges and vehicle hull and jet pump water intake nozzle and vehicle hull. Slide jet pump assembly off rear of drive shaft. Note shims located under jet pump housing mounting flanges. Use a suitable tool and rotate impeller counterclockwise to remove from drive shaft.

Remove intermediate housing (H—Fig. JS1-36) four mounting cap screws. Withdraw intermediate housing with drive flange and drive shaft. Note shims located behind intermediate housing mounting flanges and label for installation in original locations.

Hold drive shaft with Kawasaki tool W56019-003 or a suitable equivalent, then use Kawasaki tool T57001-276 or a suitable equivalent to rotate drive flange off drive shaft. Remove three front cover retaining cap screws then withdraw front cover. Remove any shims located between front cover and drive shaft front bearing. Use a soft-faced mallet and tap intermediate housing off rear of drive shaft. Use correct fixtures and press drive shaft bearings and spacer off drive shaft if needed. Inspect all components for excessive wear or any other damage and renew if needed. Drive shaft runout should not exceed 0.1 mm (0.004 in.) when measured in intermediate housing area and 0.5 mm (0.020 in.) when measured midway between shaft ends. Renew all seals and "O" ring during reassembly. Apply Shell MP or Alvania EP1 grease on front cover and intermediate housing grease seals prior to installation. Install grease seals with open side facing away from drive shaft bearings. Fill gap between seals with previously recommended grease. Apply recommended grease onto drive shaft bearings. Slide intermediate housing onto rear of drive shaft and tap intermediate housing onto drive shaft bearings with a soft-faced mallet until seated. If original intermediate housing and original drive shaft bearings are

used, then original shim located between front cover and front drive shaft bearing can be used. If intermediate housing or drive shaft bearings have been renewed, then proceed as follows. Measure distance (D—Fig. JS1-37) from surface of intermediate housing (H) to surface of drive shaft front bearing (B). If distance measured is between 12.90 mm (0.5079 in.) and 13.05 mm (0.5138 in.), no shims need to be added between front cover and bearing. If distance measured is between 13.06 mm (0.5142 in.) and 13.20 mm (0.5197 in.), add Kawasaki shim 92025-502 between front cover and bearing. If distance measured is between 13.21 mm (0.5201 in.) and 13.32 mm (0.5244 in.), add Kawasaki shim 92025-503 between front cover and bearing. Install front cover and tighten cap screws to 16 N·m (12 ft.-lbs.). Install drive flange on drive shaft and tighten to 98 N·m (72 ft.-lbs.).

Install shims in their original locations between intermediate housing mounting flanges and vehicle hull. If vehicle hull has been renewed, then the drive shaft must be properly aligned to mate with jet pump. The drive shaft must be positioned so drive shaft center is 77 mm (3.03 in.) from top of jet pump mounting surface and equally centered from side-to-side. Adjust thickness of shims located under intermediate housing mounting flanges until correct drive shaft alignment is obtained. Tighten intermediate housing mounting cap screws to 16 N·m (12 ft.-lbs.) and recheck drive shaft alignment.

Remove grease fitting (G—Fig. JS1-38) at rear of jet pump housing. Install impeller on drive shaft and tighten using hand pressure. Do not overtighten impeller. Lightly grease lips of jet pump housing grease seals and rear surface of drive shaft with Shell MP or Alvania EP1 grease. Apply Loctite Superflex or a suitable RTV silicone sealer on mounting flanges of jet pump housing and on jet pump intake area where intake mates with vehicle hull. Slide jet pump

assembly onto drive shaft. Thickness of shims located under jet pump housing mounting flanges must be adjusted so clearance (C—Fig. JS1-39) between impeller and impeller housing is at least 0.1 mm (0.004 in.) measured throughout entire impeller circumference. Tighten jet pump housing mounting cap screws, then recheck impeller-to-impeller housing clearance. After recommended clearance is obtained, remove each jet pump housing mounting cap screw and apply Loctite Stud N'Bearing Mount or a suitable equivalent on threads of each screw, then install and tighten to 22 N·m (16 ft.-lbs.). Install grease fitting (G—Fig. JS1-38) and inject Shell MP or Alvania EP1 grease through grease fitting as needed. Reconnect bilge siphon hose and cooling system supply hose onto fittings on jet pump. Reattach steering linkage joint (J) onto ball joint on steering nozzle (N). Install jet pump cover (R) and water intake grill (W) and tighten retaining screws to 10 N·m (88 in.-lbs.).

Use a suitable lifting device to hoist engine assembly into vehicle. Make sure coupler is located between engine drive flange and drive shaft drive flange. Install shims into original locations under engine mounts. Lay a straightedge (S—Fig. JS1-27) across top of engine drive flange and drive shaft drive flange. Engine drive flange should be 0-0.3 mm (0-0.012 in.) higher than drive shaft drive flange. Measure distance (A—Fig. JS1-28) and distance (B). Distance (B) should not exceed distance (A) by more than 0.6 mm (0.024 in.). Measure clearance between engine drive flange and coupler and drive shaft drive flange and coupler. Total of the two clearance measurements should not exceed 0.5 mm (0.020 in.). If recommended settings are not measured, then adjust thickness of shims located under engine mounts until recommended settings are obtained. Apply Loctite Lock N'Seal or a suitable equivalent on threads of four cap screws (C—Fig. JS1-26) and tighten cap screws to 37 N·m (27 ft.-lbs.). Remeasure as previously outlined to verify engine drive flange to drive shaft flange settings are as recommended. Adjust shim thickness if needed.

Complete reassembly in reverse order of disassembly.

JET PUMP

All Models

R&R AND OVERHAUL. Disconnect battery cables from battery. Remove jet pump water intake grill (W-Fig. JS1-38) and cover (R). Detach steering linkage joint (J) at ball joint on steering nozzle (N). Remove bilge siphon hose and cooling system supply hose from fittings on

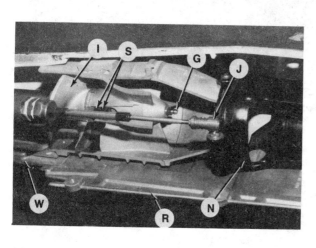

Fig. JS1-38—Cutaway view of jet pump assembly and related components.
G. Grease fitting
I. Impeller
J. Steering linkage joint
N. Steering nozzle
R. Jet pump cover
S. Seals
W. Water intake grill

48

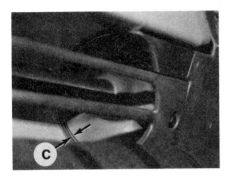

Fig. JS1-39—Clearance (C) between impeller and impeller housing should be at least 0.1 mm (0.004 in.) and should not exceed 0.87 mm (0.034 in.) measured throughout entire impeller circumference.

jet pump housing. Remove four jet pump mounting cap screws (two at front and two at rear). Be careful and use a suitable sharp tool and cut silicone sealer between jet pump mounting flanges and vehicle hull and jet pump water intake nozzle and vehicle hull. Slide jet pump assembly off rear of drive shaft. Note shims located under jet pump housing mounting flanges. Label shims for reassembly in original locations. Use a suitable tool and rotate impeller counterclockwise to remove from drive shaft.

Inspect impeller and impeller housing for excessive wear or any other damage. Diameter of impeller housing should not exceed 122.7 mm (4.83 in.). Renew jet pump housing if impeller housing is worn beyond limits or any other damage is noted. Minimum impeller diameter is 120 mm (4.72 in.). Inspect all other components for any type of damage. Remove snap ring and withdraw seals (S) using a suitable slide hammer. Diameter of drive shaft bushing in jet pump housing should not exceed 20.2 mm (0.79 in.). Renew bushing if worn beyond limit. Cool bushing and warm bushing area of jet pump to 93°C (200°F) to ease installation. Install Shell MP or Alvania EP1 grease on seals in jet pump housing prior to installation. Install thick seal next to bushing and install both seals with open side facing toward snap ring groove. Install snap

ring. Fill gap between seals with previously recommended grease. If output nozzle was removed, apply a thin coating of Loctite Superflex or a RTV silicone sealer on jet pump housing surface where output nozzle mates and install output nozzle. Apply Loctite Stud N'Bearing Mount on threads of output nozzle mounting cap screws and tighten in a crisscross pattern to 16 N·m (12 ft.-lbs.).

Remove grease fitting (G) at rear of jet pump housing. Install impeller on drive shaft and tighten using hand pressure. Do not overtighten impeller. Lightly grease lips of jet pump housing grease seals and rear surface of drive shaft with Shell MP or Alvania EP1 grease. Apply Loctite Superflex or a suitable RTV silicone sealer on mounting flanges of jet pump housing and on jet pump intake area where intake mates with vehicle hull. Slide jet pump assembly onto drive shaft. Install shims located under jet pump housing mounting flanges in original locations. Tighten jet pump housing mounting cap screws, then check impeller-to-impeller housing clearance. Clearance (C—Fig. JS1-39) should not exceed 0.87 mm (0.034 in.) measured between impeller and impeller housing throughout entire impeller circumference. Adjust thickness of shims located under jet pump housing mounting flanges if measured clearance is not equal around impeller circumference. If measured clearance is beyond recommended limit, then renew excessively worn or damaged component. After correct setting is obtained, remove each jet pump housing mounting cap screw and apply Loctite Stud N'Bearing Mount or a suitable equivalent on threads of each screw, then install and tighten to 22 N·m (16 ft.-lbs.). Install grease fitting (G—Fig. JS1-38) and inject Shell MP or Alvania EP1 grease through grease fitting as needed. Reconnect bilge siphon hose and cooling system supply hose onto fittings on jet pump. Reattach steering linkage joint (J) onto ball joint on steering nozzle (N). Install jet pump cover (R) and water intake grill (W) and tighten retaining screws to 10 N·m (88 in.-lbs.).

Fig. JS1-41—Loosen locknut (L) and remove joint (T) from ball joint on handlebar pivot plate and rotate joint (T) up or down on threaded end of steering cable as needed to center jet pump steering nozzle when steering handle bar is in a straight ahead position.

STEERING

All Models

ADJUSTMENT. With steering handlebar in straight ahead position, jet pump steering nozzle (N—Fig. JS1-38) should be centered or at a 90 degree angle to stern of vehicle. If not, raise handle pole and loosen locknut (L—Fig. JS1-41) below steering linkage joint (T). Remove joint (T) from ball joint on handlebar pivot plate. Rotate joint (T) up or down threaded end of steering cable as needed to properly center jet pump steering nozzle. After correct adjustment is obtained, reinstall steering linkage joint (T) onto ball joint and tighten locknut (L).

NOTE: If steering linkage joint (T) must be rotated out to where minimal threads on steering cable engage joint (T), then rotate joint (T) onto threaded end of steering cable to obtain safe thread engagement and complete adjustment on joint (J—Fig. JS1-38) at jet pump.

JET SKI
JS440 AND JS550

NOTE: Metric fasteners are used throughout vehicle.

General

Engine Make.................................Own
Engine Type....................Two-Stroke;
                             Water-Cooled
Number of Cylinders...........................2
Bore:
  JS440............................... 68 mm
                          (2.68 in.)
  JS550............................... 75 mm
                          (2.95 in.)
Stroke................................. 60 mm
                          (2.36 in.)
Displacement:
  JS440.............................436 cc
                      (26.6 cu. in.)
  JS550.............................531 cc
                      (32.4 cu. in.)
Compression Ratio:
  JS440................................ 6.1:1
  JS550.....................6.0:1 (Prior to 1986)
                      5.7:1 (After 1985)
Engine Lubrication......................Pre-Mix
Fuel:Oil Ratio.............................40:1*
Engine Oil Recommendation........Kawasaki Jet Ski
                      or Two-Stroke;
                    BIA Certified TC-W
*On models after 1985, manufacturer recommends using
a fuel:oil ratio of 24:1 when ambient temperature is 15°C
(59°F) or below.

Tune-Up

Engine Idle Speed:
  JS440....................1700-1900 rpm
  JS550....................1400-1600 rpm
Spark Plug:
  NGK B7ES
  Champion...........................N4G
  Electrode Gap...................0.7-0.8 mm
                  (0.027-0.031 in.)
Ignition:
  Type..............................CDI
  Timing:
    JS440................25° BTDC @ 6000 rpm
    JS550................28° BTDC @ 6000 rpm
                 (Prior to 1986)
          21° BTDC @ 6000 rpm
                 (After 1985)
Carburetor:
  Make...........................Mikuni
  Model:
    JS440....................BN38 Diaphragm
    JS550....................BN38 Diaphragm
                 (Prior to 1986)
          BN44 Diaphragm
                 (After 1985)
  Bore Size:
    BN38................................34 mm
                  (1.3 in.)
    BN44................................40 mm
                  (1.6 in.)

Sizes—Clearances

Cylinder Bore:
  JS440..................... 68.075-68.094 mm
                (2.6801-2.6809 in.)
    Service Limit..................... 68.17 mm
                (2.684 in.)
  JS550 ....75.075-75.094 mm
                (2.9557-2.9564 in.)
    Service Limit.....................75.17 mm
                (2.959 in.)
Piston Diameter Measured
5 mm (0.2 in.) from
Skirt Bottom and 90° to
Pin Bore:
  JS440..................... 67.79-67.98 mm
                (2.669-2.676 in.)
    Service Limit.....................67.79 mm
                (2.669 in.)
  JS550..................... 74.921-74.940 mm
                (2.949-2.950 in.)
    Service Limit.....................74.78 mm
                (2.944 in.)
Piston-to-Cylinder Wall
Clearance:
  JS440.........................0.095-0.133 mm
                (0.0037-0.0052 in.)
  JS550.........................0.135-0.173 mm
                (0.0053-0.0068 in.)
Piston Ring Side
Clearance........................... 0.12-0.17 mm
                (0.0048-0.0067 in.)
  Service Limit.....................0.22 mm
                (0.0087 in.)
Piston Ring End Gap .... 0.2-0.4 mm
                (0.008-0.016 in.)
  Service Limit.....................0.7 mm
                (0.027 in.)
Maximum Cylinder Head
Warp........................... 0.25 mm
                (0.01 in.)
Connecting Rod Radial
Clearance....................0.02-0.03 mm
                (0.0008-0.0012 in.)
  Service Limit.....................0.08 mm
                (0.003 in.)
Connecting Rod Side
Clearance........................... 0.4-0.5 mm
                (0.016-0.020 in.)
  Service Limit.....................0.7 mm
                (0.027 in.)
Maximum Connecting Rod
Bend or Twist Measured
Over a 100 mm (3.9 in.)
Length.................................0.2 mm
                (0.008 in.)
Maximum Crankshaft Runout
at Main Bearing Journal.............0.08 mm
                (0.003 in.)

Capacities
Fuel Tank. . . . . 13 L
(3.5 gal.)

Tightening Torques
Carburetor Mounting Nuts. . . . . .10 N·m
(88 in.-lbs.)

Cylinder Head Nuts. .22 N·m
(16 ft.-lbs.)

Crankcase Cap Screws:
Large. . . . . .22 N·m
(16 ft.-lbs.)
Small. . . . . .6 N·m
(53 in.-lbs.)

Engine-to-Engine Mounting
Plate Cap Screws. .48 N·m
(35 ft.-lbs.)

Engine Mounting Cap Screws. . . . . .37 N·m
(27 ft.-lbs.)

Engine Drive Flange. . . . . .27 N·m
(20 ft.-lbs.)

Drive Shaft Drive Flange. . . . . .27 N·m
(20 ft.-lbs.)

Intermediate Housing
Mounting Cap Screws. . . . . .16 N·m
(12 ft.-lbs.)

Intermediate Housing Front
Cover Cap Screws. .16 N·m
(12 ft.-lbs.)

Jet Pump Impeller:
JS440. . . . . .Hand Pressure
JS550. . . . . .20 N·m
(14 ft.-lbs.)

Jet Pump Mounting Cap Screws. . . . . .22 N·m
(16 ft.-lbs.)

Flywheel Nut. . . . . .160 N·m
(115 ft.-lbs.)

Spark Plug. . . . . .28 N·m
(21 ft.-lbs.)

Standard Fasteners:
5 mm. . . . . .3.4-4.9 N·m
(30-43 in.-lbs.)
6 mm. . . . . .5.9-7.8 N·m
(52-69 in.-lbs.)
8 mm. . . . . .14-19 N·m
(10-14 ft.-lbs.)
10 mm. . . . . .25-39 N·m
(18-29 ft.-lbs.)
12 mm. . . . . .44-61 N·m
(32-45 ft.-lbs.)
14 mm. . . . . .73-98 N·m
(54-72 ft.-lbs.)
16 mm. . . . . .115-155 N·m
(85-114 ft.-lbs.)
18 mm. . . . . .165-225 N·m
(121-165 ft.-lbs.)
20 mm. . . . . .225-325 N·m
(165-239 ft.-lbs.)

LUBRICATION

All Models

The engine is lubricated by oil mixed with the fuel. Fuel:oil ratio should be 40:1 for both engine break-in and normal service when using Kawasaki Jet Ski Oil or a BIA certified two-stroke TC-W engine oil. During break-in (first five hours or three tankfuls) of a new or rebuilt engine, throttle opening should not exceed ¾ and throttle position should be constantly varied.

NOTE: On models after 1985, manufacturer recommends using a fuel:oil ratio of 24:1 when ambient temperature is 15°C (59°F) or below.

Manufacturer recommends regular or no-lead automotive gasoline having a minimum octane rating of 87. Gasoline and oil should be thoroughly mixed.
Grease intermediate housing through grease fitting (F—Fig. JS2-1) with Shell MP or Alvania EP1 grease every 25 hours or more frequent if needed. Inject Shell MP or Alvania EP1 grease into grease fitting (G—Fig. JS2-2) at rear of jet pump housing every 25 hours or more frequent if needed to grease rear bushing on JS440 models and two guide vane ball bearings on JS550 models. On JS550 models, an Allen head wrench must be used to remove grease fitting cover to expose grease fitting (G).

Lubricate all cables, linkage and pivots with WD-40 or Bel-Ray 6 in 1 every 25 hours or more frequent if needed.

Fig. JS2-1—Intermediate housing is greased through grease fitting (F).

Fig. JS2-2—Jet pump rear bushing on JS440 models and two guide vane ball bearings on JS550 models are greased through grease fitting (G). On JS550 models, an Allen head wrench must be used to remove grease fitting cover to expose grease fitting (G).

FUEL SYSTEM

All Models

CARBURETOR. Refer to Fig. JS2-4 for an exploded view of Mikuni type BN38 diaphragm carburetor used on all JS440 models and JS550 models prior to 1986. On JS550 models after 1985, a Mikuni type BN44 diaphragm carburetor is used. BN44 carburetor is similar to type shown in Fig. JS2-4. Choke plate (21—Fig. JS2-4) is actuated by choke knob (K—Fig. JS2-5) on control panel via a cable and linkage.

On JS440 models and JS550 models prior to 1986, initial setting of low speed mixture needle (22—Fig. JS2-6) is 1 turn out from a lightly seated position. Initial setting of high speed mixture needle (29—Fig. JS2-7) is 5/8 to 7/8 turn out

from a lightly seated position. On JS550 models after 1985, initial setting of pilot needle (P—Fig. JS2-8) is 1-5/16 turns out from a lightly seated position. Initial setting of low speed mixture needle (22—Fig. JS2-9) is 1-1/16 turns out from a lightly seated position. Initial setting of high speed mixture needle (29—Fig.

Fig. JS2-5—View identifies location of choke knob (K) and fuel selector valve (V).

JS2-8) is 15/16 turn out from a lightly seated position. Final carburetor adjustments must be made with engine at normal operating temperature and running. Adjust pilot needle (P), on models so equipped, until a smooth idle is noted. Adjust low speed mixture needle (22—Fig. JS2-6 or Fig. JS2-9) until smooth acceleration from the idle position is noted. After adjusting low speed mixture needle, adjust idle speed screw (37—Fig. JS2-6 or Fig. JS2-9) until engine idle speed is approximately 1700-1900 rpm on JS440 models or 1400-1600 rpm on JS550 models with throttle lever completely released. To adjust high speed fuel:air mixture, the engine spark plugs must be removed and insulator tip color noted.

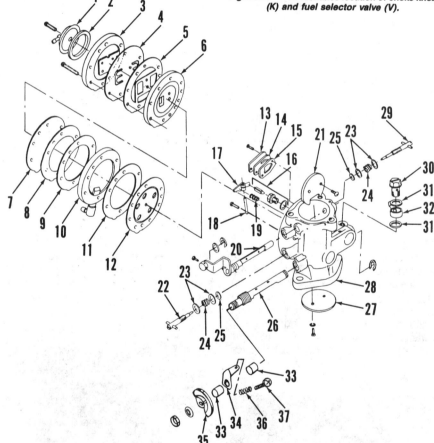

Fig. JS2-6—View identifies location of low speed mixture needle (22) and idle speed screw (37) on JS440 models and JS550 models prior to 1986.

Fig. JS2-7—View identifies location of high speed mixture needle (29) on JS440 models and JS550 models prior to 1986.

Fig. JS2-8—View identifies location of pilot needle (P) and high speed mixture needle (29) on JS550 models after 1985.

Fig. JS2-4—Exploded view of Mikuni type BN38 diaphragm carburetor used on all JS440 models and JS550 models prior to 1986. On JS550 models after 1985, a Mikuni type BN44 diaphragm carburetor is used. BN44 carburetor is similar. Refer to text.

1. Fuel inlet cover
2. Gasket
3. Inlet body
4. Check valve diaphragm
5. Gasket
6. Pump body
7. Diaphragm
8. Gasket
9. Gasket
10. Diaphragm cover
11. Gasket
12. Regulating diaphragm
13. Plate
14. Diaphragm
15. Gasket
16. Inlet valve assy.
17. Valve lever
18. Pivot shaft
19. Spring
20. Choke shaft
21. Choke plate
22. Low speed mixture needle
23. Washers
24. Springs
25. "O" rings
26. Throttle shaft
27. Throttle plate
28. Body
29. High speed mixture needle
30. Banjo bolt
31. Gaskets
32. Return line fitting
33. Spacers
34. Bracket
35. Cable lever
36. Spring
37. Idle screw

NOTE: Make sure that fuel tank contains a 40:1 fuel mixture.

Make sure cooling system will receive an adequate supply of water, then operate and sustain engine at wide-open throttle for a suitable test period. Stop the engine with throttle in wide-open position. Remove spark plugs and note insulator tip color. Normal insulator tip color is brown to light tan. If insulator tip appears to be light tan to white in color, then mixture is too lean and high speed mixture needle (29—Fig. JS2-7 or Fig. JS2-8) should be rotated outward (counterclockwise) ¼ turn to richen mixture. If insulator tip appears to be dark brown to black in color, then mixture is too rich and high speed mixture needle (29) should be rotated inward (clockwise) ¼ turn to lean mixture. Clean, regap and reinstall spark plugs and continue test procedure until spark plug insulator tip is a normal color.

The fuel pump and regulating diaphragm (12—Fig. JS2-4) can be removed after removing the six through-bolts. Note that alignment tabs on components (3 through 12) are provided to assist in proper alignment during reassembly.

Do not remove choke plate, throttle plate or shafts unless necessary. The choke and throttle plate retaining screws are either staked or retained with a thread locking solution to prevent loosening. If screws are removed, properly stake or apply a suitable thread locking solution on threads prior to assembly. Inlet needle valve lever (17) must be flush with floor of housing recess when needle valve is seated. Refer to Fig. JS2-10. If lever must be adjusted, push down on lever immediately above spring to collapse the spring, then bend the end which contacts needle valve.

FUEL PUMP. The fuel pump is an integral part of the carburetor. The fuel pump assembly can be overhauled without overhauling the complete carburetor.

With reference to Fig. JS2-4, disassemble the fuel pump assembly. Inspect all components for excessive wear or any other damage and renew if needed. Clean components as needed with a suitable cleaning solution. Blow dry with clean compressed air. If compressed air is not available, use only lint-free cloths to wipe dry. Make sure all passages are clear of any obstructions.

With reference to Fig. JS2-4, reassemble the fuel pump assembly with new gaskets. Securely tighten the six through-bolts.

FUEL FILTER. An inline filter assembly (F—Fig. JS2-12) is located between fuel selector valve (V—Fig. JS2-5) and carburetor fuel pump intake. After every 25 hours of operation or more frequent if needed, unscrew ring nut (N—Fig. JS2-12) and withdraw cup (C) with sealing ring from base. Withdraw filter element. Clean cup (C) and filter element with a suitable cleaning solution. Renew filter element if excessive contamination or damage is noted. Allow cup and filter element to air dry or blow dry with clean, low air pressure. Renew small "O" ring in bottom of filter element, then install filter element. Make sure tension spring is positioned on bottom of filter element. Renew sealing ring and securely tighten nut (N) during installation of cup (C).

THROTTLE LEVER FREE PLAY. Throttle lever should have a small amount of free play prior to activating carburetor throttle shaft when throttle lever is in released position. To adjust, rotate locknuts (N—Fig. JS2-14) up or down cable housing end as needed until a small amount of free play is noted. Tighten locknuts (N) to retain adjustment.

FLAME ARRESTOR. On all JS440 models and JS550 models after 1985, a flame arrestor is located beneath cover (C—Fig. JS2-14). Every 25 hours or more frequent if needed, remove two screws (S) on each side of cover and withdraw cover and flame arrestor. Inspect flame arrestor for contamination and use clean compressed air to blow clean. Renew flame arrestor if damage is noted. On JS440 models after 1983 and JS550 models after 1985, install flame arrestor with curved side facing down. Apply Loctite Lock N'Seal or a suitable equivalent on threads of the four cap screws retaining cover (C) and securely tighten.

NOTE: If lower cover is removed, make sure gasket between cover and carburetor top is installed.

On JS550 models prior to 1986, flame arrestor assembly (A—Fig. JS-15) is used. Every 100 hours or more frequent if needed, remove three cap screws (S) and withdraw assembly. Split cover halves and remove flame arrestor. Clean flame arrestor using a suitable cleaning solution and blow dry with clean com-

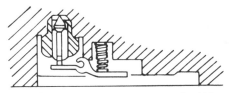

Fig. JS2-10—Inlet needle valve lever should be flush with floor of housing recess as shown.

Fig. JS2-9—View identifies location of low speed mixture needle (22) and idle speed screw (37) on JS550 models after 1985.

Fig. JS2-12—An inline fuel filter assembly (F) is used on all models. Unscrew ring nut (N) to withdraw cup (C) with sealing ring. Filter element is now accessible.

Fig. JS2-14—Rotate locknuts (N) up or down cable housing end as needed to adjust throttle lever free play. On all JS440 models and JS550 models after 1985, remove two cap screws (S) on each side of cover (C) to withdraw cover (C) and flame arrestor.

pressed air. Renew flame arrestor if damage is noted. Reassemble flame arrestor assembly. Position gasket beneath lower flame arrestor cover and carburetor top. Apply Loctite Lock N' Seal or a suitable equivalent on threads of the three cap screws (S) retaining flame arrestor assembly (A) and securely tighten.

IGNITION

All Models

All models are equipped with a simultaneous capacitor discharge ignition system. The ignition timing is electronically advanced as the magneto base plate is fixed. Ignition timing should not require adjustment, after first being correctly set, unless magneto base plate is moved or an ignition component is renewed.

IGNITION TIMING. Ignition timing should be 25 degrees or 3.53 mm (0.14 in.) before top dead center (BTDC) at 6000 rpm on all JS440 models. Ignition timing should be 28 degrees or 4.42 mm (0.17 in.) BTDC at 6000 rpm on JS550 models prior to 1986. Ignition timing should be 21 degrees or 2.52 mm (0.10 in.) BTDC at 6000 rpm on JS550 models after 1985. Ignition timing can be checked using a suitable power timing light. Remove fuel tank and place to the side of vehicle. Remove flywheel cover

(F—Fig. JS2-17). Note flywheel timing marks "T" (TDC) and "F" (recommended timing BTDC).

Detach spark plug leads from spark plugs and ground terminals ends. Remove number one cylinder (forward cylinder) spark plug. Position a suitable dial indicator so indicator needle projects through number one cylinder spark plug hole. Rotate flywheel until piston in cylinder is positioned at TDC. Mount a suitable wire pointer (P—Fig. JS2-18) on the engine and position pointer end so "T" (TDC) on flywheel is aligned with pointer end. Remove dial indicator assembly. Reinstall spark plugs and attach spark plug leads. Use two short flywheel cover retaining cap screws and remount starter motor.

Use an adapter and connect a supplemental water supply to cooling system supply hose (H—Fig. JS2-20), leading to fitting on exhaust manifold, after removing hose (H) from jet pump supply line.

NOTE: When using a supplemental water supply, do not turn on water until engine is ready to be started as exhaust flooding could occur. Operate engine only at low rpm or during a test, do not exceed recommended high rpm and only operate for a short period of time.

Connect a tachometer to engine. Start engine, then turn on supplemental water supply. Accelerate engine to 6000 rpm. Use power timing light and check alignment of flywheel timing mark (F—Fig. JS2-18) with wire pointer (P) end. Allow engine to return to idle position, then turn off supplemental water supply and stop engine.

NOTE: Make sure engine is not operated without a supply of water longer than 10-15 seconds or damage to engine and/or exhaust components could result.

NOTE: If ignition timing test must be reperformed, allow engine to idle for a short

period with supplemental water supply circulating through cooling system. Do not sustain engine at a high rpm for an extended period when not operated under a load and do not exceed the recommended testing rpm of 6000.

If ignition timing is incorrect, remove flywheel retaining nut and washer then use a suitable puller and withdraw flywheel. Loosen magneto base plate screws and rotate base plate as needed. Tighten magneto base plate screws, then reinstall flywheel and tighten retaining nut to 160 N·m (115 ft.-lbs.).

Recheck ignition timing. Continue procedure until correct ignition timing is obtained. Bend tabs on flywheel washer to retain position of flywheel securing nut after correct ignition timing is obtained. Apply a water-resistant grease on flywheel cover (F—Fig. JS2-17) "O" ring. Apply a suitable thread locking solution on threads of flywheel cover retaining screws, then install flywheel cover (F) and securely tighten screws. Reinstall and properly secure fuel tank and hoses.

TROUBLE-SHOOTING. If ignition malfunction occurs, use only approved procedures to prevent damage to the components. The fuel system should be checked first to make certain that faulty running is not caused by con-

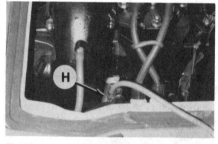

Fig. JS2-20—A supplemental water supply can be connected to cooling system supply hose (H), leading to fitting on exhaust manifold, after removing cooling system supply hose (H) from jet pump supply line.

Fig. JS2-15—On JS550 models prior to 1986, remove three cap screws (S) to withdraw flame arrestor assembly (A).

Fig. JS2-17—Engine flywheel is located behind flywheel cover (F).

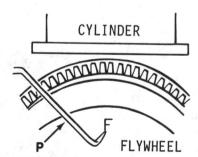

CYLINDER

P   FLYWHEEL

Fig. JS2-18—Mark "F" on flywheel represents recommended ignition timing BTDC when engine is operated at 6000 rpm. Wire pointer (P) end must be positioned as outlined in text in order to correctly verify ignition timing.

Fig. JS2-22—Remove cap (C) to expose six-wire connector. Refer to text.

taminated fuel. Make sure malfunction is not due to spark plugs, wiring or wiring connection failure. Trouble-shoot ignition circuit using a suitable ohmmeter as follows:

Remove cap (C—Fig. JS2-22) and withdraw six-wire connector. Separate connector halves to expose terminal ends of wires leading to pulser coil (1—Fig. JS2-23) and exciter coil (2). Check condition of pulser coil (1) by attaching one tester lead to terminal end of red wire (R) and attaching other tester lead to terminal end of gray wire (Gr). Pulser coil can be considered satisfactory if resistance reading is within the limits of 20-30 ohms. Check condition of exciter coil (2) by attaching one tester lead to terminal end of red wire (R) and attaching other tester lead to terminal end of black wire (B). Exciter coil can be considered satisfactory if resistance reading is within the limits of 216-324 ohms. Pulser coil and exciter coil are serviceable after removing flywheel cover and flywheel. Make sure a suitable puller is used to withdraw flywheel. Tighten flywheel retaining nut to 160 N·m (115 ft.-lbs.). Recheck ignition timing as previously outlined under IGNITION TIMING. Apply a water-resistant grease on flywheel cover ''O'' ring. Apply a suitable thread locking solution on threads of flywheel cover retaining screws, then install flywheel cover and securely tighten screws.

Ignition coil secondary winding resistance should be 4500-6700 ohms. If no components are found faulty, then renew CDI module/ignition coil assembly with a known good assembly and recheck engine operation.

CHARGING SYSTEM

All Models

All models are equipped with a charge coil, rectifier/regulator and battery. Standard battery on JS440 models prior

to 1987 and JS550 models prior to 1984 has a 16 ampere hour, 12 volt rating. Standard battery on JS440 models after 1986 and JS550 models after 1983 has a 19 ampere hour, 12 volt rating. The charge coil should produce 12-15 ac volts when engine is operated throughout rpm range. Rectifier/regulator assembly should prevent regulated voltage from exceeding 15 dc volts.

The battery electrolyte level should be checked periodically and filled to maximum level with distilled water if required. The battery should be removed from the vehicle and the battery caps removed when charging. The manufacturer recommends charging the battery at a rate of 1.6 amperes on 16 ampere hour batteries and 1.9 amperes on 19 ampere hour batteries for a period of 10 hours. Do not exceed recommended charging rate.

NOTE: Make sure battery charging area is well ventilated.

The charge coil can be statically tested using a suitable ohmmeter. Remove cap

(C—Fig. JS2-22) and withdraw six-wire connector. Separate connector halves to expose terminal ends of wires leading to charge coil. Refer to Fig. JS2-23. Check condition of charge coil (3) by attaching one tester lead to terminal end of one light green wire (Lt G) and attaching other tester lead to terminal end of remaining light green wire (Lt G). Resistance reading should be 2.4-3.6 ohms. Check resistance between each charge coil wire and black wire. Tester should show 1.2-1.8 ohms resistance at each wire. To check rectifier/regulator assembly, refer to chart shown in Fig. JS2-24. To check rectifier/regulator during operation, first make sure battery is fully charged, charge coil test good and all wiring is in good condition and all connectors fit tightly or are securely fastened. Attach test leads of a suitable voltmeter directly on battery terminals.

Use an adapter and connect a supplemental water supply to cooling system supply hose (H—Fig. JS2-20), leading to fitting on exhaust manifold, after removing hose (H) from jet pump supply line.

Fig. JS2-24—Use adjacent chart and values listed below to test condition of rectifier/regulator assembly.
A. Infinite resistance
B. Continuity

+Tester Lead / -Tester Lead	Orange	Black (Ground)	Light Green	Light Green
Orange		A	A	A
Black (Ground)	A		A	A
Light Green	B	B		A
Light Green	B	B	A	

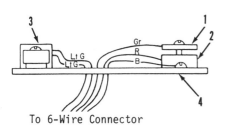

Fig. JS2-23—View identifying magneto components and color of leads.

1. Pulser coil
2. Exciter coil
3. Battery charge coil
4. Magneto base plate

B. Black
R. Red
Gr. Gray
Lt G. Light green

Fig. JS2-25—Wiring diagram typical of all JS440 models. Components (2, 5, 8 and 9) are contained within electric box. A ground wire is located between engine and electric box.

1. Battery
2. Starter solenoid
3. Starter motor
4. Magneto assy.
5. CDI module/ignition coil assy.
8. Rectifier/regulator
9. Stop switch relay
10. Start switch
11. Stop switch
B. Black
R. Red
W. White
Bl. Blue
Br. Brown
Gr. Gray
Or. Orange
B/W. Black/white
Lt G. Light green

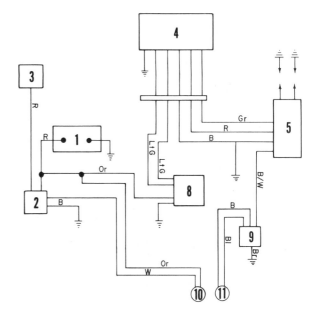

NOTE: Do not turn on water until engine is ready to be started as exhaust flooding could occur.

Start engine, then turn on supplemental water supply. Accelerate engine while observing voltmeter. The voltmeter should show approximately 15 dc volts. Allow engine to return to idle position then turn off supplemental water supply and stop engine.

NOTE: Make sure engine is not operated without a supply of water longer than 10-15 seconds or damage to engine and/or exhaust components could result.

RPM LIMITER

JS550 Models

All JS550 models are equipped with a rpm limiter to prevent engine from ex-ceeding maximum rpm when jet pump impeller is not operated under a load, e.g., breaking clear of water. Engine rpm should not exceed limit range of 6600-7500 rpm. When engine rpm is near predetermined limit, rpm limiter valve (6—Fig. JS2-26) will activate, thus opening a passage to supply additional fuel through rpm limiter hose (L—Fig. JS2-27) to the engine. The additional fuel causes a too rich condition in the engine, thus limiting engine rpm.

NOTE: If a too rich condition is noted during normal operation, rpm limiter valve could be faulty.

If a malfunction is noted, first make sure all hoses are in good condition and fit tightly onto fittings. To test rpm limiter valve, proceed as follows. Disconnect rpm limiter hose (L) and fuel return hose (R) from carburetor fittings.

Disconnect fuel return hose at fuel tank and plug hose opening. Unscrew cap (C—Fig. JS2-28) at electric box and withdraw wires to expose wire connectors. Disconnect orange/white and black/red wires at connectors. Connect a pressure pump or a low air pressure supply to fuel return hose (R—Fig. JS2-27) and blow air through hose into rpm limiter valve (V). No air should be felt expelling out rpm limiter hose (L). Connect terminal end of orange/white wire, leading to rpm limiter valve, to the positive terminal of a 12 volt battery. Connect terminal end of black/red wire, leading to rpm limiter valve, to the negative terminal of a 12 volt battery.

NOTE: DO NOT connect rpm limiter valve wires to a 12 volt battery supply until test is ready to be performed. If wires are connected directly to 12 volt battery supply longer than 15 seconds, damage to rpm limiter valve could result.

Blow air into valve through fuel return hose (R). Air should be felt expelling out rpm limiter hose (L). If rpm limiter valve (V) does not correctly restrict and permit air flow, then valve must be renewed. If rpm limiter valve tests good and rpm limiter circuit still malfunctions, then renew rpm limiter relay (7—Fig. JS2-26).

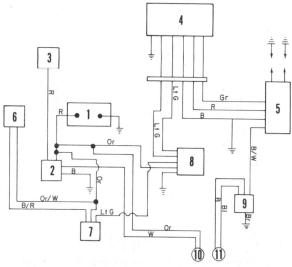

Fig. JS2-26—Wiring diagram typical of all JS550 models. Components (2, 5, 7, 8 and 9) are contained within electric box. A ground wire is located between engine and electric box.

1. Battery
2. Starter solenoid
3. Starter motor
4. Magneto assy.
5. CDI module/ignition coil assy.
6. Rpm limiter valve
7. Rpm limiter relay
8. Rectifier/regulator
9. Stop switch relay
10. Start switch
11. Stop switch
B. Black
R. Red
W. White
Bl. Blue
Br. Brown
Gr. Gray
Or. Orange
B/W. Black/white
B/R. Black/red
Or/W. Orange/white
Lt G. Light green

Fig JS2-28—Unscrew cap (C) and withdraw wires to expose wire connectors to test rpm limiter valve on JS550 models. Refer to text.

Fig. JS2-30—View identifies jet pump cooling system supply hose (H) and bilge siphon hose (S).

Fig. JS2-27—View identifies rpm limiter hose (L), fuel return hose (R) and location of rpm limiter valve (V) used on JS550 models.

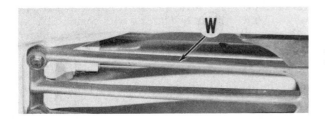

Fig. JS2-31—Jet pump water intake grill (W) must be kept clean of all foreign debris.

COOLING SYSTEM

All Models

All models are water-cooled. Forced water is supplied to the engine through jet pump outlet fitting and directed through hose (H—Fig. JS2-30) to fitting on exhaust manifold. As jet pump impeller rpm increases, so does water circulation through cooling system.

Make sure jet pump water intake grill (W—Fig. JS2-31) is kept clean. Inspect all hoses periodically for cracks, kinks or any other damage and renew if needed. The cooling system should be flushed out after each operating period when vehicle is used in contaminated or salt water. The cooling system should be flushed out prior to extended periods of storage and prior to usage after extended periods of storage.

To flush the cooling system, use an adapter and connect a supplemental water supply to cooling system supply hose (H—Fig. JS2-20), leading to fitting on exhaust manifold, after removing hose (H) from jet pump supply line. Use only clean, fresh water.

NOTE: Do not turn on water until engine is ready to be started as exhaust flooding could occur. Operate engine only at low rpm.

Start engine, then turn on supplemental water supply. Allow water to circulate through system for several minutes. Turn off supplemental water supply. If vehicle is to be stored for an extended period, raise rear of vehicle and quickly accelerate engine between idle and one-quarter throttle a couple of times. This is to force out all water within exhaust system, thus preventing damage from developing contaminates or freezing.

NOTE: Make sure engine is not operated without a supply of water longer than 10-15 seconds or damage to engine and/or exhaust components could result.

ENGINE

All Models

REMOVE AND REINSTALL. Disconnect battery cables from battery and remove battery from vehicle. Remove throttle cable and choke cable from carburetor. Remove hoses from carburetor, label if needed and plug openings. Remove exhaust manifold. Remove cap (C—Fig. JS2-22) and withdraw six-wire connector. Separate connector halves. Detach spark plug leads, disconnect starter motor lead and all other electrical wiring that will interfere with engine removal and label for reassembly. Remove drive coupler shield (S—Fig. JS2-46). Remove four cap screws and washers retaining engine to vehicle hull. Note shims located under engine mounts and identify each shim for installation in original location. Remove any other components that will interfere with engine removal. Use a suitable lifting device to hoist engine assembly from vehicle. Place engine assembly on a clean work bench.

Use a suitable lifting device to hoist engine assembly into vehicle. Make sure coupler is located between engine drive flange and drive shaft drive flange. Install shims into original locations under engine mounts. Lay a straightedge (S—Fig. JS2-33) across top of engine drive flange and drive shaft drive flange. Engine drive flange should be 0-0.3 mm (0-0.012 in.) higher than drive shaft drive flange. Measure distance (A—Fig. JS2-34) and distance (B). Distance (B) should not exceed distance (A) by more than 0.6 mm (0.024 in.). Measure clearance between engine drive flange and coupler and drive shaft drive flange and coupler. Total of the two clearance measurements should not exceed 0.5 mm (0.020 in.). If recommended settings are not measured, then adjust thickness of shims located under engine mounts until recommended settings are obtained. Apply Loctite Lock N'Seal or a suitable equivalent on threads of four engine retaining cap screws and tighten cap screws to 37 N·m (27 ft.-lbs.). Remeasure as previously outlined to verify engine drive flange to drive shaft flange settings are as recommended. Adjust shim thickness if needed.

Complete reassembly in reverse order of disassembly. Make sure "O" ring is positioned between cap (C—Fig. JS2-22) and electric box.

DISASSEMBLY. Remove engine mounting plate. Remove flame arrestor assembly, carburetor and spark plugs. Remove cylinder head nuts, then tap cylinder head with a soft-faced mallet to separate components and lift cylinder head off cylinder block. Tap cylinder block with a soft-faced mallet to break loose from top crankcase half, then carefully withdraw cylinder block. Rotate crankshaft to position piston for number one cylinder (front) at top of stroke. Remove piston pin retaining clips. Use a suitable piston pin puller and extract piston pin. Lift piston off connecting rod. Remove needle bearing from small end of connecting rod. Keep piston components together and place to the side. Label components "number one cylinder" for reference during reassembly. Repeat procedure to remove piston for number two cylinder and label accordingly.

Remove flywheel cover. Hold flywheel with a suitable tool and rotate engine drive flange off crankshaft using Kawasaki tool 57001-276. Remove electric starter motor. Remove nut and washer retaining flywheel, then use a suitable puller and withdraw flywheel. Note mark on magneto base plate that aligns with split line of crankcase halves. If magneto base plate position has been altered during ignition timing adjustment, then a new mark should be scribed in magneto base plate to align with split line of crankcase halves to ensure correct position during reassembly. Remove magneto base plate with ignition components. Stand crankcase assembly on ends of cylinder studs. Remove ten large cap screws and washers and three small cap screws and washers securing crankcase halves together. Use a soft-faced mallet and tap

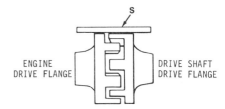

Fig. JS2-33—Engine drive flange should be 0-0.3 mm (0-0.012 in.) higher than drive shaft drive flange. Lay straightedge (S) across components and use a feeler gage to measure.

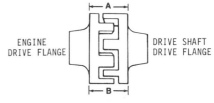

Fig. JS2-34—Distance (B) should not exceed distance (A) by more than 0.6 mm (0.024 in.).

crankcase halves to separate. Lift bottom crankcase half off top crankcase half. Crankshaft assembly can now be withdrawn from top crankcase half.

Engine components are now ready for overhaul as outlined in the appropriate following paragraphs. Refer to the following section for assembly procedure.

ASSEMBLY. Make sure all joint and gasket surfaces are clean, free from nicks and burrs and hardened cement or carbon.

Whenever the engine is disassembled, it is recommended that all gasket surfaces and mating surfaces without gaskets be carefully checked for nicks, burrs and warped surfaces which might interfere with a tight seal. Cylinder head and mating surfaces of crankcase halves should be checked on a surface plate and lapped, if necessary, to provide a smooth surface. Do not remove any more metal than is necessary.

When assembling engine, first lubricate all friction surfaces and bearings with engine oil. Apply a high temperature grease on lip and outside surface of seals. Properly assemble components on crankshaft. Install crankshaft assembly into top crankcase half. Make sure two bearing stop rings (8 and 18—Fig. JS2-38) are properly seated in grooves and pin (14) in center oil seal assembly properly seats in hole in top crankcase half. Wipe mating surfaces of crankcase halves clean and make sure surfaces are dry. Apply a coating of Kawasaki Bond or a suitable form-in-place gasket compound on crankcase mating surface of bottom crankcase

half. Position bottom crankcase half onto top crankcase half. Install ten large cap screws and washers and three small cap screws and washers which secure crankcase halves together. Use tightening sequence shown in Fig. JS2-36 and tighten ten large cap screws in increments of 7 N·m (5 ft.-lbs.) until a final torque of 22 N·m (16 ft.-lbs.) is obtained. Tighten three small cap screws to 6 N·m (53 in.-lbs.).

Install magneto base plate with ignition components and properly align mark on magneto base plate with split line of crankcase halves. Apply Loctite Superflex or a suitable equivalent on threads of magneto base plate retaining screws, then install screws with flat washers and lockwashers and securely tighten. Install flywheel, tab washer and retaining nut. Tighten nut to 160 N·m (115 ft.-lbs.). Bend tabs on flywheel washer to retain position of nut. Install engine drive flange and tighten to 27 N·m (20 ft.-lbs.) using Kawasaki tool 57001-276. Apply a water-resistant grease on flywheel cover "O" ring. Apply a suitable thread locking solution on threads of flywheel cover retaining screws, then install flywheel cover and securely tighten screws.

Rotate crankshaft to position connecting rod for number two cylinder (rear) at top of stroke. Install needle bearing

in small end of connecting rod and liberally lubricate with engine oil. Position piston assembly on connecting rod with arrow on piston crown facing cylinder exhaust port side and lubricate piston pin bores with engine oil. Use a suitable tool and install piston pin. Install new piston pin retaining clips with openings facing top or bottom of piston. Repeat procedure to install number one cylinder piston assembly. Install cylinder block base gasket. Install piston supports under piston skirts. Use suitable ring compressors and compress piston rings. Liberally lubricate cylinder bores with engine oil. Slide cylinder block onto top crankcase half and remove piston ring compressors as piston assemblies slide into cylinders. Remove piston supports. Apply a thin coating of Loctite Superflex or a suitable RTV silicone sealer onto both sides of cylinder head gasket. Use care not to block passage holes in gasket. Install cylinder head gasket with reference tab facing front of engine and aligned with cylinder head water hose fitting. Install cylinder head and tighten retaining nuts first to 14 N·m (10 ft.-lbs.) then to a final torque of 22 N·m (16 ft.-lbs.) following tightening sequence shown in Fig. JS2-37.

Complete remainder of assembly by reversing disassembly procedure.

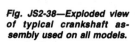

Fig. JS2-38—Exploded view of typical crankshaft assembly used on all models.

1. Piston ring
2. Piston
3. Piston pin
4. Retaining clip
5. Needle bearing
6. Crankshaft & connecting rod assy.
7. Seal
8. Stop ring
9. "O" ring
10. Bearing
11. Shim
12. Spacer shim
13. Key
14. Pin
15. Shim
16. Bearing
17. "O" ring
18. Stop ring
19. "O" ring
20. Spacer
21. Seal
22. Seal
23. Washer

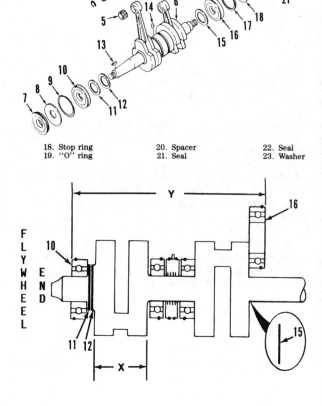

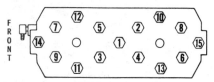

Fig. JS2-36—Tighten ten large crankcase cap screws in sequence shown. Refer to text for tightening torque specification.

Fig. JS2-37—Tighten cylinder head nuts in sequence shown. Refer to text for tightening torque specifications.

Fig. JS2-40—Refer to text for procedures in determining correct thickness of shims (11 and 15) for obtaining recommended crankshaft end play. Spacer shim (12) is a standard thickness of 1.0 mm (0.04 in.).

PISTONS, PINS, RINGS AND CYLINDERS. Recommended piston skirt-to-cylinder clearance is 0.095-0.133 mm (0.0037-0.0052 in.) on JS440 models and 0.135-0.173 mm (0.0053-0.0068 in.) on JS550 models. Bore cylinder to 0.50 mm (0.020 in.) oversize if measured piston skirt-to-cylinder clearance is beyond limit. Piston and piston ring are available in 0.50 mm (0.020 in.) oversize. Inspect cylinder walls for scoring. If minor scoring is noted, cylinders should be honed to smooth out cylinder walls.

Recommended piston ring end gap is 0.2-0.4 mm (0.008-0.016 in.) with a service limit of 0.7 mm (0.027 in.). Install piston ring on piston with manufacturer's mark facing top of piston. Make sure piston ring properly aligns with locating pin in ring groove.

When reassembling, install piston on connecting rod so arrow on top of piston faces toward exhaust side of cylinder after assembly. Install new piston pin retaining clips; openings of retaining clips must face top or bottom of piston. Coat bearings, pistons, rings and cylinder bores with engine oil during assembly.

CONNECTING RODS, CRANKSHAFT AND BEARINGS. The crankshaft assembly should only be disassembled if the necessary tools and experience are available to service this type of crankshaft. Connecting rods, crankpins and crank halves are only available as a complete crankshaft assembly.

Maximum crankshaft runout measured at main bearing journals with crankshaft ends supported in lathe centers is 0.08 mm (0.003 in.). Connecting rod radial clearance should be 0.02-0.03 mm (0.0008-0.0012 in.) with a service limit of 0.08 mm (0.003 in.). Connecting rod side clearance should be 0.4-0.5 mm (0.016-0.020 in.) with a service limit of 0.7 mm (0.027 in.). Maximum allowable connecting rod bend or twist measured over a 100 mm (3.9 in.) length is 0.2 mm (0.008 in.).

The crankshaft end play must be properly adjusted or premature failure of crankshaft and/or main bearings

Fig. JS2-42—Use "TABLE B" to determine correct thickness of shim (15—Fig. JS2-40). Refer to text.

TABLE B

Distance "Y"	Recommended Shim Thickness
188.77 - 188.98 mm (7.432 - 7.440 in.)	No Shim
188.67 - 188.76 mm (7.428 - 7.431 in.)	0.1 mm (0.004 in.)
188.57 - 188.66 mm (7.424 - 7.427 in.)	0.2 mm (0.008 in.)
188.47 - 188.56 mm (7.420 - 7.423 in.)	0.3 mm (0.012 in.)
188.37 - 188.46 mm (7.416 - 7.419 in.)	0.4 mm (0.016 in.)
188.27 - 188.36 mm (7.412 - 7.415 in.)	0.5 mm (0.020 in.)
188.17 - 188.26 mm (7.408 - 7.411 in.)	0.6 mm (0.024 in.)
188.07 - 188.16 mm (7.404 - 7.407 in.)	0.7 mm (0.028 in.)
187.97 - 188.06 mm (7.400 - 7.403 in.)	0.8 mm (0.032 in.)
187.87 - 187.96 mm (7.396 - 7.399 in.)	0.9 mm (0.036 in.)
187.77 - 187.86 mm (7.392 - 7.395 in.)	1.0 mm (0.040 in.)
187.67 - 187.76 mm (7.388 - 7.391 in.)	1.1 mm (0.044 in.)
187.57 - 187.66 mm (7.384 - 7.387 in.)	1.2 mm (0.048 in.)

could result. If the crankshaft is disassembled or the front and rear main bearings are renewed, then refer to Fig. JS2-40 and the following procedure to properly set crankshaft end play. Measure distance "X" and refer to "TABLE A" in Fig. JS2-41. Install recommended thickness of shim (11—Fig. JS2-40) between spacer shim (12) and main bearing (10). Place pto end main bearing (16) against crankshaft as shown in Fig. JS2-40 and measure distance "Y." Refer to "TABLE B" in Fig. JS2-42. Install recommended thickness of shim (15—Fig. JS2-40) between crankshaft and main bearing. Shim (15) is available in thicknesses of 0.1 mm (0.004 in.) through 0.6 mm (0.024 in.) in increments of 0.1 mm (0.004 in.). When required thickness exceeds 0.6 mm (0.024 in.), then shims must be stacked to obtain recommended thickness. Installed crankshaft end play should be less than 0.75 mm (0.029 in.).

ELECTRIC STARTER

All Models

All models are equipped with electric starter shown in Fig. JS2-44. Disassembly is evident after inspection of unit and reference to exploded view.

When servicing starter motor, scribe reference marks across motor frame to aid in reassembly.

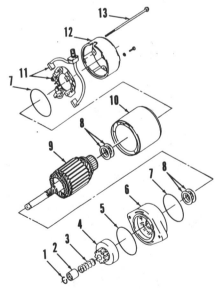

Fig. JS2-44—Exploded view of electric starter motor.

1. "C" ring
2. Stop
3. Spring
4. Drive
5. "O" ring
6. Frame head
7. "O" ring
8. Thrust washers
9. Armature
10. Frame
11. Brush assy.
12. End housing
13. Through-bolt

TABLE A

Distance "X"	Recommended Shim Thickness
49.66 - 49.87 mm (1.955 - 1.963 in.)	No Shim
49.45 - 49.65 mm (1.946 - 1.954 in.)	0.2 mm (0.008 in.)
49.22 - 49.44 mm (1.938 - 1.945 in.)	0.4 mm (0.016 in.)

Fig. JS2-41—Use "TABLE A" to determine correct thickness of shim (11—Fig. JS2-40). Refer to text.

Starter brushes have a standard length of 15 mm (0.47 in.) and should be renewed if worn to 9 mm (0.33 in.). Commutator undercut should be 0.5-0.8 mm (0.02-0.03 in.). If under is 0.2 mm (0.007 in.) or less, then use a suitable tool to remove mica between commutator sections until undercut between each section is within the recommended range. Armature end play should be 0.05-0.30 mm (0.002-0.012 in.) with a limit of 1.0 mm (0.04 in.). To check, remove components (1 through 4) and use a suitable dial indicator to measure end play. If end play is not within limits, then remove or add thrust washers (8), as needed, at brush end of armature until end play is within recommended range.

During reassembly, apply Loctite Superflex or a suitable RTV silicone sealer around frame opening for terminal end of positive brush assembly and on sealing surfaces of frame, frame head and end housing where components mate. After reassembly, bench test starter motor before installing on engine.

BILGE PUMP

All Models

When the vehicle is operated, the jet pump forces water past siphon hose (S—Fig. JS2-30) opening. The passing force of water creates a vacuum effect, thus drawing (siphoning) any water out of vehicle bilge. Make sure all hoses and strainer (R—Fig. JS2-46) are kept clean of all foreign debris. Disassemble and clean or renew components if needed. Make sure all hose connections are tight or vacuum loss will result in siphoning system malfunction. An antisiphon loop is positioned at top, rear of engine compartment to prevent water from being drawn into hull when engine is not being operated. Make sure small breather hole in plastic fitting of antisiphon loop

is clear. If hole is plugged, water could be drawn into engine compartment when engine is stopped or idling. Clean hole only with compressed air. Using a tool to clean hole could enlarge hole size, thus causing a vacuum loss at bilge strainer during operation. The lower vacuum will result in a decrease in bilge siphoning efficiency.

INTERMEDIATE HOUSING AND DRIVE FLANGE

All Models

R&R AND OVERHAUL. Disconnect battery cables from battery and remove battery from vehicle. Remove throttle cable and choke cable from carburetor. Remove hoses from carburetor, label if needed and plug openings. Remove exhaust manifold. Remove cap (C—Fig. JS2-22) and withdraw six-wire connector. Separate connector halves. Detach spark plug leads, disconnect starter motor lead and all other electrical wiring that will interfere with engine removal and label for reassembly. Remove drive coupler shield (S—Fig. JS2-46). Remove four cap screws and washers retaining engine to vehicle hull. Note shims located under engine mounts and identify each shim for installation in original location. Remove any other components that will interfere with engine removal. Use a suitable lifting device to hoist engine assembly from vehicle. Place engine assembly on a clean work bench.

Remove jet pump water intake grill (W—Fig. JS2-51) and cover (R). Detach steering linkage joint (J) at ball joint on steering nozzle (N). Remove bilge siphon hose and cooling system supply hose from fittings on jet pump housing. Remove four jet pump mounting cap

screws (two at front and two at rear). Be careful and use a suitable sharp tool and cut silicone sealer between jet pump water intake nozzle and vehicle hull. Slide jet pump assembly off rear of drive shaft. Note shims located under jet pump housing mounting flanges.

On JS440 models, use a suitable tool and rotate impeller counterclockwise to remove from drive shaft.

On all models, remove intermediate housing (H—Fig. JS2-48) four mounting cap screws. Withdraw intermediate housing with drive flange and drive shaft. Note shims located behind intermediate housing mounting flanges and label for installation in original locations.

Hold drive shaft with Kawasaki tool W56019-003 or a suitable equivalent, then use Kawasaki tool T57001-276 or a suitable equivalent to rotate drive flange off drive shaft. Remove three front cover retaining cap screws then withdraw front cover. Remove any shims located between front cover and drive shaft front bearing. Use a soft-faced mallet and tap intermediate housing off rear of drive shaft. Use correct fixtures and press drive shaft bearings and spacer off drive shaft if needed. Inspect all components for excessive wear or any other damage and renew if needed. Drive shaft runout should not exceed 0.1 mm (0.004 in.) when measured in intermediate housing area and 0.5 mm (0.020 in.) when measured midway between shaft ends. Renew all seals and "O" ring during reassembly. Apply Shell MP and Alvania EP1 grease on front cover and intermediate housing grease seals prior to installation. Install grease seals with open sides facing away from drive shaft bearings. Fill gap between seals with previously recommended grease. Apply recommended grease onto drive shaft bearings. Slide intermediate housing onto rear of drive shaft and tap intermediate housing onto drive shaft bearings with a soft-faced mallet until seated. If original in-

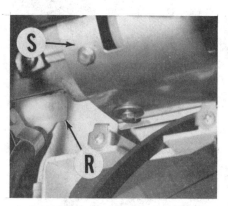

Fig. JS2-46—View identifies drive coupler shield (S) and location of bilge strainer (R).

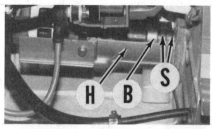

Fig. JS2-48—Cutaway view showing a typical intermediate housing setup. After removing intermediate housing assembly as outlined in text, remove drive shaft drive flange and front cover. Tap intermediate housing (H) off rear of drive shaft using a soft-faced mallet. Bearing (B) is located on drive shaft at front and rear of intermediate housing. Two seals (S) are located in rear of intermediate housing and two seals are located in front cover. An "O" ring is used around outside of front cover. A shim may be used between front cover and front drive shaft bearing.

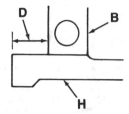

Fig. JS2-49—Refer to text after reassembling intermediate housing. Measure distance (D) between surface of intermediate housing (H) and surface of drive shaft front bearing (B) to determine if a shim is needed between front cover and bearing.

termediate housing and original drive shaft bearings are used, then original shim located between front cover and front drive shaft bearing can be used. If intermediate housing or drive shaft bearings have been renewed, then proceed as follows. Measure distance (D—Fig. JS2-49) from surface of intermediate housing (H) to surface of drive shaft front bearing (B). If distance measured is between 12.90 mm (0.5079 in.) and 13.05 mm (0.5138 in.), no shims need to be added between front cover and bearing. If distance measured is between 13.06 mm (0.5142 in.) and 13.20 mm (0.5197 in.), add Kawasaki shim 92025-502 between front cover and bearing. If distance measured is between 13.21 mm (0.5201 in.) and 13.32 mm (0.5244 in.), add Kawasaki shim 92025-503 between front cover and bearing. Install front cover and tighten cap screws to 16 N·m (12 ft.-lbs.). Install drive flange on drive shaft and tighten to 27 N·m (20 ft.-lbs.).

Install shims in their original locations between intermediate housing mounting flanges and vehicle hull. If vehicle hull has been renewed, then the drive shaft must be properly aligned to mate with jet pump. The drive shaft must be positioned so drive shaft center is 77 mm (3.03 in.) from top of jet pump mounting surface and equally centered from side-to-side. Adjust thickness of shims located under intermediate housing mounting flanges until correct drive shaft alignment is obtained. Tighten intermediate housing mounting cap screws to 16 N·m (12 ft.-lbs.) and recheck drive shaft alignment.

On JS440 models, remove grease fitting (G—Fig. JS2-51) at rear of jet pump housing. Install impeller on drive shaft and tighten using hand pressure. Do not overtighten impeller. Lightly grease lips of jet pump housing grease seals and rear surface of drive shaft with Shell MP or Alvania EP1 grease.

On JS550 models, apply Shell MP or Alvania EP1 grease on drive shaft

splines. Make sure "O" ring is located inside impeller shaft and is in good condition.

On all models, apply Loctite Superflex or a suitable RTV silicone sealer on jet pump inlet area where intake mates with vehicle hull. Slide jet pump assembly onto drive shaft.

On JS440 models, thickness of shims located under jet pump housing mounting flanges must be adjusted so clearance (C—Fig. JS2-52) between impeller and impeller housing is at least 0.1 mm (0.004 in.) measured throughout entire impeller circumference. Tighten jet pump housing mounting cap screws, then recheck impeller-to-impeller housing clearance. After recommended clearance is obtained, remove each jet pump housing mounting cap screw and apply Loctite Stud N'Bearing Mount or a suitable equivalent on threads of each screw, then install and tighten to 22 N·m (16 ft.-lbs.). Install grease fitting (G—Fig. JS2-51) and inject Shell MP or Alvania EP1 grease through grease fitting as needed.

On JS550 models, install shims in original locations under jet pump housing mounting flanges. Apply Loctite Stud N'Bearing Mount or a suitable equivalent on threads of each jet pump housing mounting cap screw, then install and tighten to 22 N·m (16 ft.-lbs.).

On all models, reconnect bilge siphon hose and cooling system supply hose onto fittings on jet pump. Reattach steering linkage joint (J) onto ball joint on steering nozzle (N). Install jet pump cover (R) and water intake grill (W) and tighten retaining screws to 10 N·m (88 in.-lbs.).

Use a suitable lifting device to hoist engine assembly into vehicle. Make sure coupler is located between engine drive flange and drive shaft drive flange. Install shims into original locations under engine mounts. Lay a straightedge (S—Fig. JS2-33) across top of engine drive flange and drive shaft drive flange. Engine drive flange should be 0-0.3 mm

(0-0.012 in.) higher than drive shaft drive flange. Measure distance (A—Fig. JS2-34) and distance (B). Distance (B) should not exceed distance (A) by more than 0.6 mm (0.024 in.). Measure clearance between engine drive flange and coupler and drive shaft drive flange and coupler. Total of the two clearance measurements should not exceed 0.5 mm (0.020 in.). If recommended settings are not measured, then adjust thickness of shims located under engine mounts until recommended settings are obtained. Apply Loctite Lock N'Seal or a suitable equivalent on threads of four engine retaining cap screws and tighten cap screws to 37 N·m (27 ft.-lbs.). Remeasure as previously outlined to verify engine drive flange to drive shaft flange settings are as recommended. Adjust shim thickness if needed.

Complete reassembly in reverse order of disassembly. Make sure "O" ring is positioned between cap (C—Fig. JS2-22) and electric box.

JET PUMP

Model JS440

R&R AND OVERHAUL. Disconnect battery cables from battery. Remove jet pump water intake grill (W—Fig. JS2-51) and cover (R). Detach steering linkage joint (J) at ball joint on steering nozzle (N). Remove bilge siphon hose and cooling system supply hose from fittings on jet pump housing. Remove four jet pump mounting cap screws (two at front and two at rear). Be careful and use a suitable sharp tool and cut silicone sealer between jet pump intake nozzle and vehicle hull. Slide jet pump assembly off rear of drive shaft. Note shims located under jet pump housing mounting flanges. Label shims for

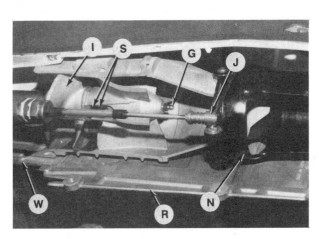

Fig. JS2-51—Cutaway view of jet pump assembly used on JS440 models and related components common to both JS440 and JS550 models.

G. Grease fitting
I. Impeller
J. Steering linkage joint
N. Steering nozzle
R. Jet pump cover
S. Seals
W. Water intake grill

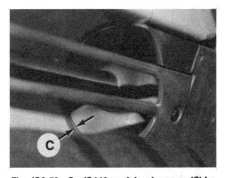

Fig. JS2-52—On JS440 models, clearance (C) between impeller and impeller housing should be at least 0.1 mm (0.004 in.) and should not exceed 0.87 mm (0.034 in.) measured throughout entire impeller circumference. On JS550 models, clearance between impeller and impeller housing should be at least 0.2-0.3 mm (0.008-0.012 in.) and should not exceed 0.6 mm (0.024 in.) measured throughout entire impeller circumference.

reassembly in original locations. Use a suitable tool and rotate impeller counterclockwise to remove from drive shaft.

Inspect impeller and impeller housing for excessive wear or any other damage. Diameter of impeller housing should not exceed 122.7 mm (4.83 in.). Renew jet pump housing if impeller housing is worn beyond limit or any other damage is noted. Minimum impeller diameter is 120 mm (4.72 in.). Inspect all other components for any type of damage. Remove snap ring and withdraw seals (S) using a suitable slide hammer. Diameter of drive shaft bushing in jet pump housing should not exceed 20.2 mm (0.79 in.). Renew bushing if worn beyond limit. Cool bushing and warm bushing area of jet pump to 93° C (200°F) to ease in installation. Install Shell MP or Alvania EP1 grease on seals in jet pump housing prior to installation. Install thick seal next to bushing and install both seals with open side facing toward snap ring groove. Install snap ring. Fill gap between seals with previously recommended grease. If output nozzle was removed, apply a thin coating of Loctite Superflex or a RTV silicone sealer on jet pump housing surface where output nozzle mates and install output nozzle. Apply Loctite Stud N'Bearing Mount or a suitable equivalent on threads of output nozzle mounting cap screws and tighten in a crisscross pattern to 16 N·m (12 ft.-lbs.).

Remove grease fitting (G) at rear of jet pump housing. Install impeller on drive shaft and tighten using hand pressure. Do not overtighten impeller. Lightly grease lips of jet pump housing grease seals and rear surface of drive shaft with Shell MP or Alvania EP1 grease. Apply Loctite Superflex or a suitable RTV silicone sealer on jet pump intake area where intake mates with vehicle hull. Slide jet pump assembly onto drive shaft. Install shims located under jet pump housing mounting flanges in

original locations. Tighten jet pump housing mounting cap screws, then check impeller-to-impeller housing clearance. Clearance (C—Fig. JS2-52) should not exceed 0.87 mm (0.034 in.) measured between impeller and impeller housing throughout entire impeller circumference. Adjust thickness of shims located under jet pump housing mounting flanges if measured clearance is not equal around impeller circumference. If measured clearance is beyond recommended limit, then renew excessively worn or damaged component. After correct setting is obtained, remove each jet pump housing mounting cap screw and apply Loctite Stud N'Bearing Mount or a suitable equivalent on threads of each screw, then install and tighten to 22 N·m (16 ft.-lbs.). Install grease fitting (G—Fig. JS2-51) and inject Shell MP or Alvania EP1 grease through grease fitting as needed. Reconnect bilge siphon hose and cooling system supply hose onto fittings on jet pump. Reattach steering linkage joint (J) onto ball joint on steering nozzle (N). Install jet pump cover (R) and water intake grill (W) and tighten retaining screws to 10 N·m (88 in.-lbs.).

Model JS550

R&R AND OVERHAUL. Disconnect battery cables from battery. Remove jet pump water intake grill (W—Fig. JS2-51) and cover (R). Detach steering linkage joint (J) at ball joint on steering nozzle (N). Remove bilge siphon hose and cool-

ing system supply hose from fittings on jet pump housing. Remove four jet pump mounting cap screws (two at front and two at rear). Be careful and use a suitable sharp tool and cut silicone sealer between jet pump intake nozzle and vehicle hull. Slide jet pump assembly off rear of drive shaft. Note shims located under jet pump housing mounting flanges. Label shims for reassembly in original locations. Place jet pump assembly on a clean work bench.

Remove steering nozzle (N—Fig. JS2-54). Remove four through-bolts (B), two on top and two on bottom, then separate inlet housing (1) and outlet nozzle (0) and vane housing (6). Insert Kawasaki impeller shaft holder 57001-3005 into impeller shaft (9—Fig. JS2-55) end. Position a suitable tool on impeller (2) nut and rotate impeller clockwise (L.H. threads), while not permitting impeller shaft to rotate, to remove impeller (2) from impeller shaft (9). Note shims (3) located behind impeller (2). Remove grease fitting cover (18) with "O" ring (17), grease fitting (16) and three cap screws to remove cap (15) with "O" ring (14) and cap plug (13). Place Kawasaki impeller shaft seal protector 57001-3003 on shaft end, then tap impeller shaft (9) with two roller bearings (7 and 11) out rear of vane housing (6). If plug (10) must be removed, use a suitable punch and hammer and drive plug (10) out rear of impeller shaft (9). Remove seals (4 and 5) from vane housing (6) using a suitable slide hammer. Use a suitable press and fixtures to remove bearings (7 and 11) from impeller shaft (9).

Inspect impeller (2) and impeller case of inlet housing (1) for excessive wear or any other damage. Manufacturer recommends renewing inlet housing (1) if any scratches noted in impeller case are deeper than 1 mm (0.04 in.). Inspect all other components for any type of damage. Renew components as needed.

Apply Shell MP or Alvania EP1 grease on seals (4 and 5) prior to installation. Install seal (5) (plain outer circumference) into vane housing (6), until seated, with open side facing toward impeller. Fill seal with previously recommended grease. Install seal (4) (ribbed outer circumference) into vane housing

Fig. JS2-55—Exploded view showing correct arrangement of jet pump components on JS550 models.

1. Inlet housing
2. Impeller
3. Shim
4. Seal
5. Seal
6. Vane housing
7. Bearing
8. "O" ring
9. Impeller shaft
10. Plug
11. Bearing
12. Shim
13. Cap plug
14. "O" ring
15. Cap
16. Grease fitting
17. "O" ring
18. Cover

Fig. JS2-54—On JS550 models, jet pump inlet housing (1), vane housing (6) and outlet nozzle (0) are held together by four through-bolts (B), two on top and two on bottom. Steering nozzle (N) pivots on outlet nozzle (0).

(6), until rib fits into stopper groove, with open side facing toward impeller. Fill seal with previously recommended grease.

Install plug (10) into pump shaft (9) with flat side of plug facing down. Do not lubricate plug prior to installation. Press bearings (7 and 11) onto impeller shaft (9) making sure bearings properly seat against large center section of impeller shaft. Place Kawasaki seal protector 57001-3003 onto impeller shaft end and install impeller shaft assembly into vane housing (6). Use a soft-faced mallet and tap impeller shaft end to properly seat assembly in vane housing. Measure distance from vane housing (6) surface to bearing (11) surface and record as measurement "A." Measure distance end of cap (15) will protrude into vane housing (6) when assembled and record as measurement "B." Subtract measurement "B" from measurement "A" and refer to "TABLE C" in Fig. JS2-56. Install recommended thickness of shim (12—Fig. JS2-55) between bearing (11) and cap (15). Shim (12) is available in thicknesses of 0.15 mm (0.006 in.) and 0.30 mm (0.012 in.). When required thickness exceeds 0.30 mm (0.012 in.), then shims must be stacked to obtain recommended thickness. Install cap (15) with "O" ring (14) and cap plug (13) and tighten retaining cap screws to 6 N·m (52 in.-lbs.). Install grease fitting (16) and inject Shell MP or Alvania EP1 grease through grease fitting opening until grease expels out from around lip of grease seal (4). Install grease fitting cover (18) with "O" ring (17) and securely tighten.

Lightly grease impeller shaft (9) threads with previously recommended grease. Install original thickness of shims (3) onto impeller shaft, then position impeller (2) on impeller shaft and rotate counterclockwise to thread onto impeller shaft. Insert Kawasaki impeller shaft holder 57001-3005 into impeller shaft (9) end. Position a suitable torque wrench and tool onto impeller (2) nut and rotate impeller counterclockwise, while not permitting impeller shaft to rotate, until a torque of 20 N·m (14 ft.-lbs.) is obtained on impeller. Temporarily reassemble inlet housing (1—Fig. JS2-54) and outlet nozzle (0) onto vane housing (6). Install four through-bolts (B) and slowly tighten bolts in a crisscross pattern while rotating impeller to be sure free rotation is noted. Tighten bolts to 5.5 N·m (48 in.-lbs.) if no binding is noted prior to final tightening. If binding is noted, repair cause or decrease shim (3—Fig. JS2-55) thickness as needed until no binding is obtained. Measure clearance between impeller (2) and impeller case of inlet housing (1). Recommended clearance is 0.2-0.3 mm

(0.008-0.012 in.) and should not exceed 0.6 mm (0.024 in.) measured throughout entire impeller circumference. If measured clearance is beyond recommended limit, then adjust thickness of shims (3) until clearance is less than 0.6 mm (0.024 in.) limit. Adding a 1 mm (0.04 in.) thick shim will reduce clearance approximately 0.144 mm (0.0057 in.).

After correct setting is obtained, disassemble inlet housing (1—Fig. JS2-54) and outlet nozzle (0) from vane housing (6). Apply a thin coating of Loctite Superflex or a suitable RTV silicone sealer onto inlet housing (1) and outlet nozzle (0) where surfaces mate with vane housing (6). Reinstall components and place Loctite Lock N'Seal or a suitable equivalent onto threads of through-bolts (B) and tighten to 5.5 N·m (48 in.-lbs.) using a crisscross pattern. Install steering nozzle (N).

Apply Shell MP or Alvania EP1 grease on drive shaft splines. Make sure "O" ring (8—Fig. JS2-55) is located inside of impeller shaft (9). Apply Loctite Superflex or a suitable RTV silicone sealer onto jet pump intake area where intake mates with vehicle hull. Slide jet pump assembly onto drive shaft. Install shims located under jet pump housing mounting flanges in original locations. Apply Loctite Stud N'Bearing Mount or a suitable equivalent on threads of each jet pump housing mounting cap screw, then install and tighten to 22 N·m (16 ft.-lbs.). Reconnect bilge siphon hose and cooling system supply hose onto fit-

tings on jet pump. Reattach steering linkage joint (J—Fig. JS2-51) onto ball joint on steering nozzle (N). Install jet pump cover (R) and water intake grill (W) and tighten retaining screws to 10 N·m (88 in.-lbs.).

STEERING

All Models

ADJUSTMENT. With steering handlebar in straight ahead position, jet pump steering nozzle (N—Fig. JS2-51)

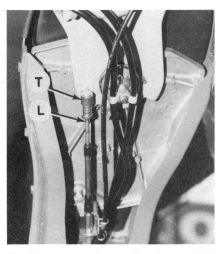

Fig. JS2-58—Loosen locknut (L) and remove joint (T) from ball joint on handlebar pivot plate and rotate joint (T) up or down on threaded end of steering cable as needed to center jet pump steering nozzle when steering handlebar is in a straight ahead position.

Fig. JS2-56—Use "TABLE C" to determine correct thickness of shim (12—Fig. JS2-55). Refer to text.

TABLE C

"A" Minus "B" Equals	Recommended Shim Thickness
0.10 - 0.25 mm (0.004 - 0.009 in.)	No Shim
0.26 - 0.40 mm (0.010 - 0.015 in.)	0.15 mm (0.006 in.)
0.41 - 0.55 mm (0.016 - 0.021 in.)	0.30 mm (0.012 in.)
0.56 - 0.70 mm (0.022 - 0.027 in.)	0.45 mm (0.018 in.)
0.71 - 0.85 mm (0.028 - 0.033 in.)	0.60 mm (0.024 in.)
0.86 - 0.94 mm (0.034 - 0.037 in.)	0.75 mm (0.030 in.)

should be centered or at a 90 degree angle to stern of vehicle. If not, raise handle pole and loosen locknut (L—Fig. JS2-58) below steering linkage joint (T). Remove joint (T) from ball joint on handlebar pivot plate. Rotate joint (T) up or down threaded end of steering cable as needed to properly center jet pump steering nozzle. After correct adjustment is obtained, reinstall steering linkage joint (T) onto ball joint and tighten locknut (L).

NOTE: If steering linkage joint (T) must be rotated out to where minimal threads on steering cable engage joint (T), then rotate joint (T) onto threaded end of steering cable to obtain safe thread engagement and complete adjustment on joint (J—Fig. JS2-51) at jet pump.

JET SKI
JF650 (X-2) AND JS650SX
NOTE: Metric fasteners are used throughout vehicle.

General

Engine Make.................................Own
Engine Type.........................Two-Stroke;
Water-Cooled
Number of Cylinders...........................2
Bore......................................76 mm
(3.0 in.)
Stroke ....70 mm
(2.75 in.)
Displacement............................635 cc
(38.7 cu. in.)
Compression Ratio.......................7.2:1
Engine Lubrication...............Oil Injection
Engine Oil Recommendation........Kawasaki Jet Ski
or Two-Stroke;
BIA Certified TC-W

Tune-Up

Engine Idle Speed.................1150-1350 rpm
Spark Plug:
NGK B7ES
Champion................................N4G
Electrode Gap..................0.7-0.8 mm
(0.027-0.031 in.)
Ignition:
Type ....CDI
Timing.................17° BTDC @ 6000 rpm
Carburetor:
Make ....Keihin
Model.............CDK34 Diaphragm
Bore Size.........................28 mm
(1.1 in.)

Sizes—Clearances

Cylinder Bore...................76.050-76.065 mm
(2.9941-2.9947 in.)
Service Limit.............................76.10
(2.996 in.)
Piston Diameter Measured
18 mm (0.7 in.) from Skirt
Bottom and 90° to Pin Bore......75.961-75.976 mm
(2.990-2.991 in.)
Service Limit.........................75.81 mm
(2.985 in.)
Piston-to-Cylinder Wall Clearance:
JF650...................0.074-0.104 mm
(0.0029-0.0041 in.)
JS650SX.................0.074-0.084 mm
(0.0029-0.0033 in.)
Piston Ring End Gap.................0.2-0.4 mm
(0.008-0.016 in.)
Service Limit............................0.7 mm
(0.027 in.)
Maximum Cylinder Head Warp............0.05 mm
(0.002 in.)
Connecting Rod Radial Clearance.....0.045-0.055 mm
(0.0018-0.0022 in.)
Service Limit...........................0.11 mm
(0.004 in.)
Connecting Rod Side Clearance........0.45-0.55 mm
(0.018-0.022 in.)

Sizes—Clearances (Cont.)

Service Limit............................0.8 mm
(0.031 in.)
Maximum Connecting Rod Bend or
Twist Measured Over a 100 mm
(3.9 in.) Length........................0.2 mm
(0.008 in.)
Maximum Crankshaft Runout at
Main Bearing Journal.................0.10 mm
(0.004 in.)

Capacities

Fuel Tank:
JF650............................. 16 L
(4.2 gal.)
JS650SX.......................... 17.5 L
(4.6 gal.)
Engine Oil Tank:
JF650............................. 2.7 L
(0.71 gal.)
JS650SX.......................... 2.8 L
(0.74 gal.)

Tightening Torques

Carburetor Mounting Nuts.................7.8 N·m
(69 in.-lbs.)
Cylinder Head Nuts:
JF650.............................25 N·m
(18 ft.-lbs.)
JS650SX.......................... 23 N·m
(17 ft.-lbs.)
Cylinder Block Nuts.....................34 N·m
(25 ft.-lbs.)
Crankcase Cap Screws:
6 mm.............................7.8 N·m
(69 in.-lbs.)
8 mm............................. 25 N·m
(18 ft.-lbs.)
Engine-to-Engine Mounting Plate
Cap Screws:
JF650.............................23 N·m
(17 ft.-lbs.)
JS650SX.......................... 36 N·m
(26 ft.-lbs.)
Engine Mounting Cap Screws..............36 N·m
(26 ft.-lbs.)
Engine Drive Flange:
JF650.............................98 N·m
(72 ft.-lbs.)
JS650SX.......................... 27 N·m
(20 ft.-lbs.)
Drive Shaft Drive Flange:
JF650.............................98 N·m
(72 ft.-lbs.)
JS650SX..........................27 N·m
(20 ft.-lbs.)
Drive Shaft Bearing Housing.............22 N·m
(16 ft.-lbs.)
Jet Pump Mounting Cap Screws...........25 N·m
(18 ft.-lbs.)

Tightening Torques (Cont.)

Jet Pump Impeller.........................98 N·m
(72 ft.-lbs.)
Flywheel Cap Screw:
JF650.................................69 N·m
(51 ft.-lbs.)
JS650SX.............................98 N·m
(72 ft.-lbs.)
Spark Plug............................27 N·m
(20 ft.-lbs.)
Standard Fasteners:
5 mm..........................3.4-4.9 N·m
(30-43 in.-lbs.)
6 mm..........................5.9-7.8 N·m
(52-69 in.-lbs.)

Tightening Torques (Cont.)

8 mm..................................14-19 N·m
(10-14 ft.-lbs.)
10 mm................................25-39 N·m
(18-29 ft.-lbs.)
12 mm................................44-61 N·m
(32-45 ft.-lbs.)
14 mm................................73-98 N·m
(54-72 ft.-lbs.)
16 mm..............................115-155 N·m
(85-114 ft.-lbs.)
18 mm..............................165-225 N·m
(121-165 ft.-lbs.)
20 mm..............................225-325 N·m
(165-239 ft.-lbs.)

LUBRICATION

All Models

The engine is lubricated by oil mixed with the fuel. All models are equipped with oil injection. The manufacturer recommends using Kawasaki Jet Ski Oil or a BIA certified two-stroke TC-W engine oil. During break-in (first five hours or three tankfuls) of a new or rebuilt engine, mix fuel with oil in fuel tank at a ratio of 40:1. Switch to straight fuel in fuel tank at the completion of the break-in period. Manufacturer recommends regular or no-lead automotive gasoline having a minimum octane rating of 87. Gasoline and oil should be thoroughly mixed in fuel tank when used during break-in period.

Lubricate all cables, linkage and pivots with WD-40 or Bel-Ray 6 in 1 every 25 hours or more frequent if needed.

Fig. JS3-1—View identifies location of choke lever (L) on JF650 models.

FUEL SYSTEM

All Models

CARBURETOR. A Keihin type CDK34 diaphragm carburetor is used on all models. Carburetor choke plate is actuated by choke lever (L—Fig. JS3-1) on JF650 models and by choke knob (K—Fig. JS3-2) on JS650SX models via a cable and linkage.

Initial setting of low speed mixture needle (L—Fig. JS3-3) is one turn out from a lightly seated position on all models. Initial setting of high speed mixture needle (H) is 5/8 turn out from a lightly seated position on all models. Final carburetor adjustments must be made with engine at normal operating temperature and running. Clockwise rotation of either needle leans the mixture. Adjust low speed mixture needle (L) until smooth acceleration from the idle position is noted. After adjusting low speed mixture needle, adjust idle speed screw (I—Fig. JS3-4) until engine idle speed is approximately 1150-1350 rpm with throttle lever completely released. To adjust high speed fuel:air mixture, the engine spark plugs must be removed and insulator tip color noted.

NOTE: Make sure that fuel tank contains straight fuel.

Make sure cooling system will receive an adequate supply of water, then operate and sustain engine at wide-

Fig. JS3-2—View identifies location of choke knob (K) and fuel selector valve (V) on JS650SX models.

open throttle for a suitable test period. Stop the engine with throttle in wide-open position. Remove spark plugs and note insulator tip color. Normal insulator tip color is brown to light tan. If insulator tip appears to be light tan to white in color, then mixture is too lean and high speed mixture needle (H—Fig. JS3-3) should be rotated out-

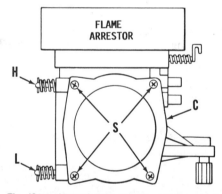

Fig. JS3-3—View identifies location of low speed mixture needle (L) and high speed mixture needle (H). Remove four corner screws (S) and withdraw cover (C) to service regulating diaphragm or check inlet needle valve lever (L—Fig. JS3-5) setting.

Fig. JS3-4—View identifies location of idle speed screw (I).

ward (counterclockwise) ¼ turn to richen mixture. If insulator tip appears to be dark brown to black in color, then mixture is too rich and high speed mixture needle (H) should be rotated inward (clockwise) ¼ turn to lean mixture. Clean, regap and reinstall spark plugs and continue test procedure until spark plug insulator tip is a normal color.

Carburetor regulating diaphragm can be serviced after removing four cover screws (S) and withdrawing cover (C). Inspect diaphragm for damage and renew if needed. Install diaphragm with a new gasket between diaphragm and cover.

Inlet needle valve lever (L—Fig. JS3-5) should be 1-2 mm (0.04-0.08 in.) below surface of carburetor housing when needle valve is seated as shown in Fig. JS3-5. If lever must be adjusted, push down on lever immediately above spring to collapse the spring, then bend the end which contacts needle valve.

REED VALVES. A vee type reed valve assembly is located between the intake manifold and crankcase for each cylinder. Remove intake manifold for access to reed valve assemblies.

Renew reeds if petals are broken, cracked, warped or bent. Do not attempt to bend or straighten reeds. Reed

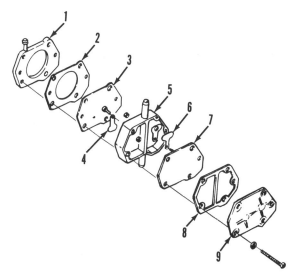

Fig. JS3-8—Exploded view of fuel pump assembly.
1. Base
2. Gasket
3. Diaphragm
4. Check valve
5. Body
6. Check valve
7. Diaphragm
8. Gasket
9. Cover

seating surface on reed blocks should be smooth and flat. Maximum allowable reed petal stand open is 0.2 mm (0.008 in.). Install reed valve assemblies into crankcase intakes with small hole in reed valve holder on bottom.

FUEL PUMP. A diaphragm type fuel pump assembly (F—Fig. JS3-7) is used on all models. Refer to Fig. JS3-8 for an exploded view of fuel pump assembly. Alternating pressure and vacuum pulsations in the crankcase actuates the diaphragms and check valves in the pump. Fuel pump assembly uses reed valve type check valves.

With reference to Fig. JS3-8, disassemble fuel pump assembly. Inspect body (5), diaphragms (3 and 7) and check valves (4 and 6) for damage and renew if needed. Renew gaskets (2 and 8) during reassembly. Reassemble components, then securely and evenly tighten cover (9) retaining screws.

FUEL TANK AND FUEL FILTER. A fuel strainer is attached on the bottom of the "ON" fuel tank pickup line and on the bottom of the "RES" fuel tank pickup line. The pickup lines are contained within fuel tank pickup assembly

(P—Fig. JS3-10). On JS650SX models, an inline sediment bowl (I) is used to prevent entrance of water into fuel tank. Occasionally or if water is noted, unscrew ring nut (N) and withdraw cup (C) with sealing ring from base. Clean cup with a suitable cleaning solution. Renew sealing ring and securely tighten nut (N) during installation of cup (C). On all models, after every 25 hours of operation or more frequent if needed, fuel tank strainers (S—Fig. JS3-11)

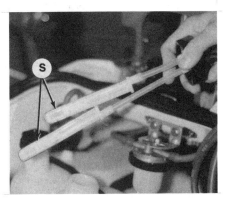

Fig. JS3-11—View identifies fuel tank strainers (S). Reserve "RES" is longest pickup line.

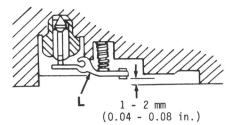

Fig. JS3-5—Inlet needle valve lever (L) should be 1-2 mm (0.04-0.08 in.) below surface of carburetor housing when needle valve is seated.

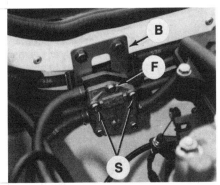

Fig. JS3-7—View identifies fuel pump assembly (F) used on all models. Remove two screws (S) to withdraw fuel pump assembly from mounting bracket (B).

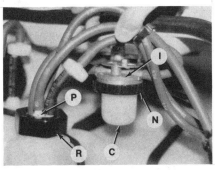

Fig. JS3-10—Ring nut (R) secures pickup assembly (P) in fuel tank. On JS650SX models, a sediment bowl assembly (I) is used. Unscrew ring nut (N) to withdraw cup (C) with sealing ring.

Fig. JS3-13—Rotate locknuts (N) up or down cable housing end as needed to adjust throttle lever free play. Model JF650 is shown. Throttle cable on Model JS650SX is routed from the bottom.

should be cleaned. Unscrew ring nut (R—Fig. JS3-10) and withdraw pickup assembly (P). Clean strainers (S—Fig. JS3-11) with a suitable cleaning solution and a soft-bristled brush if needed. Renew sealing ring and securely tighten nut (R—Fig. JS3-10) during installation of pickup assembly (P).

THROTTLE LEVER FREE PLAY. Throttle lever should have a small amount of free play prior to activating carburetor throttle shaft when throttle lever is in released position. To adjust, rotate locknuts (N—Fig. JS3-13) up or down cable housing end as needed until a small amount of free play is noted. Tighten locknuts (N) to retain adjustment.

FLAME ARRESTOR. A flame arrestor is located beneath cover (C—Fig. JS3-15). Every 25 hours or more frequent if needed, remove two cap screws (S) and withdraw cover and flame arrestor. Inspect flame arrestor for contamination and use clean compressed air to blow clean. Renew flame arrestor if damage is noted. Install flame arrestor while making sure gasket is located beneath flame arrestor. Apply Loctite Lock N' Seal or a suitable equivalent on threads of the two cap screws (S) retaining cover (C) and securely tighten.

OIL INJECTION

All Models

BLEEDING PUMP. To bleed trapped air from oil supply line or pump, first make sure vehicle is level and oil tank is full.

Remove bypass hose (H—Fig. JS3-30) from fitting (F) on cylinder head and exhaust pipe. Refer to Fig. JS3-31. Connect a short piece of a suitable sized hose to fitting on cylinder head and exhaust pipe, then connect hose ends to a tee

adapter. Use a suitable sized hose and an adapter and connect a supplemental water supply to tee adapter.

NOTE: When using a supplemental water supply, do not turn on water until engine is ready to be started as exhaust flooding could occur. Operate engine only at low rpm or during a test, do not exceed recommended high rpm and only operate for a short period of time.

Place a container under oil pump (P—Fig. JS3-17). Open oil pump air bleed screw (B) two or three turns to allow oil to seep out around screw threads. After no air bubbles are noticed, close air bleed screw (B).

Start engine, then turn on supplemental water supply. Adjust water pressure to where a small amount of water is being discharged out bypass outlet on side of hull. Note transparent outlet hose (T). Allow engine to idle until no air bubbles are noted in transparent outlet hose (T).

Turn off supplemental water supply and stop engine.

NOTE: Make sure engine is not operated without a supply of water longer than 10-15 seconds or damage to engine and/or exhaust components could result.

OIL PUMP OUTPUT. Connect a supplemental water supply as previously outlined under BLEEDING PUMP.

NOTE: A fuel:oil mixture of 40:1 must be supplied to engine during test.

Disconnect transparent outlet hose (T—Fig. JS3-17) from engine inlet fitting. Route end of transparent outlet hose (T) into a suitable measuring container. Connect a tachometer to engine. Start engine, then turn on supplemental water supply and properly adjust water flow. Accelerate engine to 6000 rpm and maintain for one minute. After one minute, note amount of oil in measur-

ing container. Allow engine to return to idle position, then turn off supplemental water supply and stop engine.

NOTE: If oil pump output test must be reperformed, allow engine to idle for a short period with supplemental water supply circulating through cooling system. Do not sustain engine at a high rpm for an extended period when not operated under a load and do not exceed the recommended testing rpm of 6000.

Oil pump can be considered satisfactory if measured oil is within the range of 5.9-7.2 mL (0.20-0.24 oz.). If oil pump output is not within the recommended range, then oil pump must be renewed.

IGNITION

All Models

All models are equipped with a simultaneous capacitor discharge ignition system. The ignition timing is electronically advanced as the magneto base plate is fixed. Ignition timing should not require adjustment, after first being correctly set, unless magneto base plate is moved or an ignition component is renewed.

IGNITION TIMING. Ignition timing should be 17 degrees or 2.0 mm (0.08 in.) before top dead center (BTDC) at 6000 rpm on all models. Ignition timing can be checked dynamically using a suitable power timing light. Remove plug (G—Fig. JS3-19) from flywheel cover (C).

Remove bypass hose (H—Fig. JS3-30) from fitting (F) on cylinder head and exhaust pipe. Refer to Fig. JS3-31. Connect a short piece of a suitable sized hose to fitting on cylinder head and exhaust pipe, then connect hose ends to tee adapter. Use a suitable sized hose and an adapter and connect a supplemental water supply to tee adapter.

NOTE: When using a supplemental water supply, do not turn on water until engine is ready to be started as exhaust flooding could occur. Operate engine only at low rpm or during a test, do not exceed recommended high rpm and only operate for a short period of time.

Connect a tachometer to engine. Start engine, then turn on supplemental water supply. Adjust water pressure to where a small amount of water is being discharged out bypass outlet on side of hull. Accelerate engine to 6000 rpm. Point timing light so strobe light flashes into plug opening (O—Fig. JS3-19). Note if timing mark on flywheel aligns with

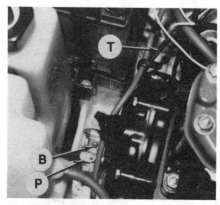

Fig JS3-15—Remove two cap screws (S) to withdraw cover (C) and flame arrestor.

Fig. JS3-17—View identifies oil injection pump assembly (P), air bleed screw (B) and transparent outlet hose (T).

notch (N) in flywheel cover. Allow engine to return to idle position, then turn off supplemental water supply and stop engine.

NOTE: Make sure engine is not operated without a supply of water longer than 10-15 seconds or damage to engine and/or exhaust components could result.

NOTE: If ignition timing test must be reperformed, allow engine to idle for a short period with supplemental water supply circulating through cooling system. Do not sustain engine at a high rpm for an extended period when not operated under a load and do not exceed the recommended testing rpm of 6000.

If ignition timing is incorrect, first disconnect battery cables from battery and remove battery from vehicle. Remove fuel tank hoses, as needed, and oil tank hose and plug openings to allow removal of respective tank. Remove fuel tank and oil tank. Remove oil injection pump assembly (P). Remove flywheel cover (C). Remove flywheel retaining cap screw then use a suitable puller and withdraw flywheel. Loosen magneto base plate screws and rotate base plate as needed. Tighten magneto base plate screws, then reinstall flywheel and tighten retaining cap screw to 69 N·m (51 ft.-lbs.) on JF650 models and 98 N·m (72 ft.-lbs.) on JS650SX models.

Apply a suitable thread locking solution on threads of flywheel cover retaining screws, then install flywheel cover (C) with "O" ring seal and tighten screws to 7.8 N·m (69 in.-lbs.). Reinstall oil injection pump assembly (P), fuel tank and oil tank and reconnect hoses. Reinstall battery and connect battery cables. Bleed air from oil supply line or oil injection pump as outlined under BLEEDING PUMP in OIL INJECTION section.

Recheck ignition timing. Continue previously outlined adjustment procedure until correct ignition timing is obtained.

If accuracy of timing mark on flywheel is questioned, then detach spark plug leads from spark plugs and ground terminal ends. Disconnect battery cables from battery and remove battery from vehicle. Remove fuel tank hoses, as needed, and oil tank hose and plug openings to allow removal of respective tank and oil tank. Remove oil injection pump assembly (P). Remove flywheel cover (C). Remove number one cylinder (forward cylinder) spark plug. Position a suitable dial indicator so indicator needle projects through number one cylinder spark plug hole. Rotate flywheel until piston in cylinder is posi-

tioned at TDC. Zero dial indicator face with needle, then rotate flywheel clockwise until 2.0 mm (0.08 in.) is read on dial indicator.

Apply a suitable thread locking solution on threads of flywheel cover retaining screws, then install flywheel cover (C) with "O" ring seal and tighten screws to 7.8 N·m (69 in.-lbs.). Reinstall oil injection pump assembly (P), fuel tank and oil tank and reconnect hoses. Reinstall battery and connect battery cables.

Note if original mark on flywheel aligns with notch (N) in flywheel cover. If not, scribe a new mark on flywheel in alignment with notch. Remove dial indicator and reinstall spark plug. Reconnect spark plug leads.

Bleed air from oil supply line or oil injection pump as outlined under BLEEDING PUMP in OIL INJECTION section. Recheck ignition timing as previously outlined. New scribe mark should align with notch (N) in flywheel cover if ignition timing is correct.

TROUBLE-SHOOTING. If ignition malfunction occurs, use only approved procedures to prevent damage to the components. The fuel system should be checked first to make certain that faulty running is not caused by contaminated fuel. Make sure malfunction is not due to spark plugs, wiring or wiring connection failure. Trouble-shoot ignition circuit using a suitable ohmmeter as follows:

Disconnect battery cables from battery terminals. On JS650SX models, remove electric box cover mounting cap screws and withdraw cover to expose wire connectors. On JF650 models, disconnect black/red wire and black wire at connectors leading to exciter coil mounted on magneto base plate. On JS650SX models, disconnect black/yellow wire and black/red wire at connectors leading to exciter coil mounted on magneto base plate. Check condition of exciter coil by attaching a tester lead

to terminal end of each wire leading to exciter coil. Exciter coil can be considered satisfactory if resistance reading is within the limits of 250-380 ohms. Exciter coil is renewable as an assembly with battery charge coil and magneto base plate.

To renew magneto base plate assembly, first remove battery from vehicle. Remove fuel tank hoses, as needed, and oil tank hose and plug openings to allow removal of respective tank. Remove fuel tank and oil tank. Remove oil injection pump assembly (P—Fig. JS3-19). Remove flywheel cover (C). Remove flywheel retaining cap screw, then use a suitable puller and withdraw flywheel. Renew magneto base plate asembly. Align mark (M—Fig. JS3-20) on magneto base plate with mark (K) on crankcase, then securely tighten retaining screws. Install flywheel and tighten retaining cap screw to 69 N·m (51 ft.-lbs.) on JF650 models and 98 N·m (72 ft.-lbs.) on JS650SX models.

Apply a suitable thread locking solution on threads of flywheel cover (C—Fig. JS3-19) retaining screws, then install

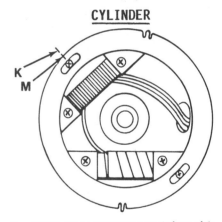

Fig. JS3-20—When renewing magneto base plate, align mark (M) on magneto base plate with mark (K) on crankcase.

Fig. JS3-19—View identifies flywheel cover (C), plug (G) and oil injection pump assembly (P). With plug (G) removed, notch (N) in flywheel cover opening (O) is exposed. Refer to text.

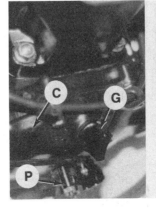
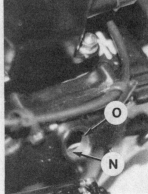

flywheel cover with "O" ring seal and tighten screws to 7.8 N·m (69 in.-lbs.). Reinstall oil injection pump assembly (P), fuel tank and oil tank and reconnect hoses. Reinstall battery and connect battery cables. Bleed air from oil supply line and oil injection pump as outlined under BLEEDING PUMP in OIL INJECTION section. Recheck and adjust igni-

tion timing as previously outlined under IGNITION TIMING.

To check CDI module/ignition coil assembly on JF650 models, refer to Fig. JS3-21. To check CDI module/ignition coil assembly on JS650SX models, refer to Fig. JS3-22. Ignition coil secondary winding resistance should be 2100-3100 ohms.

+Tester Lead / −Tester Lead	Black /Red	Black /White	Black /Yellow
Black /Red		B	C
Black /White	A		A
Black /Yellow	B	D	

Fig. JS3-21—Use adjacent chart and values listed below to test CDI module/ignition coil unit on JF650 models.
A. Infinite
B. 1,000-5,000 ohms
C. 500,000-Infinite ohms
D. 5,000-17,000 ohms

+Tester Lead / −Tester Lead	Brown	Black /Yellow	Black	Blue
Brown		E	A	E
Black /Yellow	C		A	B
Black	D	D		D
Blue	C	B	A	

Fig. JS3-22—Use adjacent chart and values listed below to test CDI module/ignition coil unit on JS650SX models.
A. Infinite
B. Zero ohms
C. 3,000-6,000 ohms
D. Initial: 15,000-25,000 ohms; Charging capacitor: 50,000-100,000 ohms*
E. 500,000-Infinite ohms*
*If test must be reperformed to obtain value, a 30 second gap must be existent between tests.

CHARGING SYSTEM

All Models

All models are equipped with a charge coil, rectifier/regulator and battery. Standard battery has a 19 ampere hour, 12 volt rating on all models. The charge coil should produce 38 ac volts when engine is operated at approximately 3000 rpm. Rectifier/ regulator assembly should prevent regulated voltage from exceeding 15 dc volts.

The battery electrolyte level should be checked periodically and filled to maximum level with distilled water if required. The battery should be removed from the vehicle and the battery caps removed when charging. The manufacturer recommends charging the battery at a rate of 1.9 amperes for a period of 10 hours. Do not exceed recommended charging rate.

NOTE: Make sure battery charging area is well ventilated.

The charge coil can be statically tested using a suitable ohmmeter. Disconnect battery cables from battery terminals. On JS650SX models, remove electric box cover mounting cap screws and withdraw cover to expose wire connectors. On all models, disconnect two yellow wires at connectors leading to charge coil mounted on magneto base plate. Refer to Fig. JS3-23 for Model JF650 and Fig. JS3-24 for Model JS650SX. Check condition of charge coil by attaching one tester lead to terminal end of one yellow wire and attaching other tester lead to terminal end of remaining yellow wire. Resistance reading should be 1.5-2.3 ohms. Check resistance between each charge coil wire and black wire. Tester should show 0.7-1.3 ohms resistance at each wire. Charge coil is renewable as an assembly with ignition exciter coil and magneto base plate.

To renew magneto base plate assembly, first remove battery from vehicle. Remove fuel tank hoses, as needed, and oil tank hose and plug openings to allow removal of respective tank. Remove fuel tank and oil tank. Remove oil injection pump assembly (P—Fig. JS3-19). Remove flywheel cover (C). Remove flywheel retaining cap screw, then use a suitable puller and withdraw flywheel. Renew magneto base plate assembly. Align mark (M—Fig. JS3-20) on magneto base plate with mark (K) on crankcase, then securely tighten retaining screws. Install flywheel and tighten retaining cap screw to 69 N·m (51 ft.-lbs.) on JF650 models and 98 N·m (72 ft.-lbs.) on JS650SX models.

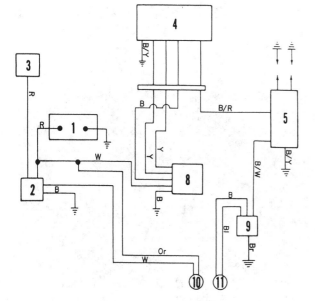

Fig. JS3-23—Wiring diagram typical of all JF650 models.
1. Battery
2. Starter solenoid
3. Starter motor
4. Magneto assy
5. CDI module/ignition coil assy.
8. Rectifier/regulator
9. Stop switch relay
10. Start switch
11. Stop switch
B. Black
R. Red
W. White
Y. Yellow
Bl. Blue
Br. Brown
Or. Orange
B/R. Black/red
B/W. Black/white
B/Y. Black/yellow

Apply a suitable thread locking solution on threads of flywheel cover (C—Fig. JS3-19) retaining screws, then install flywheel cover with "O" ring seal and tighten screws to 7.8 N·m (69 in.-lbs.) Reinstall oil injection pump assembly (P), fuel tank and oil tank and reconnect hoses. Reinstall battery and connect battery cables. Bleed air from oil supply line and oil injection pump as outlined under BLEEDING PUMP in OIL INJECTION section. Recheck and adjust ignition timing as outlined under IGNITION TIMING in IGNITION section.

To check rectifier/regulator assembly, refer to chart shown in Fig. JS3-26. To check rectifier/regulator during operation, first make sure battery is fully charged, charge coil test good and all wiring is in good condition and all connectors fit tightly or are securely fastened. Attach test leads of a suitable voltmeter directly on battery terminals.

Remove bypass hose (H—Fig. JS3-30) from fitting (F) on cylinder head and exhaust pipe. Refer to Fig. JS3-31. Connect a short piece of a suitable sized hose to fitting on cylinder head and exhaust pipe, then connect hose ends to a tee adapter. Use a suitable sized hose and an adapter and connect a supplemental water supply to tee adapter.

NOTE: When using a supplemental water supply, do not turn on water until engine is ready to be started as exhaust flooding could occur. Operate engine only at low rpm or during a test, do not exceed recommended high rpm and only operate for a short period of time.

Start engine, then turn on supplemental water supply. Adjust water pressure to where a small amount of water is being discharged out bypass outlet on side of hull. Accelerate engine while observing voltmeter. The voltmeter should show approximately 15 dc volts. Allow engine to return to idle position then turn off supplemental water supply and stop engine.

NOTE: Make sure engine is not operated without a supply of water longer than 10-15 seconds or damage to engine and/or exhaust components could result.

COOLING SYSTEM

All Models

All models are water-cooled. Forced water is supplied to the engine through jet pump outlet fitting and directed through hose (T—Fig. JS3-28) to fitting on exhaust manifold. As jet pump impeller rpm increases, so does water circulation through cooling system.

Make sure jet pump water intake grill

(W—Fig. JS3-29) is kept clean. Inspect all hoses periodically for cracks, kinks or any other damage and renew if needed. The cooling system should be flushed out after each operating period when the vehicle is used in contaminated or salt water. The cooling system should be flushed out prior to extended periods of storage and prior to usage after extended periods of storage.

To flush the cooling system, remove bypass hose (H—Fig. JS3-30) from fitting

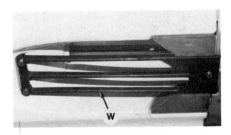

Fig. JS3-29—Jet pump water Intake grill (W) must be kept clean of all foreign debris.

Fig. JS3-24—Wiring diagram typical of all JS650SX models.
1. Battery
2. Starter solenoid
3. Starter motor
4. Magneto assy.
5. CDI module/ignition coil assy.
8. Rectifier/regulator
10. Start switch
11. Stop switch
B. Black
R. Red
W. White
Y. Yellow
Bl. Blue
Or. Orange
B/R. Black/red
B/Y. Black/yellow

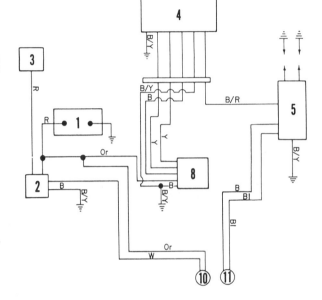

Fig. JS3-26—Use adjacent chart and values listed below to test condition of rectifier/regulator assembly.
A. Infinite resistance
B. 1,000-5,000 ohms
C. 2,000-10,000 ohms

+Tester Lead / -Tester Lead	White (JF650) Orange (JS650SX)	Black	Yellow	Yellow
White (JF650) Orange (JS650SX)		A	A	A
Black	A		A	A
Yellow	B	C		A
Yellow	B	C	A	

Fig. JS3-28—View identifies jet pump cooling system supply hose (T) and bilge siphon hose (S).

(F) on cylinder head and exhaust pipe. Refer to Fig. JS3-31. Connect a short piece of a suitable sized hose to fitting on cylinder head and exhaust pipe, then connect hose ends to a tee adapter. Use a suitable sized hose and an adapter and connect a supplemental water supply to tee adapter.

NOTE: Do not turn on water until engine is ready to be started as exhaust flooding could occur. Operate engine only at low rpm.

Start engine, then turn on supplemental water supply. Adjust water pressure to where a small amount of water is being discharged out bypass outlet on side of hull. Allow water to circulate through system for several minutes. Turn off supplemental water supply. If vehicle is to be stored for an extended period, raise rear of vehicle and quickly accelerate engine between idle and one-quarter throttle a couple of times. This is to force out all water within exhaust system, thus preventing damage from developing contaminates or freezing.

NOTE: Make sure engine is not operated without a supply of water longer than 10-15 seconds or damage to engine and/or exhaust components could result.

Fig. JS3-30—View identifies bypass hose (H) and fitting (F) on cylinder head and exhaust pipe. Knob (K) controls operation of water drain valve via a cable.

WATER DRAIN VALVE

All Models

A reed valve type water drain valve is mounted on the lower crankcase half. Water drain valve is provided to allow crankcase to be easily drained when contaminated with water. Knob (K—Fig. JS3-30) is used to operate a control valve in water drain valve assembly via a cable. The positioning of the control valve will allow operation or restrict operation of reed valve in water drain valve assembly. To drain crankcase of any water, remove spark plug leads and properly ground. Pull knob (K) up to allow operation of reed valve. Crank engine over with electric starter to expel water from crankcase. To restrict operation of reed valve, push knob (K) down to seated position.

ENGINE

All Models

REMOVE AND REINSTALL. Disconnect battery cables from battery and remove battery from vehicle. Remove oil tank and on Model JF650, remove fuel tank. Plug all hose and fitting openings. Remove throttle cable and choke cable from carburetor. Remove hoses from carburetor, label if needed and plug openings. Remove exhaust pipe from exhaust manifold. Separate wires at connectors leading to exciter coil and battery charge coil mounted on magneto base plate.

Detach spark plug leads, disconnect starter motor lead and all other electrical wiring that will interfere with engine removal and label for reassembly. Remove fuel pump pulse line from crankcase fitting. Remove cooling system supply hose (P—Fig. JS3-32) from fitting on bottom of exhaust manifold. Remove four cap screws (C—Fig. JS3-33) and washers retaining engine to vehicle hull. Note shims located under engine mounts and identify each shim for installation in original location. Remove any other components that will interfere with engine removal. Use a suitable lifting device to hoist engine assembly from vehicle. Place engine assembly on a clean work bench.

Use a suitable lifting device to hoist engine assembly into vehicle. Make sure coupler is located between engine drive flange and drive shaft drive flange. Install shims into original locations under engine mounts. Align cast protrusion (P—Fig. JS3-34) on flywheel cover with arrow (A) molded into vehicle hull. Check for clearance between engine mounting plate and shims on top of vehicle hull mounts by attempting to rock engine with light hand pressure. If rocking is noted, indicating clearance, then adjust thickness of shims until engine will not rock on mounts. Apply Loctite Lock N'Seal or a suitable equivalent on threads of four engine retaining cap screws (C—Fig. JS3-33) and tighten cap screws to 36 N·m (26 ft.-lbs.).

Complete reassembly in reverse order of disassembly. Bleed air from oil supply line or oil injection pump as outlined under BLEEDING PUMP in OIL INJECTION section.

DISASSEMBLY. Remove engine mounting plate. Remove flame arrestor assembly, carburetor and spark plugs. Remove water drain valve cable from mounting bracket. Remove cylinder

Fig. JS3-32—View identifying cooling system supply hose (P) routed from jet pump and bypass hose (B) routed to fitting in side of hull.

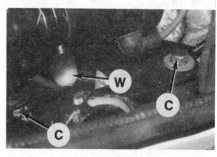

Fig. JS3-33—Engine is retained to vehicle hull by front and rear cap screws (C) on each side of engine. A lockwasher and flat washer is used on each cap screw. View identifies location of water drain valve (W) on port side of engine.

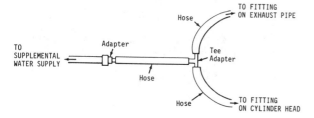

Fig. JS3-31—Remove bypass hose (H—Fig. JS3-30), then connect components as shown to fitting (F—Fig. JS3-30) on cylinder head and exhaust pipe to connect a supplemental water supply.

head nuts, then tap cylinder head with a soft-faced mallet to separate components and lift cylinder head off cylinder block. Remove cylinder block nuts, then tap cylinder block with a soft-faced mallet to break loose from top crankcase half. Carefully withdraw cylinder block. Rotate crankshaft to position piston for number one cylinder (front) at top of stroke. Remove piston pin retaining clips. Use a suitable piston pin puller if needed and extract piston pin. Lift piston off connecting rod. Remove needle bearing from small end of connecting rod. Keep piston components together and place to the side. Label components ''number one cylinder'' for reference during reassembly. Repeat procedure to remove piston for number two cylinder and label accordingly.

Remove oil injection pump assembly. Remove flywheel cover. Hold flywheel with a suitable tool and rotate engine drive flange off crankshaft using Kawasaki tool 57001-1230. Remove electric starter motor and reduction gear assembly. Remove cap screw retaining flywheel, then use a suitable puller and withdraw flywheel. Note mark (M—Fig. JS3-20) on magneto base plate that aligns with mark (K) on crankcase. If magneto base plate position has been altered during ignition timing adjustment, then a new mark should be scribed in magneto base plate to align with mark (K) on crankcase to ensure correct position during reassembly. Remove magneto base plate with ignition components. Remove water drain valve assembly. Mount crankcase assembly in an engine holder or suitably support top of upper crankcase half so lower crankcase half faces upward. Remove seven 6 mm cap screws and washers and eight 8 mm cap screws and washers securing crankcase halves together. Use a soft-faced mallet and tap crankcase halves to separate or pry halves apart using care not to damage

mating surfaces. Lift bottom crankcase half off top crankcase half. Crankshaft assembly can now be withdrawn from top crankcase half.

Engine components are now ready for overhaul as outlined in the appropriate following paragraphs. Refer to the following section for assembly procedure.

ASSEMBLY. Make sure all joint and gasket surfaces are clean, free from nicks and burrs and hardened cement or carbon.

Whenever the engine is disassembled, it is recommended that all gasket surfaces and mating surfaces without gaskets be carefully checked for nicks, burrs and warped surfaces which might

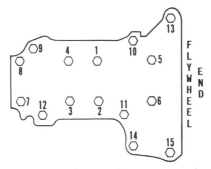

Fig. JS3-35—Tighten crankcase cap screws in sequence shown. Refer to text for tightening torque specifications.

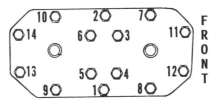

Fig. JS3-36—Tighten cylinder head nuts in sequence shown. Refer to text for tightening torque specifications.

interfere with a tight seal. Cylinder head and mating surfaces of crankcase halves should be checked on a surface plate and lapped, if necessary, to provide a smooth surface. Do not remove any more metal than is necessary.

When assembling engine, first lubricate all friction surfaces and bearings with engine oil. Apply a high temperature grease on lip of seals. Properly assemble components on crankshaft. Install crankshaft assembly into top crankcase half. Make sure pin (5—Fig. JS3-37) in top crankcase half properly seats in hole in center oil seal assembly. Wipe mating surfaces of crankcase halves clean and make sure surfaces are dry. Apply a coating of Kawasaki Bond or a suitable form-in-place gasket compound on crankcase mating surfaces of bottom crankcase half. Position bottom crankcase half onto top crankcase half. Apply a suitable thread locking solution on threads of crankcase halves securing cap screws, then install the seven 6 mm cap screws and washers and the eight 8 mm cap screws and washers. Use tightening sequence shown in Fig. JS3-35 and tighten 6 mm cap screws to 7.8 N·m (69 in.-lbs.) and 8 mm cap screws to 25 N·m (18 ft.-lbs.).

Install water drain valve assembly. Install magneto base plate with ignition components and properly align mark (M—Fig. JS3-20) on magneto base plate with mark (K) on crankcase, then securely tighten retaining screws. Install flywheel and tighten retaining cap screw to 69 N·m (51 ft.-lbs.) on JF650 models and 98 N·m (72 ft.-lbs.) on JS650SX models. Install engine drive flange and tighten to 98 N·m (72 ft.-lbs.) on JF650 models and 27 N·m (20 ft.-lbs.) on JS650SX models using Kawasaki 57001-276. Apply a suitable thread locking solution on threads of flywheel cover retaining screws, then install

Fig. JS3-37—Exploded view of typical crankshaft assembly used on all models. Pin (5) is located in top crankcase half.

1. Seal
2. Bearing
3. Key
4. Crankshaft & connecting rod assy.
5. Pin
6. Bearing
7. "O" ring
8. Collar
9. Seal
10. Seal
11. Needle bearing
12. Retaining clip
13. Piston pin
14. Piston rings
15. Piston

Fig. JS3-34—Protrusion (P) on flywheel cover must align with arrow (A) molded into vehicle hull.

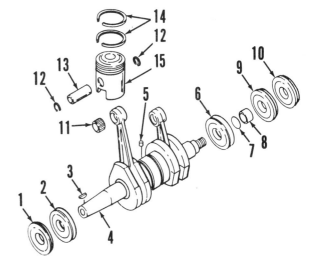

flywheel cover with "O" ring seal and tighten screws to 7.8 N·m (69 in.-lbs.).

Rotate crankshaft to position connecting rod for number two cylinder (rear) at top of stroke. Install needle bearing in small end of connecting rod and liberally lubricate with engine oil. Position piston assemby on connecting rod with arrow on piston crown facing cylinder exhaust port side and lubricate piston pin bores with engine oil. Use a suitable tool if needed and install piston pin. Install new piston pin retaining clips with openings facing top or bottom of piston. Repeat procedure to install number one cylinder piston assembly. Install cylinder block base gasket. Position a suitable tool on engine drive flange to prevent crankshaft rotation. Use suitable ring compressors and compress piston rings. Liberally lubricate cylinder bores with engine oil. Slide cylinder block onto top of crankcase half and remove piston ring compressors as piston assemblies slide into cylinders. Use a crisscross pattern and tighten cylinder block retaining nuts to 34 N·m (25 ft.-lbs.). Install cylinder head gasket with "UP" mark facing upward and "EX" mark facing exhaust port side of cylinder block. Install cylinder head and tighten retaining nuts to 25 N·m (18 ft.-lbs.) on JF650 models and to 23 N·m (17 ft.-lbs.) on JS650SX models following tightening sequence shown in Fig. JS3-36.

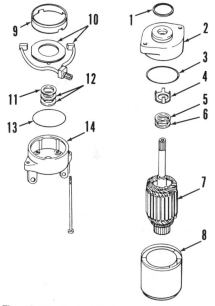

Fig. JS3-39—Exploded view of typical electric starter assembly.

1. "O" ring
2. Frame head
3. Seal ring
4. Tab washer
5. Insulator
6. Thrust washer
7. Armature
8. Frame
9. Brush plate holder
10. Brush assy.
11. Thick thrust washer
12. Thinner thrust washers
13. Seal ring
14. End housing

Complete remainder of assembly by reversing disassembly procedure.

PISTONS, PINS, RINGS AND CYLINDERS. Recommended piston skirt-to-cylinder clearance is 0.074-0.104 mm (0.0029-0.0041 in.) on JF650 models and 0.074-0.084 mm (0.0029-0.0033 in.) on JS650SX models. Bore cylinder to 0.50 mm (0.020 in.) or 1.0 mm (0.040 in.) oversize if measured piston skirt-to-cylinder clearance is beyond limit. Piston and piston rings are available in 0.50 mm (0.020 in.) and 1.0 mm (0.040 in.) oversizes. Inspect cylinder walls for scoring. If minor scoring is noted, cylinders should be honed to smooth out cylinder walls.

Recommended piston ring end gap is 0.2-0.4 mm (0.008-0.016 in.) with a service limit of 0.7 mm (0.027 in.). Install piston rings on piston so locating pin notch in piston ring ends faces top of piston. Make sure piston rings properly align with locating pins in ring grooves.

When reassembling, install piston on connecting rod so arrow on top of piston faces toward exhaust side of cylinder after assembly. Install new piston pin retaining clips; openings of retaining clips must face top or bottom of piston. Coat bearings, pistons, rings and cylinder bores with engine oil during assembly.

CONNECTING RODS, CRANKSHAFT AND BEARINGS. The crankshaft assembly should only be disassembled if the necessary tools and experience are available to service this type of crankshaft. Connecting rods, crankpins and crank halves are only available as a complete crankshaft assembly.

Maximum crankshaft runout measured on outer surface of outside main bearings with crankshaft center main bearings supported on vee blocks is 0.10 mm (0.004 in.). Connecting rod radial clearance should be 0.045-0.055 mm (0.0018-0.0022 in.) with a service limit of 0.11 mm (0.004 in.). Connecting rod side clearance should be 0.45-0.55 mm (0.018-0.022 in.) with a service limit of 0.8 mm (0.031 in.). Maximum allowable connecting rod bend or twist measured over a 100 mm (3.9 in.) length is 0.2 mm (0.008 in.).

ELECTRIC STARTER

All Models

All models are equipped with electric starter shown in Fig. JS3-39. Disassembly is evident after inspection of unit and reference to exploded view. When servicing starter motor, scribe reference marks across motor frame to aid in reassembly.

Starter brushes have a standard length of 12.5 mm (0.49 in.) and should be renewed if worn to 6.5 mm (0.26 in.). Commutator has a standard diameter of 28 mm (1.10 in.) and should be renewed if worn to a diameter of 27 mm (1.06 in.). During reassembly, apply Loctite Superflex or a suitable RTV silicone sealer around frame opening for terminal end of positive brush assembly and on sealing surfaces of frame, frame head and end housing where components mate.

BILGE PUMP

All Models

When the vehicle is operated, the jet pump forces water past siphon hose (S—Fig. JS3-28) opening. The passing force of water creates a vacuum effect, thus drawing (siphoning) any water out of vehicle bilge. Make sure all hoses and bilge strainer (S—Fig. JS3-40) are kept clean of all foreign debris. Disassemble and clean or renew components if needed. Make sure all hose connections are tight or vacuum loss will result in siphoning system malfunction.

An antisiphon loop is positioned at top, rear of engine compartment to prevent water from being drawn into hull when engine is not being operated. Make sure small breather hole in plastic fitting (F) of antisiphon loop is clear. If hole is plugged, water could be drawn into engine compartment when engine is stopped or idling. Clean hole only with compressed air. Using a tool to clean hole could enlarge hole size, thus causing a vacuum loss at bilge strainer during operation. The lower vacuum

Fig. JS3-40—View identifies location of bilge strainer (S). Plastic fitting (F) of antisiphon loop is located as shown on JS650SX models. On JF650 models, plastic fitting is located near top of main bulkhead.

will result in a decrease in bilge siphoning efficiency.

DRIVE SHAFT AND BEARING CARRIER

All Models

R&R AND OVERHAUL. Disconnect battery cables from battery and remove battery from vehicle. Remove oil tank and on Model JF650, remove fuel tank. Plug all hose and fitting openings. Remove throttle cable and choke cable from carburetor. Remove hoses from carburetor, label if needed and plug openings. Remove exhaust pipe from exhaust manifold. Separate wires at connectors leading to exciter coil and battery charge coil mounted on magneto base plate.

Detach spark plug leads, disconnect starter motor lead and all other electrical wiring that will interfere with engine removal and label for reassembly. Remove fuel pump pulse line from crankcase fitting. Remove cooling system supply hose (P—Fig. JS3-32) from fitting on bottom of exhaust manifold. Remove four cap screws (C—Fig. JS3-33) and washers retaining engine to vehicle hull. Note shims located under engine mounts and identify each shim for installation in original location. Remove any other components that will interfere with engine removal. Use a suitable lifting device to hoist engine assembly from vehicle. Place engine assembly on a clean work bench.

Withdraw drive shaft with drive flange from jet pump impeller and drive shaft bearing carrier (R—Fig. JS3-41). To remove drive shaft drive flange, hold drive shaft with Kawasaki tool W56019-003 and adapter 57001-1231 or a suitable equivalent tool, then rotate drive flange off drive shaft using Kawasaki tool 57001-1230 or a suitable equivalent. Remove four bearing carrier assembly mounting cap screws (S), then withdraw bearing carrier assembly (R).

On JF650 models, pry out two seals (3—Fig. JS3-42) in each end of bearing carrier (1) and press ball bearing (4) out of carrier if needed. On JS650SX models, remove snap ring (6—Fig. JS3-43) in front of large seals (3), then press two large seals (3), ball bearing (4) and two small seals (5) out front of carrier (1).

Inspect all components for excessive wear or any other damage and renew if needed. Drive shaft runout should not exceed 0.5 mm (0.020 in.) on JF650 models and 0.6 mm (0.024 in.) on JS650SX models with drive shaft supported on vee blocks on each end and midway between shaft ends. Measure drive shaft runout midway between center vee block and end vee block on each side of drive shaft.

Install seals in bearing carrier with open sides facing away from center ball bearing. Fill inner seals with a suitable high temperature grease. Install a nonpermanent thread locking solution on threads of bearing carrier mounting cap screws (S—Fig. JS3-41), then install bearing carrier (R) and tighten cap screws (S) to 22 N·m (16 ft.-lbs.). Hold drive shaft with Kawasaki tool W56019-003 and adapter 57001-1231 or a suitable equivalent tool, then use Kawasaki tool 57001-1230 or a suitable equivalent and tighten drive flange to 98 N·m (72 ft.-lbs.) on JF650 models and to 27 N·m (20 ft.-lbs.) on JS650SX models. Grease drive shaft splines, then install drive shaft through bearing carrier and engage drive shaft splines with splines in jet pump impeller.

Use a suitable lifting device to hoist engine assembly into vehicle. Make sure coupler is located between engine drive

flange and drive shaft drive flange. Install shims into original locations under engine mounts. Align cast protrusion (P—Fig. JS3-34) on flywheel cover with arrow (A) molded into vehicle hull. Check for clearance between engine mounting plate and shims on top of vehicle hull mounts by attempting to rock engine with light hand pressure. If rocking is noted, indicating clearance, then adjust thickness of shims until engine will not rock on mounts. Apply Loctite Lock N'Seal or a suitable equivalent on threads of four engine retaining cap screws (C—Fig. JS3-33) and tighten cap screws to 36 N·m (26 ft.-lbs.).

Complete reassembly in reverse order of disassembly. Bleed air from oil supply line or oil injection pump as outlined under BLEEDING PUMP in OIL INJECTION section.

JET PUMP

All Models

R&R AND OVERHAUL. Disconnect battery cables from battery. Remove jet pump water intake grill (W—Fig. JS3-45)

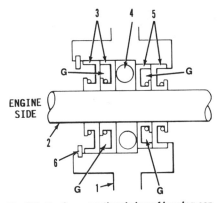

Fig JS3-43—Cross-sectional view of bearing carrier assembly used on JS650SX models. Fill area (G) between inner and outer seals with a suitable high temperature grease.

1. Bearing carrier	4. Ball bearing
2. Drive shaft	5. Seals
3. Seals	6. Snap ring

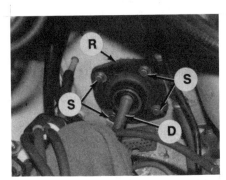

Fig. JS3-41—After withdrawing drive shaft (D) as outlined in text, remove cap screws (S) to withdraw bearing carrier assembly (R).

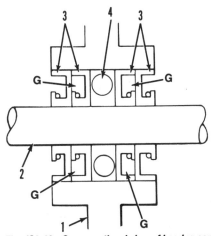

Fig. JS3-42—Cross-sectional view of bearing carrier assembly used on JF650 models. Fill area (G) between inner and outer seals with a suitable high temperature grease.

1. Bearing carrier	3. Seals
2. Drive shaft	4. Ball bearing

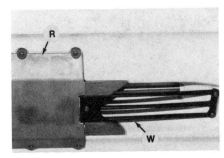

Fig. JS3-45—View identifying jet pump water intake grill (W) and cover (R).

and cover (R). Detach steering linkage joint (J—Fig. JS3-46) from ball joint on steering nozzle. On JF650 models, detach trim linkage joint from ball joint on trim nozzle. Remove bilge siphon hose (S) and cooling system supply hose (T) from fittings on jet pump housing. Remove four jet pump mounting cap screws (two at front and two at rear). Be careful and use a suitable sharp tool and cut silicone sealer between jet pump intake nozzle and vehicle hull. Slide jet pump assembly off rear of drive shaft. Place jet pump assembly on a clean work bench.

On JS650SX models, remove steering nozzle (N). On JF650 models, remove steering nozzle and trim nozzle as an assembly. Remove four cap screws, two on top and two on bottom, to remove outlet nozzle (O). Remove two cap screws to remove cap (12—Fig. JS3-47) with "O" ring (11). Insert rear of impeller shaft (10) into a suitable soft-jawed vise and tighten vise jaws to prevent impeller rotation. Insert Kawasaki impeller tool 57001-1228 into drive shaft splines in impeller (2) and rotate impeller tool counterclockwise (R.H. threads) to remove impeller (2) from impeller shaft (10). Lift pump housing (6) off impeller shaft (10). Extract collar (3), then use a suitable slide hammer and finger assembly to withdraw seals (4). Use a suitable punch and hammer and drive bearing (5) out front of pump housing. Remove spacer (7), then drive bearing (8) out rear of pump housing.

Inspect impeller (2) and impeller case of pump housing (6) for excessive wear or any other damage. Diameter of impeller case in pump housing should not exceed 141.1 mm (5.55 in.). Renew jet pump housing if impeller case is worn beyond limit or any other damage is

noted. Minimum impeller diameter is 138.5 mm (5.453 in.). Manufacturer recommends renewing pump housing (6) if any deep scratches are noted in impeller case. Inspect all other components for any type of damage. Renew components as needed.

Drive rear bearing (8) into pump housing (6) until seated using a suitable bearing driver and hammer. Install spacer (7), then drive front bearing (5) into pump housing until properly seated. Apply Shell MP or Alvania EP1 grease onto seals (4), then install seals into pump housing with open side facing toward impeller. Make sure seals properly seat. Fill seals with previously recommended grease. Push collar (3) into grease seals. Renew "O" rings (9) on impeller shaft (10). Apply Shell MP or Alvania EP1 grease onto impeller shaft, then slide pump housing (6) with assembled components onto impeller shaft (10). With rear of impeller shaft (10) mounted in a suitable soft-jawed vise, install impeller onto impeller shaft and tighten (rotate clockwise) impeller to 98 N·m (72 ft.-lbs.) using Kawasaki impeller tool 57001-1228 and a suitable torque wrench. Renew impeller grease seal (1) if needed. Fill grease seal with Shell MP or Alvania EP1 grease. Install cap (12) with "O" ring (11). Apply Loctite N'Seal or a suitable equivalent onto threads of cap (12) retaining screws, then install screws and securely tighten. Apply Loctite N'Seal or a suitable equivalent onto threads of outlet nozzle (O—Fig. JS3-46) retaining screws, then install outlet nozzle and securely tighten retaining screws. On JS650SX models, install steering nozzle (N). On JF650 models, install steering nozzle and trim nozzle as an assembly.

Apply Shell MP or Alvania EP1 grease on drive shaft splines. Apply Loctite Superflex or a suitable RTV silicone sealer onto jet pump intake area where intake mates with vehicle hull. Slide jet pump assembly onto drive shaft. Apply Loctite Stud N'Bearing Mount or a suitable equivalent on threads of each jet pump housing mounting cap screw, then install and tighten to 25 N·m (18 ft.-lbs.). Reconnect bilge siphon hose (S) and cooling system supply hose (T) on-

to fittings on jet pump. Reattach steering linkage joint (J) onto ball joint on steering nozzle (N). On JF650 models, reattach trim linkage joint onto ball joint on trim nozzle. Install jet pump cover (R—Fig. JS3-45) and water intake grill (W) and tighten retaining screws to 10 N·m (88 in.-lbs.).

STEERING

Model JS650SX

ADJUSTMENT. With steering handlebar in straight ahead position, jet pump steering nozzle (N—Fig. JS3-46) should be centered or at a 90 degree angle to stern of vehicle. If not, raise handle pole and loosen locknut (L—Fig. JS3-49) below steering linkage joint (G). Remove joint (G) from ball joint on handlebar pivot plate. Rotate joint (G) up or down threaded end of steering cable as needed to properly center jet pump steering nozzle. After correct adjustment is obtained, reinstall steering linkage joint (G) on ball joint and tighten locknut (L).

NOTE: If steering linkage joint (G) must be rotated out to where minimal threads on steering cable engage joint (G), then rotate joint (G) onto threaded end of steering cable to obtain safe thread engagement and complete adjustment on joint (J—Fig. JS3-46) at jet pump.

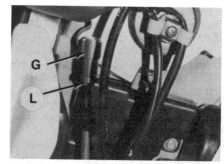

Fig. JS3-49—On JS650SX models, loosen locknut (L) and remove joint (G) from ball joint on handlebar pivot plate and rotate joint (G) up or down on threaded end of steering cable as needed to center jet pump steering nozzle when steering handlebar is in a straight ahead position.

Fig. JS3-46—View of rear jet pump components used on all models. On Model JF650, an adjustable trim nozzle is located between outlet nozzle (O) and steering nozzle (N).

J. Steering linkage joint
N. Steering nozzle
O. Outlet nozzle
S. Bilge siphon hose
T. Cooling system supply hose

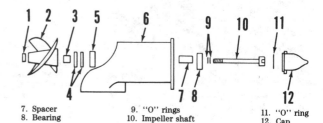

Fig. JS3-47—Exploded view showing correct arrangement of jet pump components on all models.

1. Seal
2. Impeller
3. Collar
4. Seals
5. Bearing
6. Pump housing
7. Spacer
8. Bearing
9. "O" rings
10. Impeller shaft
11. "O" ring
12. Cap

Model JF650

ADJUSTMENT. With steering handlebar in straight ahead position, jet pump steering nozzle (N—Fig. JS3-46) should be centered or at a 90 degree angle to stern of vehicle. If not, remove engine cover and loosen locknut (L—Fig. JS3-50) below steering linkage joint (R). Remove joint (R) from ball joint on steering arm. Rotate joint (R) up or down threaded end of steering cable as needed to properly center jet pump steering

Fig. JS3-50—On JF650 models, loosen locknut (L) and remove joint (R) from ball joint on steering arm and rotate joint (R) up or down on threaded end of steering cable as needed to center jet pump steering nozzle when steering handlebar is in a straight ahead positon.

nozzle. After correct adjustment is obtained, reinstall steering linkage joint (R) on ball joint and tighten locknut (L).

NOTE: If steering linkage joint (R) must be rotated out to where minimal threads on steering cable engage joint (R), then rotate joint (R) onto threaded end of steering cable to obtain safe thread engagement and complete adjustment on joint (J—Fig. JS3-46) at jet pump.

TRIM

Model JF650

ADJUSTMENT. With trim knob (K—Fig. JS3-51) rotated complete clockwise (down), jet pump steering nozzle (N—Fig. JS3-46) should almost touch jet pump cover (R—Fig. JS3-45). If not,

Fig. JS3-51—View identifies trim knob (K) on JF650 models.

remove engine cover and adjust steering handlebar to highest position. Loosen locknut (N—Fig. JS3-52) below trim linkage joint (M). Remove joint (M) from ball joint on lever. Rotate joint (M) up or down threaded end of trim cable as needed so steering nozzle almost touches jet pump cover. After correct adjustment is obtained, reinstall trim linkage joint (M) onto ball joint and tighten locknut (N).

NOTE: If trim linkage joint (M) must be rotated out to where minimal threads on trim cable engage joint (M), then rotate joint (M) onto threaded end of steering cable to obtain safe thread engagement and complete adjustment on trim linkage joint at jet pump.

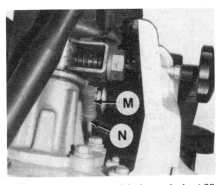

Fig. JS3-52—On JF650 models, loosen locknut (N) and remove joint (M) from ball joint on lever and rotate joint (M) up or down on threaded end of trim cable as needed to correctly position steering nozzle (N—Fig. JS3-46) as outlined in text.

SCAT HOVERCRAFT

SCAT HOVERCRAFT
10621 North Kendall Drive, Suite 208
Miami, FL 33176

SCAT I (1986-1988)

NOTE: Metric fasteners are used throughout engine.

General

Engine Make	Rotax
Engine Type	Two-Stroke; Air-Cooled
HP/Rated Rpm	23/6500
Number of Cylinders	1
Bore	72 mm (2.834 in.)
Stroke	66 mm (2.598 in.)
Displacement	268.7 cc (16.4 cu. in.)
Compression Ratio	6.7:1
Engine Lubrication	Pre-Mix
Fuel:Oil Ratio	50:1
Engine Oil Recommendation	Two-Stroke; Air-Cooled
Drive Ratio Between Engine And Fan	2:1
Maximum Fan Rpm	3250
Fan Blade Pitch	31°

Tune-Up

Engine Idle Speed	1100-1300 rpm
Spark Plug:	
NGK	BR8ES
Champion	RN3C
Electrode Gap	0.40 mm (0.016 in.)
Ignition:	
Type	Nippondenso CDI
Timing (BTDC)	2.31 mm (0.091 in.)
Carburetor Make	Bing

Sizes—Clearances

Maximum Cylinder Taper	0.08 mm (0.0031 in.)

Sizes—Clearances (Cont.)

Maximum Cylinder Out-of-Round	0.05 mm (0.0018 in.)
Piston-to-Cylinder Wall Standard Clearance	0.070-0.090 mm (0.0027-0.0035 in.)
Maximum Clearance	0.20 mm (0.0079 in.)
Piston Ring Standard Side Clearance	0.04-0.11 mm (0.0016-0.0043 in.)
Maximum Limit	0.20 mm (0.0079 in.)
Piston Ring Standard End Gap— Top and Second	0.20-0.35 mm (0.0079-0.0138 in.)
Maximum Limit	1.0 mm (0.039 in.)
Connecting Rod Big End Axial Play:	
Standard	0.20-0.53 mm (0.0079-0.0208 in.)
Maximum Limit	1.0 mm (0.0394 in.)
Crankshaft End Play	0.20-0.40 mm (0.008-0.016 in.)
Maximum Crankshaft Runout	0.08 mm (0.003 in.)

Capacities

Fuel Tank	22.7 L (6 gal.)

Tightening Torques

Cylinder Head Nuts	21 N·m (15 ft.-lbs.)
Crankcase Cap Screws	21 N·m (15 ft.-lbs.)
Flywheel Nut	85 N·m (63 ft.-lbs.)

LUBRICATION

All Models

The engine is lubricated by oil mixed with the fuel. Fuel:oil ratios should be 32:1 during break-in of a new or rebuilt engine and 50:1 for normal service when using a two-stroke air-cooled engine oil. Manufacturer recommends regular or no lead automotive gasoline having a minimum octane rating of 87. Gasoline and oil should be thoroughly mixed.

FUEL SYSTEM

All Models

CARBURETOR. All models are e-quipped with a Bing slide-valve type carburetor as shown in Fig. SH-1. Adjust idle speed screw (I—Fig. SH-1) until engine idle speed is between 1100-1300 rpm with throttle lever completely released. Choke lever (C—Fig. SH-2) is used to actuate starter valve (V) for cold engine starts. Push choke lever (C) down to actuate starter valve. Choke lever should be in complete up position (starter valve "OFF" position) prior to operating vehicle.

A slight amount of free play should be noted in throttle cable. If no free play or an excessive amount is noted, then slide dust boot (B) up cable and loosen locknut (N) and rotate cable adjuster (A) until a slight amount of free play is noted. Tighten locknut (N) to secure adjustment and reinstall dust boot (B).

FUEL PUMP. A Mikuni diaphragm type fuel pump (P—Fig. SH-4) is mounted on the bottom of the engine crankcase and is actuated by pressure and vacuum pulsations from the engine crankcase through hose (H).

When servicing pump, scribe reference marks across pump body to aid in reassembly. Defective or questionable parts should be renewed. Diaphragm should be renewed if air leaks or cracks are noted, or if deterioration is evident.

FUEL TANK. Fuel tank assembly (1—Fig. SH-5) is located under seat. Seat can be removed to service or withdraw fuel tank. Fuel tank is retained in position by strap assembly (2). A fuel strainer is located on the bottom of fuel tank pickup line (3). Strainer should not need to be removed and cleaned unless contamination is suspected.

AIR FILTER. An air filter assembly (F—Fig. SH-7) is mounted on the side of the carburetor. Air filter element (E) should be removed at least every five operating hours or more frequent if needed and cleaned and inspected for damage. To remove, loosen top and bottom wires (W) and rotate element (E) counterclockwise to remove. Wash element (E) with clean, fresh water. Allow element to drip dry or use low, clean air pressure to blow dry before reinstalling. Inspect element for any damage and renew if needed. Make sure top and bottom wires (W) are tight after installation.

IGNITION

All Models

All models are equipped with a capacitor discharge ignition system. The ignition timing is electronically advanced as the magneto base plate is fixed.

IGNITION TIMING. To check ignition timing, remove engine cover, fan cover assembly and spark plug. Install Top Dead Center (TDC) gage in cylinder head. Set gage to zero, then rotate crankshaft counterclockwise until a reading of 2.31 mm (0.091 in.) Before Top Dead Center (BTDC) is obtained. Crankcase mark (1—Fig. SH-9) and fan mark (2) must be aligned. If marks do not align, then reinstall fan cover and check to see if yellow pawl mark (3) aligns with cover mark. If marks align, then remove cover and make a new mark on outer circumference of fan in line with crankcase mark. If yellow pawl mark and cover mark do not align, then make a new mark on fan cover in line with yellow pawl mark.

Using a timing light with a separate battery source, run the engine at 6000 rpm and check timing mark alignment. If marks do not align, then magneto base will need to be adjusted. Remove fan cover assembly and starter pulley. Turn magneto base plate clockwise to retard timing and counterclockwise to advance timing. Reinstall removed components, then recheck engine timing.

Fig. SH-1—View identifies idle speed screw (I).

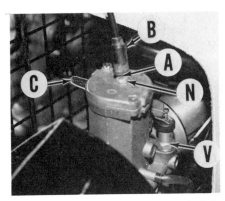

Fig. SH-2—For cold engine starts, push choke lever (C) down to actuate starter valve (V). Slide dust boot (B) up cable and loosen locknut (N) and rotate adjuster (A) to adjust throttle cable free play.

Fig. SH-4—View identifying Mikuni diaphragm type fuel pump (P). Crankcase pressure and vacuum pulsations are transmitted to fuel pump through hose (H).

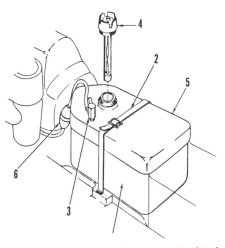

Fig. SH-5—View of fuel tank and related components.

1. Fuel tank
2. Strap assy.
3. Pickup line
4. Cap with gage & breather valve
5. Cover
6. Priming bulb

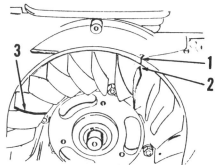

Fig. SH-7—Air filter element (E) is contained within assembly (F). Top and bottom wires (W) secure element. On some models, air filter element assembly is mounted vertically on top of an air silencer. Incoming air passes through element (E) and air silencer prior to entering carburetor.

Fig. SH-9—View showing timing marks. Refer to text for ignition timing procedures.

1. Crankcase mark
2. Fan mark
3. Fan pawl (Yellow Mark)

NOTE: Ignition timing should be checked with engine cold. Temperature variations may affect components.

TROUBLE-SHOOTING. If ignition malfunction occurs, use only approved procedures to prevent damage to the components. The fuel system should be checked first to make certain that faulty running is not caused by incorrect mixture or contaminated fuel. Make sure malfunction is not due to spark plug, wiring or wiring connection failure. Trouble-shoot ignition circuit using a suitable ohmmeter as follows:

Separate the wires at the connector between magneto components and CDI module. Refer to Fig. SH-10. Check condition of low speed charge coil (L) by attaching one tester lead to black wire leading to magneto assembly and attaching other tester lead to black/red wire leading to magneto assembly. Low speed charge coil can be considered satisfactory if resistance reading is within the limits of 120-180 ohms. Check condition of high speed charge coil (H) by attaching one tester lead to black/white wire leading to magneto assembly and attaching other tester lead to black/red wire leading to magneto assembly. High speed charge coil can be considered satisfactory if resistance reading is within the limits of 2.8-4.2 ohms. Low speed charge coil (L) and high speed charge coil (H) are serviceable after removing engine cover, fan cover assembly and flywheel. Make sure a suitable puller is used to withdraw flywheel. Tighten flywheel nut to 85 N·m (63 ft.-lbs.).

To check ignition coil primary winding resistance, separate the white/blue wire and black wire at connector. Attach one tester lead to terminal end of white/blue wire leading to coil and other tester lead to terminal end of black wire leading to

coil. Primary winding resistance reading should be within the limits of 0.23-0.43 ohms.

If no components are found defective in the previous tests and ignition malfunction is still suspected, then install a known good CDI module and recheck engine operation.

COOLING SYSTEM

All Models

All models are air-cooled. Make sure blades on engine cooling fan are not plugged from foreign debris, cracked or broken. Clean blades if needed and renew engine cooling fan if damage is noted.

ENGINE

All Models

REMOVE AND REINSTALL. To remove engine, first disconnect fuel supply line from fuel pump and plug openings. Remove seat and withdraw fuel tank assembly. Remove supply hose to carburetor, then remove carburetor assembly with air filter assembly. Remove engine cover and fan guard. Remove exhaust pipe from engine cylinder. Remove bolts and nuts retaining engine frame at six mounting locations. Lean assembly backward while suitably supporting components or withdraw complete assembly.

Remove fasteners securing fan assembly to fan hub (8—Fig. SH-16) and withdraw fan assembly. Remove dust cap (3) and cotter pin (4). Rotate castle nut (5) off fan shaft (2). Hold drive belt

and withdraw fan hub (8) with components (6 through 10). Remove drive belt. Remove four engine mounting cap screws (2—Fig. SH-12) and two drive belt adjusting cap screws (5). Place engine assembly on a clean work bench.

Installation is reverse order of removal while observing the following: Apply Loctite 242 or a suitable equivalent to threads of engine mounting cap screws prior to installation. Drive belt should deflect 6.35 mm (0.25 in.) with 18 N (4 lbs.) force applied to belt at midpoint between engine pulley and fan pulley. Adjust drive belt tension by loosening four engine mounting cap screws (2) and repositioning engine with cap screws (5) and jam nuts (8). After obtaining correct drive belt tension, tighten four engine mounting cap screws (2) to 22 N·m (16 ft.-lbs.). Remove engine spark plug and ground terminal end of spark plug lead. Castle nut (5—Fig. SH-16) should be tightened to seat bearings (7), then loosened so fan assembly will rotate one-half revolution when turned by normal hand pressure. Zero fan hub endplay should be noted. Reinstall engine spark plug and attach spark plug lead. Make sure engine frame mounts are in good condition and engine frame fasteners are securely tightened.

DISASSEMBLY. Remove tapered pulley lock assembly (12—Fig. SH-16), engine pulley (13) and adapter (14). Remove cylinder head cover, fan cover, starter cup, fan and flywheel nut and lockwasher. Use a suitable puller to extract flywheel from crankshaft end. Remove flywheel key and magneto base plate with ignition components. Remove cylinder head and cylinder. Remove five

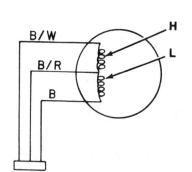

Fig. SH-10—Refer to procedures outlined in text to test high speed charge coil (H) and low speed charge coil (L).

B. Black
B/R. Black/red
B/W. Black/white

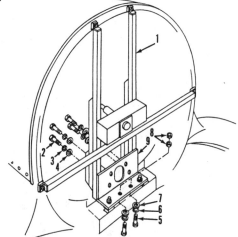

Fig. SH-12—View depicting engine frame (1), engine mounting plate (9), engine retaining cap screws (2), lockwashers (3) and flat washers (4) and drive belt tension adjuster cap screws (5), lockwashers (6), flat washers (7) and jam nuts (8).

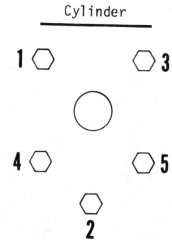

Fig. SH-13—Tighten crankcase screws in progressive increments following sequence shown until a final torque of 21 N·m (15 ft.-lbs.) is obtained.

crankcase cap screws located on flywheel side. Separate crankcase halves. Crankshaft and piston assembly can now be removed from crankcase half.

Engine components are now ready for overhaul as outlined in the appropriate following paragraphs. Refer to the following section for assembly procedure.

ASSEMBLY. Refer to specific service sections when assembling internal engine components. Make sure all joint and gasket surfaces are clean, free from nicks, burrs and carbon deposits.

Whenever the engine is disassembled, it is recommended that all gasket surfaces be carefully checked for nicks, burrs and warped surfaces which might interfere with a tight seal. Cylinder head, head end of cylinder and mating surfaces of crankcase halves should be check on a surface plate and lapped, if necessary, to provide a smooth surface. Do not remove any more metal than is necessary.

When assembling engine, first lubricate all friction surfaces and bearings with engine oil. Crankshaft end play should be carefully adjusted by varying thickness of shim or shims (15—Fig. SH-14). Selection of shim thickness can be accomplished by measuring depth of crankcase halves from mating surfaces to main bearing seats and adding totals together plus thickness of crankcase gasket (23) to obtain measurement "X." Add thickness of main bearings (14 and 20), distance of crankshaft between main bearing seats, thickness of spacers (16 and 19) and thickness of original shims (15) to obtain measurement "Y." Subtract measurement "Y" from measurement "X" to obtain crankshaft end play. Recommended crankshaft end play should be between 0.20-0.40 mm (0.008-0.016 in.). Install the correct amount of shims so end play is within recommended range. Shim (15) will usually not need to be changed unless crankshaft or crankcase is renewed.

Reassemble components with reference to Fig. SH-14. Tighten crankcase screws in progressive increments following sequence shown in Fig. SH-13 until a final torque of 21 N·m (15 ft.-lbs.) is obtained. Tighten cylinder head nuts to 21 N·m (15 ft.-lbs.) using a crisscross pattern.

PISTON, PIN, RINGS AND CYLINDER. The piston can be removed after removing exhaust pipe, carburetor, cylinder head and cylinder. Piston and rings are available in standard size and oversizes. Arrow and "AUS" mark on piston crown must be toward exhaust

port in cylinder when engine is assembled. The piston pin retaining clips should be installed so open section is toward bottom of piston. On all models, rebore or renew cylinder if out-of-round more than 0.05 mm (0.0018 in.) or if tapered more than 0.08 mm (0.0031 in.). Piston-to-cylinder wall clearance should be measured 16 mm (0.63 in.) above lower edge of piston skirt. Piston-to-cylinder wall clearance should be 0.070-0.090 mm (0.0027-0.0035 in.) with a maximum clearance limit of 0.20 mm (0.0079 in.). Ring side clearance in groove should be 0.04-0.11 mm

(0.0016-0.0043 in.) with a maximum limit of 0.20 mm (0.0079 in.). Ring end gap should be 0.20-0.35 mm (0.0079-0.0138 in.) with a maximum limit of 1.0 mm (0.039 in.).

CRANKSHAFT AND CONNECTING ROD ASSEMBLY. The crankshaft and connecting rod assembly is available only as a complete unit and should not be disassembled. Main bearings must be removed using a suitable puller assembly. Heat bearings in a container of engine oil to 100° C (210° F) to ease installation. Install bearings with groove

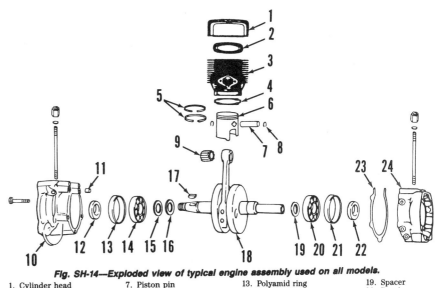

Fig. SH-14—Exploded view of typical engine assembly used on all models.

1. Cylinder head	7. Piston pin	13. Polyamid ring	19. Spacer
2. Gasket	8. Clips	14. Bearing	20. Bearing
3. Cylinder	9. Needle bearing	15. Shim	21. Polyamid ring
4. Gasket	10. Crankcase half	16. Spacer	22. Seal
5. Piston rings	11. Dowel pin	17. Key	23. Gasket
6. Piston	12. Seal	18. Crankshaft assy.	24. Crankcase half

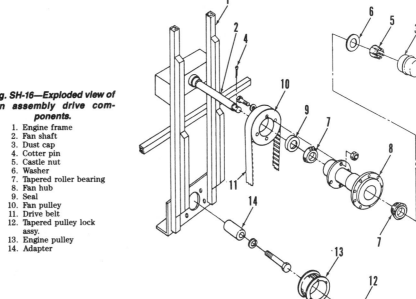

Fig. SH-16—Exploded view of fan assembly drive components.

1. Engine frame
2. Fan shaft
3. Dust cap
4. Cotter pin
5. Castle nut
6. Washer
7. Tapered roller bearing
8. Fan hub
9. Seal
10. Fan pulley
11. Drive belt
12. Tapered pulley lock assy.
13. Engine pulley
14. Adapter

facing outward. To check crankshaft and connecting rod assembly, mount the unit on vee blocks and check shaft ends for runout. Measure pto end 6 mm (0.236 in.) from shaft end and flywheel end behind flywheel key groove. Runout should not exceed 0.08 mm (0.003 in.). Standard connecting rod big end axial play is 0.20-0.53 mm (0.0079-0.0208 in.) with a maximum limit of 1.0 mm (0.0394 in.). Renew crankshaft and connecting rod assembly if wear is excessive or there is any other damage.

MANUAL STARTER

All Models

An exploded view typical of rewind starter used is shown in Fig. SH-18. To overhaul starter, first remove engine cover and fan cover assembly. Remove rope handle and allow rope to rewind onto pulley (8). Remove snap ring (1), lock spring (2), "E" clip (3), pawl lock (4) and pawl (5). Pull rope (6) out of pulley (8) until rope is fully extended. Disengage key (7) and pull rope completely out of pulley. Withdraw pulley (8), spring guide (9) and spring (10). Use extreme care when removing spring (10). Inspect all parts for damage and renew as needed.

Reassembly is reverse order of disassembly. Apply a marine type water-resistant grease to rewind spring (10) area of fan housing. Starter rope is wound around pulley (8) in a counterclockwise direction as viewed with pulley in housing. Rotate pulley (8) six turns counterclockwise before passing rope through fan housing so rewind spring is preloaded, then complete reassembly. Make sure rope handle returns to proper released position. Apply additional tension on rewind spring if required.

DRIVE BELT

All Models

A Kevlar type drive belt is used. Make sure drive belt guard is properly installed to prevent foreign debris from

Fig. SH-20—View identifying fan assembly components. Note scribe mark (S) at base of blade jig tool (8).

1. Inner bolt
2. Locknut
3. Outer bolt
4. Locknut
5. Fan blade
6. Flat washers
7. Fan hub halves
8. Blade jig tool

reaching drive belt and related components.

RENEW. First disconnect fuel supply line from fuel pump and plug openings. Remove seat and withdraw fuel tank assembly. Remove engine cover and fan guard. Remove exhaust pipe from engine cylinder. Remove bolts and nuts retaining engine frame at six mounting locations. Lean assembly backward while suitably supporting components.

Remove fasteners securing fan assembly to fan hub (8—Fig. SH-16) and withdraw fan assembly. Remove dust cap (3) and cotter pin (4). Rotate castle nut (5) off fan shaft (2). Hold drive belt and withdraw fan hub (8) with components (6 through 10). Remove drive belt.

Inspect engine pulley and fan hub pulley for excessive wear or any other damage and renew if needed. Clean and inspect bearings (7) and their respective cups. Renew if excessive wear, pitting, binding or any other damage is noted. Repack bearings with a suitable marine type water-resistant grease prior to reassembly.

NOTE: Only a Kevlar type drive belt, available through a Scat Hovercraft authorized dealer, can be used. Any other type drive belt will result in premature failure.

Reassembly is reverse order of disassembly while observing the following: Drive belt should deflect 6.35 mm (0.25 in.) with 18 N (4 lbs.) force applied at belt at midpoint between engine pulley and fan pulley. Adjust drive belt tension by loosening four engine mounting cap screws (2—Fig. SH-12) and repositioning engine with cap screws (5) and jam nuts (8). After obtaining correct drive belt tension, tighten four engine mounting cap screws (2) to 22 N·m (16 ft.-lbs.). Remove engine spark plug and ground terminal end of spark plug lead. Castle nut (5—Fig. SH-16) should be tightened to seat bearings (7), then loosened so fan assembly will rotate one-half revolution when turned by normal hand pressure. Zero fan hub endplay should be noted. Reinstall engine spark plug and attach spark plug lead. Make sure engine frame mounts are in good condition and engine frame fasteners are securely tightened.

FAN ASSEMBLY

All Models

R&R AND OVERHAUL. First disconnect fuel supply line from fuel pump and plug openings. Remove seat and withdraw fuel tank assembly. Remove engine cover and fan guard. Remove exhaust pipe from engine cylinder. Remove bolts and nuts retaining engine frame at six mounting locations. Lean assembly backward while suitably supporting components.

Remove fasteners securing fan assembly to fan hub and withdraw fan assembly. Loosen inner row of bolts

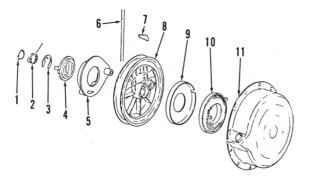

Fig. SH-18—Exploded view of manual rewind starter typical of type used on all models.

1. Snap ring
2. Lock spring
3. "E" clip
4. Pawl lock
5. Pawl
6. Rope
7. Key
8. Rope pulley
9. Spring guide
10. Rewind spring
11. Starter housing

(1—Fig. SH-20) and locknuts (2) and outer row of bolts (3) and locknuts (4) and remove fan blades (5) as needed. Completely remove inner and outer bolts, flat washers (6) and locknuts to separate fan hub halves (7).

Reassembly is the reverse order of disassembly. When reinstalling fan blades, make sure fan blades (5) face correct direction and fan blade pitch is correct.

NOTE: Incorrect fan blade pitch could cause engine to operate above recommended maximum rpm resulting in possible engine damage.

Recommended fan blade pitch is 31 degrees. Use Scat Hovercraft special tool 1614 (8) to correctly install fan blades. Scribe mark (S—Fig. SH-21) on blade jig tool should align with mating surface (M) of fan hub halves. Securely tighten all bolts and nuts to retain fan blades in fan hub.

STEERING

All Models

ADJUSTMENT. When steering handlebar is positioned in straight ahead position, rudders (R—Fig. SH-23) should be perpendicular to stern of vehicle. If not, remove cable joint end (E) from rudder ball joint and loosen locknut (L). Place steering handlebar to face straight ahead and position rudders (R) perpendicular to stern of vehicle. Rotate joint end (E) in or out on threaded cable rod as needed to align joint end (E) with rudder ball joint. Secure adjustment with locknut (L) and reattach joint end (E). Rudder angle should be equal when steering handlebar is rotated to full right and then to full left.

SKIRT

All Models

Sixty-four individual skirt segments are used around the vehicle hull. Three type of skirt segments are used. Refer to Fig. SH-25 for identification of skirt

type and number used. Each skirt segment is retained by three clips and two tie straps as shown in Fig. SH-26. To renew a skirt segment, pull trim molding from deck to expose clips. Remove three clips and two tie straps. Reverse procedure to install skirt segment.

Fig. SH-23—Rudders (R) are used to control direction of vehicle travel via steering cable and handlebar. Position of joint end (E) on steering cable is secured by locknut (L).

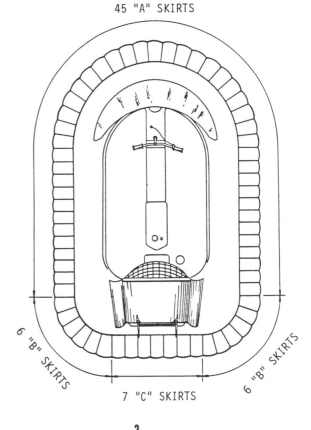

Fig. SH-25—View identifying location of skirt segment types and number used.

45 "A" SKIRTS

6 "B" SKIRTS

6 "B" SKIRTS

7 "C" SKIRTS

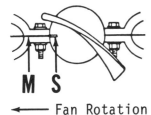

M S

◄— Fan Rotation

Fig. SH-21—When installing fan blades, scribe mark (S) on blade jig tool should align with mating surface (M) of fan hub halves to obtain recommended fan blade pitch of 31 degrees.

Fig. SH-26—Pull trim molding (2) from deck, then remove clips (3) and tie straps (5) on each side to remove skirt segment (1). Note "P" clip (4) on each side.

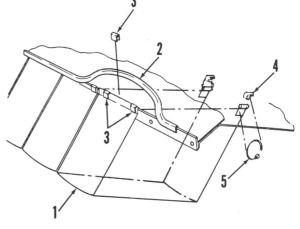

SURF-JET

PROGRESSIVE POWER CORPORATION
504 S. Washington
Janesville, WI, 53545

STANDARD (1980-1988), 275SS (1985-1988) AND 236SS (1983-1988)

NOTE: Metric fasteners are used throughout engine.

General

Engine Make................................Subaru
Engine Type........................Two-Stroke; Water-Cooled
HP/Rated Rpm......................15/4500-5500
Number of Cylinders............................2
Bore.................................57 mm (2.25 in.)
Stroke................................50 mm (1.97 in.)
Displacement.............................225 cc (13.7 cu. in.)
Compression Ratio...........................7.2:1
Engine Lubrication........................Pre-Mix
Fuel:Oil Ratio.................................50:1
Engine Oil Recommendation............Two-Stroke; BIA Certified TC-W

Tune-Up

Engine Idle Speed.....................800-1200 rpm
Spark Plug:
  NGK...................................B7HS
  Champion...............................L82C
  Electrode Gap.....................0.6-0.7 mm (0.024-0.028 in.)
Ignition Type:
  Serial No. RHT00870M82G And Prior......................Breaker Points
  After Serial No. RHT00870M82G...............CDI
Breaker Point Models:
  Breaker Point Gap.................0.30-0.40 mm (0.012-0.016 in.)
  Ignition Timing...................10°-25° BTDC
CDI Models—Ignition Timing:
  Moveable Magneto Base Plate........10°-25° BTDC
  Fixed Magneto Base Plate...........12°-22° BTDC
Carburetor:
  Make..................................Mikuni
  Model...................................BV22
  Bore Size.............................22 mm (0.87 in.)
  Low Speed Mixture Screw...............1 turn
  Pilot Jet................................#50
  Main Jet................................#130

Sizes—Clearances

Piston-to-Cylinder Wall
  Clearance......................0.10-0.14 mm (0.0039-0.0054 in.)
  Maximum Clearance.................0.25 mm (0.0098 in.)
Piston Ring Side Clearance:
  Top.............................0.06-0.10 mm (0.0024-0.0039 in.)
  Second........................0.04-0.08 mm (0.0016-0.0032 in.)
Maximum Crankshaft Runout..............0.12 mm (0.0047 in.)
Maximum Cylinder Head Warp.............0.25 mm (0.0098 in.)

Capacities

Fuel Tank...............................7.6 L (2 gal.)

Tightening Torques

Cylinder Head Cap Screws............17.7-23.1 N·m (13-17 ft.-lbs.)
Crankcase Cap Screws:
  6 mm..............................8.2-9.5 N·m (6-7 ft.-lbs.)
  8 mm.............................19.0-21.8 N·m (14-16 ft.-lbs.)
Flywheel...........................43.5-49.0 N·m (32-36 ft.-lbs.)
Spark Plug.........................24.5-29.9 N·m (18-22 ft.-lbs.)
Standard Screws:
  5 mm..............................4.3-5.4 N·m (38-48 in.-lbs.)
  7 mm..............................7.3-9.3 N·m (65-82 in.-lbs.)
  8 mm.............................17.7-23.1 N·m (13-17 ft.-lbs.)
  10 mm............................37.3-47.2 N·m (27-34 ft.-lbs.)

LUBRICATION

All Models

The engine is lubricated by oil mixed with the fuel. Fuel:oil ratios should be 25:1 during break-in (two tankfuls) of a new or rebuilt engine and 50:1 for normal service when using a BIA certified two-stroke TC-W engine oil. Manufacturer recommends regular or no-lead automotive gasoline having a minimum octane rating of 87. Gasoline and oil should be thoroughly mixed.

FUEL SYSTEM

All Models

CARBURETOR. Refer to Fig. SJ-1 for an exploded view of Mikuni type BV22 diaphragm carburetor used on all

models. A primer button (B—Fig. SJ-2) located on control panel is used for cold engine starts. When button (B) is depressed, a small amount of fuel is injected through a nozzle at the rear of the carburetor into the intake manifold.

Initial setting of low speed mixture needle (7—Fig. SJ-1) is one turn out from a lightly seated position. Final carburetor adjustments must be made with engine at normal operating temperature and running. Clockwise rotation of needle leans the mixture. Adjust low speed mixture needle (7) until smooth acceleration from the idle position is noted. After adjusting low speed mixture needle, adjust idle speed screw (4) until engine idle speed is between 800-1200 rpm with throttle lever completely released. To adjust high speed fuel:air mixture, the engine spark plugs must be removed and insulator tip color noted.

NOTE: Make sure that fuel tank contains a 50:1 fuel mixture.

Make sure cooling system will receive an adequate supply of water, then operate and sustain engine at wide-open throttle for a suitable test period. Stop the engine with throttle in wide-open position. Remove spark plugs and note insulator tip color. Normal insulator tip color is brown to light tan. If insulator tip appears to be light tan to white in color, then mixture is too lean and main jet (11) size should be increased. If insulator tip appears to be dark brown to black in color, then mixture is too rich and main jet (11) size should be decreased. Clean, regap and reinstall spark plugs and continue test procedures until spark plug insulator tips are a normal color.

To check float level, connect a clear vinyl tube (T—Fig. SJ-3) to the float bowl drain nozzle and hold the drain tube up. Open float bowl drain screw

(22). Make sure cooling system will receive an adequate supply of water, then start and run the engine at idle speed for a few minutes. Stop the engine and observe drain tube. Fuel level in drain tube should be a distance (L) of 31-33 mm (1.22-1.30 in.) below center of carburetor throttle bore. If fuel level is incorrect, float bowl (20—Fig. SJ-1) must be removed and tang (T) on float arm adjusted until the proper setting is obtained.

REED VALVES. The inlet reed valves (Fig. SJ-5) are mounted on a reed plate between the inlet manifold and crankcase. The reed petals should seat very lightly against reed plate throughout their entire length with the least possible tension.

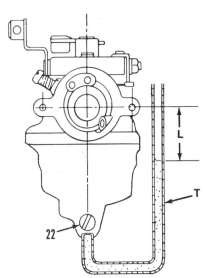

Fig. SJ-1—Exploded view of Mikuni type BV22 carburetor used on all models. Roller (23) and clip (24) are used on breaker point models.

T. Tang
1. Body
2. Pilot jet
3. Tube
4. Idle speed screw
5. Spring
6. Throttle shaft
7. Low speed mixture needle
8. Spring
9. Throttle plate
10. Gasket
11. Main jet
12. Gasket
13. Gasket
14. Inlet needle & seat
15. Nozzle
16. "O" ring
17. Plug
18. Float
19. Pin
20. Bowl
21. Spring
22. Drain screw
23. Roller
24. Clip

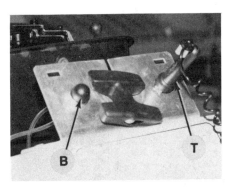

Fig. SJ-2—Figure identifying primer button (B) and ignition tether switch. Tether switch cap (T) must be snapped onto tether switch prior to attempting starting of engine.

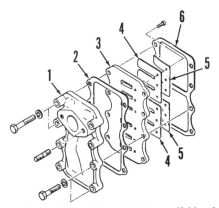

Fig. SJ-3—Fuel level in drain tube (T) should be a distance (L) of 31-33 mm (1.22-1.30 in.) below center of carburetor throttle bore. Refer to text.

Fig. SJ-5—Exploded view of intake manifold and reed valve assembly.

1. Intake manifold
2. Gasket
3. Reed plate
4. Reed petals
5. Reed stoppers
6. Gasket

Renew reeds if petals are broken, cracked, warped, rusted or bent. Never attempt to bend a reed petal or straighten a damaged reed. Never install a bent or damaged reed. Seating surface of reed plate should be smooth and flat. When installing reeds or reed stopper, make sure that petals are centered over the inlet holes in reed plate and that the reed stoppers are centered over reed petals. Apply a suitable thread locking solution to reed stopper mounting screws and securely tighten.

FUEL PUMP. A diaphragm type fuel pump (P—Fig. SJ-7) is mounted on the starboard side of engine cylinder block and is actuated by pressure and vacuum pulsations from the lower cylinder crankcase. Refer to Fig. SJ-8 for an exploded view of fuel pump assembly.

When servicing pump, scribe reference marks across pump body to aid in reassembly. Defective or questionable parts should be renewed. Diaphragm should be renewed if air leaks or cracks are noted, or if deterioration is evident.

FUEL TANK AND FUEL FILTER. Fuel strainer (4—Fig. SJ-10) is attached

on the bottom of fuel tank pickup line (3). An inline fuel filter (F—Fig. SJ-7) is located between fuel tank and fuel pump. Periodically unscrew cup (7—Fig. SJ-11) on bottom of fuel filter base (4) and withdraw sealing ring (6) and strainer (5) from base. Clean cup (7) and strainer (5) in a suitable cleaning solution and inspect strainer (5) for excessive contamination or damage. Renew sealing ring and any damaged components. Renew strainer (5) if excessive contamination is noted. Reassembly is reverse order of disassembly. Fuel tank strainer (4—Fig. SJ-10) should not need to be removed and cleaned unless contamination is suspected.

HYDRAULIC THROTTLE

All Models

All models are equipped with a throttle grip assembly (Fig. SJ-13) which hydraulically controls movement of magneto base plate on models without

a fixed magneto base plate and carburetor throttle shaft via linkage on models with a fixed magneto base plate.

NOTE: The manufacturer recommends that hydraulic control components on 1980 and 1981 models be upgraded to 1982 model year components. Consult the manufacturer or a dealer for a listing of components.

The manufacturer recommends separating throttle grip halves (1 and 3—Fig. SJ-13) and cleaning slide (2) and slide surfaces in throttle grip halves after every 25 hours of operation or more frequent if needed. Be careful not to over torque screws.

The hydraulic system and reservoir (1—Fig. SJ-16 or Fig. SJ-17) should be filled with 5W hydraulic oil, 5W motorcycle fork oil, SAE 10W nondetergent oil or Dextron II automatic transmission fluid. Maintain reservoir (1) at one-half full mark or above.

NOTE: Fluids should not be mixed.

Fig. SJ-7—View identifying diaphragm type fuel pump (P) located on starboard side of power head cylinder block. Fuel filter assembly is identified at (F).

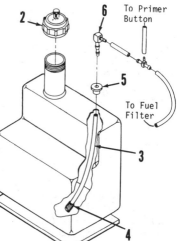

Fig. SJ-10—Exploded view of fuel tank and related components.
1. Fuel tank
2. Cap
3. Pickup hose
4. Strainer
5. Grommet
6. Elbow fitting

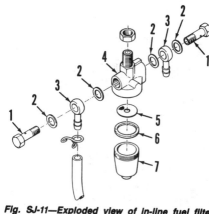

Fig. SJ-11—Exploded view of in-line fuel filter assembly.
1. Banjo bolts
2. Gaskets
3. Fittings
4. Base
5. Strainer
6. Seal ring
7. Cup

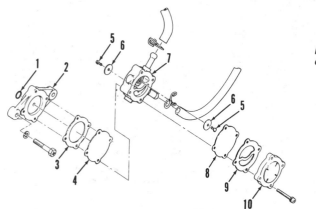

Fig. SJ-8—Exploded view of diaphragm type fuel pump assembly.
1. "O" ring
2. Base
3. Gasket
4. Diaphragm
5. Retainers
6. Check valves
7. Body
8. Diaphragm
9. Gasket
10. Cover

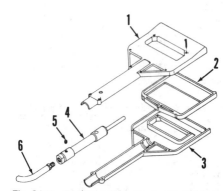

Fig. SJ-13—Exploded view of typical throttle grip assembly.
1. Throttle grip half
2. Slide
3. Throttle grip half
4. Hydraulic cylinder
5. Allen head screw
6. Hydraulic line

When throttle grip slide (2—Fig. SJ-13) is fully depressed, the magneto base plate should rotate freely on models without a fixed magneto base plate and carburetor throttle shaft should rotate freely on all models. On models without a fixed magneto base plate, magneto stop plate (9—Fig. SJ-14) should contact cylinder block pin (P). On models with a fixed magneto base plate, tab (T—Fig. SJ-15) on throttle shaft (6) should contact stop (S) on carburetor body. If tab (T) does not contact stop (S) and actuator rod in cylinder (2—Fig. SJ-17) is fully extended, then loosen nuts (5) and adjust length of cable (6) until wide-open throttle is obtained.

BLEEDING. To bleed air from throttle system, first make sure reservoir (1—Fig. SJ-16 or Fig. SJ-17) is at least one-half full. Open or remove reservoir (1) cover. Insert a suitable sized brass rod into reservoir (1) and push down on ball at base of reservoir to open check valve. Slowly depress throttle grip slide (2—Fig. SJ-13) to force oil and trapped air past check valve ball. After all air has vented out from reservoir oil, slowly release throttle grip so only oil is drawn back into system. Remove brass rod and fill reservoir to at least one-half full and check throttle system operation. Repeat bleeding procedure if needed.

On models equipped with Allen head screw (5) in throttle grip cylinder (4), loosen screw and slowly depress throttle grip until no air bubbles are noted in oil seeping from around screw (5) threads. Tighten screw (5) prior to releasing throttle grip. Fill reservoir to at least one-half full and repeat bleeding procedure if needed. If trapped air cannot be removed following bleeding procedures, then complete system must be purged of all air.

IGNITION

Breaker Point Models

The standard spark plug is NGK B7HS with an electrode gap of 0.6-0.7 mm (0.024-0.028 in.).

The breaker point gap should be 0.30-0.40 mm (0.012-0.016 in.) and can be inspected and adjusted through opening in flywheel (2—Fig. SJ-19) after removing manual rewind starter assembly, starter cup and cover (1). Two breaker point assemblies (3) and two

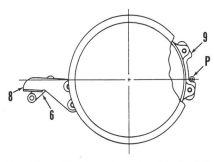

Fig. SJ-14—When throttle grip slide is fully depressed on models without a fixed magneto base plate, magneto stop plate (9) should contact cylinder block pin (P) and throttle cam (8) should rotate carburetor throttle shaft (6) to wide-open throttle.

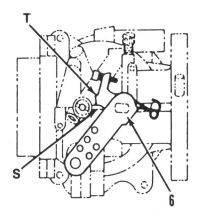

Fig. SJ-15—When throttle grip slide is fully depressed on models with a fixed magneto base plate, tab (T) on throttle shaft (6) should contact stop (S) on carburetor body.

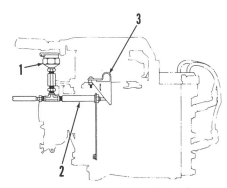

Fig. SJ-16—View depicting hydraulic throttle reservoir and related components on models without a fixed magneto base plate.

1. Reservoir
2. Cylinder
3. Magneto base plate bracket

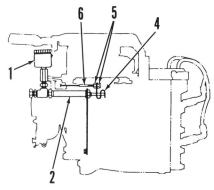

Fig. SJ-17—View depicting hydraulic throttle reservoir and related components on models with a fixed magneto base plate.

1. Reservoir
2. Cylinder
4. "S" bracket
5. Nuts
6. Cable

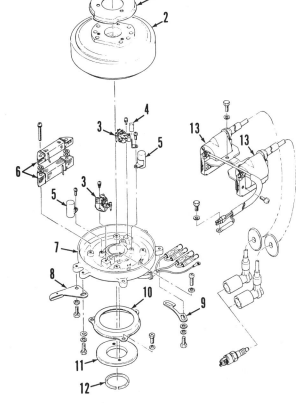

Fig. SJ-19—Exploded view of flywheel magneto unit on breaker point models.

1. Cover
2. Flywheel
3. Breaker point assys.
4. Lubricator
5. Condensers
6. Low voltage cells
7. Magneto base plate
8. Throttle cam
9. Magneto stop plate
10. Bracket
11. Retainer
12. Felt ring
13. Ignition coils

condensers (5) are used. To service breaker point assemblies, remove flywheel (2). Inspect the breaker point surfaces for excessive wear, pitting or any other damage. Clean the breaker point contact surfaces with a point file or 400 to 600 grit sandpaper. Renew breaker point assemblies if excessive wear or damage is noted.

IGNITION TIMING. Ignition timing can be statically checked and adjusted as follows: Make sure cylinder block pin (P—Fig. SJ-20) is aligned with magneto base plate mark (M) when magneto stop plate (9) is in full retarded position. If not, loosen magneto stop plate (9) retaining screws, then rotate magneto base plate (7) until mark (M) is aligned with cylinder block pin (P). Position magneto stop plate (9) against pin (P) and tighten retaining screws.

Connect the input lead of a dc voltmeter to the red wire leading to the magneto base plate and the voltmeter common lead to a suitable engine ground. Position magneto stop plate (9) against pin (P) so ignition is in full retarded position. Remove spark plugs and ground terminal ends of spark plug leads. Rotate flywheel clockwise until voltage reading on meter shows a slight jump. Then note position of magneto base plate mark (M) to low speed timing mark (R) on flywheel. If marks are aligned (10 degrees BTDC), low speed ignition timing is correct. If not, adjust the contact gap on the appropriate set of breaker points until timing marks are aligned. After adjusting low speed timing, rotate magneto base plate (7) to full advanced position and check to make sure magneto base plate mark (M) properly aligns with high speed timing mark (A) on flywheel when voltmeter shows a slight jump as flywheel is rotated clockwise.

Repeat timing procedure with dc voltmeter connected to white wire. Tim-

ing marks on opposite side of flywheel are used. After correct ignition timing is obtained, reinstall spark plugs and connect spark plug leads.

Ignition timing can be dynamically checked as follows: Connect a suitable inductive type power timing light to top (No. 1) spark plug lead. Use a suitable auxillary water supply and direct water into jet pump intake on bottom of hull. Start engine and make sure water is being discharged out jet pump outlet.

NOTE: If water is not being discharged, redirect water supply. Engine should not be run longer than 15 seconds without a sufficient supply of water or damage to the engine could result.

With engine idling, low speed timing mark (R) should align with magneto base plate mark (M). With engine accelerated to ½-¾ throttle position, high speed timing mark (A) should align with magneto base plate mark (M). Repeat procedure with timing light connected to bottom (No. 2) spark plug lead. Adjust the contact gap on the appropriate set of breaker points, as previously outlined, if timing marks are not properly aligned.

TROUBLE-SHOOTING. If ignition malfunction occurs, use only approved

procedures to prevent damage to the components. The fuel system should be checked first to make certain that faulty running is not caused by incorrect mixture or contaminated fuel. Make sure malfunction is not due to spark plug, wiring or wiring connection failure. Use a suitable ohmmeter and refer to the following specifications to trouble-shoot ignition circuit:

Low Voltage Coils
   Resistance........0.915-1.355 ohms
Ignition Coil Primary
   Resistance........0.940-1.380 ohms
Ignition Coil Secondary
   Resistance........4100-6100 ohms

CDI Models With Moveable Magneto Base Plate

All models are equipped with a simultaneous capacitor discharge ignition system. Ignition timing should be 10 degrees to 25 degrees BTDC throughout operating range. The standard spark plug is NGK B7HS with an electrode gap of 0.6-0.7 mm (0.024-0.028 in.).

IGNITION TIMING. Ignition timing can be statically checked and adjusted as follows: Make sure cylinder block pin (P—Fig. SJ-20) is aligned with magneto

Fig. SJ-22—Exploded view of flywheel magneto unit on CDI models with moveable magneto base plate.

1. Cover
2. Flywheel
3. Charge coil
4. Pulser coil
5. CDI module
7. Magneto base plate
8. Throttle cam
9. Magneto stop plate
10. Bracket
11. Retainer
12. Felt ring

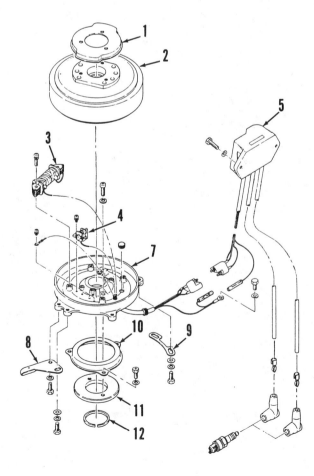

Fig. SJ-20—Refer to text for procedures to set ignition timing on breaker point models and CDI models with moveable magneto base plate.

A. High speed timing mark (25° BTDC)	R. Low speed timing mark (10° BTDC)
F. Flywheel	7. Magneto base plate
M. Magneto base plate mark	9. Magneto stop plate
P. Cylinder block pin	

-Tester Lead \ +Tester Lead		Exciter	Pulser	Ground	Tether
		Black/Red	Brown/White	White	Black
Exciter	Black /Red		A	B	C
Pulser	Brown /White	D		E	F
Ground	White	G	A		H
Tether	Black	A	A	A	

Fig. SJ-23—Use adjacent chart and values listed below to test condition of CDI module used on CDI models with a moveable magneto base plate.

A. Infinite resistance
B. 200,000 ohms
C. 3,000 ohms
D. 30,000 ohms
E. 18,000 ohms
F. 80,000 ohms
G. 2,500 ohms
H. 9,000 ohms

base plate mark (M) when magneto stop plate (9) is in full retarded position. If not, loosen magneto stop plate (9) retaining screws, then rotate magneto base plate (7) until mark (M) is aligned with cylinder block pin (P). Position magneto stop plate (9) against pin (P) and tighten retaining screws.

Ignition timing can be dynamically checked as follows: Connect a suitable inductive type power timing light to top (No. 1) spark plug lead. Use a suitable auxiliary water supply and direct water into jet pump intake on bottom of hull. Start engine and make sure water is being discharged out jet pump outlet.

NOTE: If water is not being discharged, redirect water supply. Engine should not be run longer than 15 seconds without a sufficient supply of water or damage to the engine could result.

With engine idling, low speed timing mark (R) should align with magneto base plate mark (M). With engine accelerated to ½-¾ throttle position, high speed timing mark (A) should align with magneto base plate mark (M).

TROUBLE-SHOOTING. If ignition malfunction occurs, use only approved procedures to prevent damage to the components. The fuel system should be checked first to make certain that faulty running is not caused by incorrect mixture or contaminated fuel. Make sure malfunction is not due to spark plug, wiring or wiring connection failure. Trouble-shoot ignition circuit using a suitable ohmmeter as follows:

Separate the three-wire connector between magneto components and CDI module. Refer to Fig. SJ-26. Check condition of charge coil (3) by attaching one tester lead to black/red wire leading to magneto assembly and attaching other tester lead to engine ground. Charge coil can be considered satisfactory if resistance reading is within the limits of 226-339 ohms. Check condition of pulser coil (4) by attaching one tester lead to brown/white wire leading to magneto assembly and attaching other tester lead to engine ground. Pulser coil can be considered satisfactory if

resistance reading is within the limits of 18-28 ohms.

To check secondary ignition coil resistance, attach a tester lead to terminal end of each high tension wire. Secondary coil resistance reading should be within the limits of 1360-2040 ohms.

To check condition of CDI module, use ohmmeter in conjunction with test chart shown in Fig. SJ-23. Renew CDI module if required.

CDI Models With Fixed Magneto Base Plate

All models are equipped with a simultaneous capacitor discharge ignition system. The ignition timing is electronically advanced as the magneto base plate is fixed. Ignition timing should be 12 degrees to 22 degrees BTDC throughout operating range.

IGNITION TIMING. Ignition timing can be dynamically checked as follows:

Connect a suitable inductive type power timing light to top (No. 1) spark plug lead. Use a suitable auxiliary water supply and direct water into jet pump intake on bottom of hull. Start engine and make sure water is being discharged out jet pump outlet.

NOTE: If water is not being discharged, redirect water supply. Engine should not be run longer than 15 seconds without a sufficient supply of water or damage to the engine could result.

With engine accelerated to ½-¾ throttle position, high speed timing mark (A—Fig. SJ-25) on flywheel should align with magneto base plate mark (M). If ignition timing is incorrect, trouble-shoot ignition components.

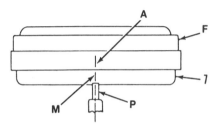

Fig. SJ-25—Refer to text for procedures to check ignition timing on CDI models with a fixed magneto base plate.

A. High speed timing mark (22° BTDC)
F. Flywheel
M. Magneto base plate mark
P. Cylinder block pin
7. Magneto base plate

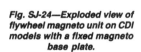

Fig. SJ-24—Exploded view of flywheel magneto unit on CDI models with a fixed magneto base plate.

2. Flywheel
3. Charge coil
4. Pulser coil
5. CDI module
7. Magneto base plate

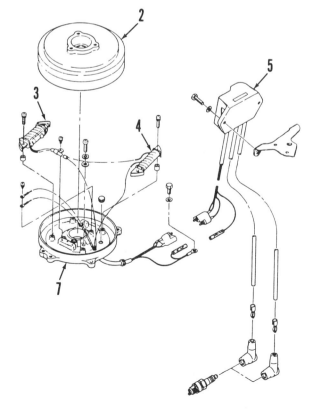

TROUBLE-SHOOTING. If ignition malfunction occurs, use only approved procedures to prevent damage to the components. The fuel system should be checked first to make certain that faulty running is not caused by incorrect mixture or contaminated fuel. Make sure malfunction is not due to spark plug, wiring or wiring connection failure. Trouble-shoot ignition circuit using a suitable ohmmeter as follows:

Separate the three-wire connector between magneto components and CDI module. Refer to Fig. SJ-26. Check condition of charge coil (3) by attaching one tester lead to black/red wire leading to magneto assembly and attaching other tester lead to engine ground. Charge coil can be considered satisfactory if resistance reading is within the limits of 128-192 ohms. Check condition of pulser coil (4) by attaching one tester lead to brown/white wire leading to magneto assembly and attaching other tester lead to engine ground. Pulser coil can be considered satisfactory if resistance reading is within the limits of 18-28 ohms.

To check secondary ignition coil resistance, attach a tester lead to terminal end of each high tension wire. Secondary coil resistance reading should be within the limits of 1360-2040 ohms.

To check condition of CDI module, use ohmmeter in conjunction with test chart shown in Fig. SJ-27. Renew CDI module if required.

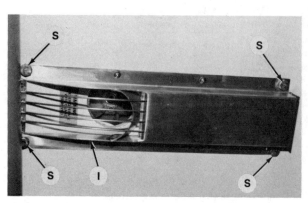

Fig. SJ-30—View identifies jet pump water intake (I) on bottom of hull. Four screws (S) mount engine and jet pump assembly to hull.

COOLING SYSTEM

All Models

All models are water-cooled. Forced water is supplied to the engine by the jet pump through a tube mounted on top of the jet pump water chamber. Thermostat (10—Fig. SJ-36) is used to regulate operating temperature. The thermostat should start to open at approximately 60° C (140° F) and be fully open at 71° C (160° F). Thermostat can be removed for inspection or renewal by removing thermostat cover (7).

Make sure jet pump water intake (I—Fig. SJ-30) is kept clean. The cooling system should be flushed out after each operating period when vehicle is used in contaminated or salt water. The cooling system should be flushed out prior to extended periods of storage and prior to usage after extended periods of storage.

To flush the cooling system, use a suitable auxiliary water supply and direct clean, fresh water into jet pump intake (I). Start engine and make sure water is being discharged out jet pump outlet.

NOTE: If water is not being discharged, redirect water supply. Engine should not be run longer than 15 seconds without a sufficient supply of water or damage to the engine could result.

Operate engine at low rpm and for a short period of time to flush system.

ENGINE

All Models

REMOVE AND REINSTALL. The engine and jet pump assembly must be removed as a complete unit. Remove fuel supply line (L—Fig. SJ-32) from fitting on fuel tank and primer hose (P)

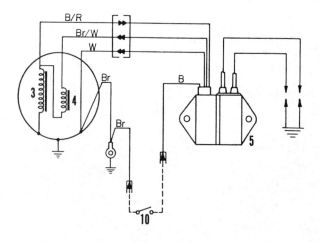

Fig. SJ-26—View showing ignition system wiring schematic on CDI models with both moveable and fixed magneto base plate.

3. Charge coil
4. Pulser coil
5. CDI module
10. Tether switch
B. Black
W. White
Br. Brown
B/R. Black with red tracer
Br/W. Brown with white tracer

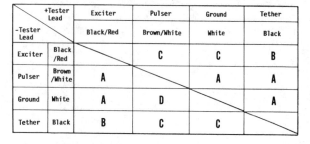

	+Tester Lead	Exciter	Pulser	Ground	Tether
−Tester Lead		Black/Red	Brown/White	White	Black
Exciter	Black /Red		C	C	B
Pulser	Brown /White	A		A	A
Ground	White	A	D		A
Tether	Black	B	C	C	

Fig. SJ-27—Use adjacent chart and values listed below to test condition of CDI module used on CDI models with a fixed magneto base plate.

A. Infinite resistance
B. Zero ohms
C. Continuity
D. 30,000 ohms

Fig. SJ-32—View identifying grommet (G), hydraulic throttle system line (H), fuel supply line (L), primer hose (P), starter rope (R) and belly pan opening (O).

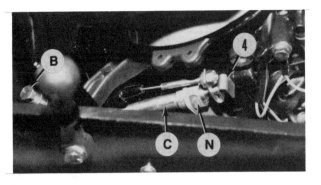

Fig. SJ-33—View identifying hydraulic throttle cylinder (C), cylinder retaining nut (N) and "S" bracket (4) used on models with a fixed magneto base plate. Install a 1/8 inch brass plug (B) into tee fitting opening when reservoir is removed.

from primer button. Remove hydraulic throttle system reservoir and install a 1/8 inch brass plug (B—Fig. SJ-33) into tee fitting opening. On models with a fixed magneto base plate, remove "S" bracket (4) from cylinder actuator rod. On nonupgraded 1980 and 1981 models, remove magneto base plate linkage from cylinder actuator rod. On all models, remove nut (N) and grommet (G—Fig. SJ-32). Remove starter handle from starter rope (R) and allow starter rope to slowly rewind onto starter pulley. Pull end of starter rope through belly pan opening (O) and tie a slip-knot in starter

rope. Disconnect tether switch wires from engine harness and feed wires through belly pan or remove tether switch from control panel. Remove four mounting screws (S—Fig. SJ-30). Break seal between exhaust housing and hull and jet pump water intake and hull, then use a suitable lifting device to hoist complete unit from hull. Feed hydraulic throttle system line (H—Fig. SJ-32) and cylinder (C—Fig. SJ-33) through opening in belly pan as engine and jet pump assembly is being withdrawn. Place complete unit on a clean work bench.

Prior to reinstalling complete unit, apply RTV silicone sealer to both sides of gasket located between exhaust housing and hull and jet pump water intake and hull. Use a suitable lifting device to hoist complete unit into hull. Guide hydraulic throttle system line (H—Fig. SJ-32) and cylinder (C—SJ-33) through opening in belly pan as unit is being installed. Install four mounting screws (S—Fig. SJ-30) and tighten to 24.5-27.2 N·m (18-20 ft.-lbs.) on models prior to 1984 and 13.6-14.9 N·m (10-11 ft.-lbs) on models after 1983. Complete

reinstallation in reverse order of removal. Refer to BLEEDING under HYDRAULIC THROTTLE section to remove any trapped air within system.

DISASSEMBLY. Remove jet pump cover (8—Fig. SJ-48). Rotate impeller (counterclockwise) to remove from engine crankshaft. Note shims (5) located above impeller and retain for reassembly.

NOTE: If Impeller cannot be rotated off of engine crankshaft, place a blunt-end brass punch at base of an impeller blade and strike punch with a suitable mallet (driving impeller counterclockwise) to break impeller loose from crankshaft.

Remove outlet nozzle (12). Remove screws retaining jet pump housing (2) to exhaust housing (6—Fig. SJ-35) and separate components. Withdraw water tube (11—Fig. SJ-48). Remove exhaust pipe (7—Fig. SJ-35) after removing two mounting screws. Remove the four engine mounting screws, then separate engine assembly from exhaust housing (6) and belly pan (2). Remove heat insulator (3) on models after 1980.

Remove rewind starter, starter cup, flywheel, magneto base plate and ignition components. Remove fuel pump and in-line fuel filter. Remove carburetor throttle shaft return spring and on models equipped with a fixed magneto base plate, the throttle shaft actuator cable. Remove carburetor retaining nuts, lockwashers and flat washers, then withdraw carburetor assembly. Remove bearing cover (3—Fig. SJ-36). Remove exhaust cover (1) and gasket (2). Remove intake manifold

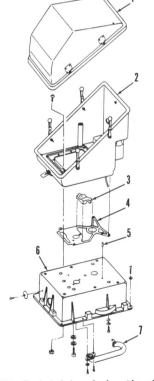

Fig. SJ-35—Exploded view of exhaust housing (6), belly pan (2) and related components. Belly pan (2) design on 1980 and 1981 models differs from type shown. Heat insulator (3) is used on models after 1980.

1. Cover
2. Belly pan
3. Heat insulator
4. Gasket
5. Pin
6. Exhaust housing
7. Exhaust pipe

Fig. SJ-36—Exploded view of cylinder block and crankcase assembly typical of all models. Bearing cover (3) will differ on CDI models with a fixed magneto base plate.

1. Exhaust cover
2. Gasket
3. Bearing cover
4. Seal
5. Gasket
6. Pin
7. Thermostat cover
8. Gasket
9. Seal ring
10. Thermostat
11. Crankcase half
12. Cylinder block
13. Cylinder head gasket
14. Cylinder head
15. Elbow
16. Hose
17. Seal

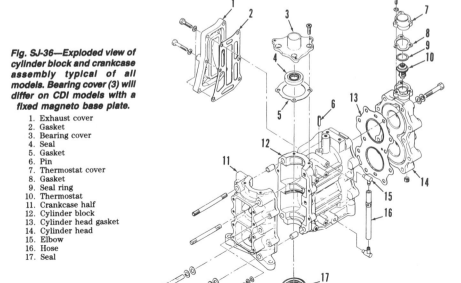

(1—Fig. SJ-5), gasket (2), reed valve assembly and gasket (6). Remove cylinder head (14—Fig. SJ-36) and cylinder head gasket (13). Clean carbon from combustion chamber and any foreign material accumulation in water passages. Remove rewind starter bracket retaining nuts, lockwashers and flat washers, then withdraw bracket. Remove crankcase half (11) retaining cap screws and separate crankcase half (11) from cylinder block (12). Crankshaft and piston assembly can now be removed from cylinder block.

Engine components are now ready for overhaul as outlined in the appropriate following paragraphs. Refer to the following section for assembly procedure.

ASSEMBLY. Refer to specific service sections when assembling the crank-

shaft, connecting rod, piston and reed valves. Make sure all joint and gasket surfaces are clean, free from nicks and burrs and hardened silicone sealer or carbon.

Whenever the engine is disassembled, it is recommended that all gasket surfaces and mating surfaces without gaskets be carefully checked for nicks, burrs and warped surfaces which might interfere with a tight seal. Cylinder head, head end of cylinder block and some mating surfaces of manifold and crankcase should be checked on a surface plate and lapped, if necessary, to provide a smooth surface. Do not remove any more metal than is necessary.

When assembling engine, first lubricate all friction surfaces and bearings with engine oil. Install crankshaft assembly with shim (4—Fig. SJ-37) into

cylinder block. Make certain main bearing locating pins engage notches in cylinder block. Apply a coat of a suitable form-in-place gasket compound on mating surfaces of crankcase and cylinder block and position crankcase on cylinder block. Install rewind starter bracket and retaining flat washers, lockwashers and nuts. Install remaining cap screws, lockwashers and flat washers securing crankcase half to cylinder block.

Using tightening sequence shown in Fig. SJ-38, tighten the crankcase fasteners in 1.36 N·m (1.0 ft.-lb.) increments until a final torque of 8.2-9.5 N·m (6-7 ft.-lbs.) is obtained on 6 mm cap screws and 19.0-21.8 N·m (14-16 ft.-

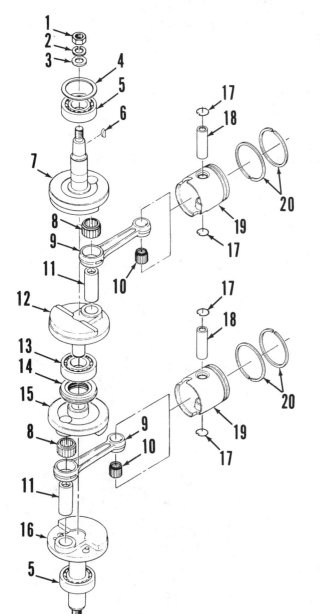

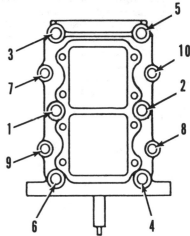

Fig. SJ-38—Crankcase cap screws and nuts should be tightened in the sequence shown. Refer to text for tightening torque specifications.

Fig. SJ-37—Exploded view of crankshaft assembly.

1. Flywheel retaining nut
2. Lockwasher
3. Flat washer
4. Shim
5. Ball bearings
6. Key
7. Upper crank half
8. Caged needle bearings
9. Connecting rods
10. Caged needle bearings
11. Crankpins
12. Upper crank half
13. Ball bearing
14. Labyrinth seal
15. Lower crank half
16. Lower crank half
17. Clips
18. Piston pins
19. Pistons
20. Piston rings

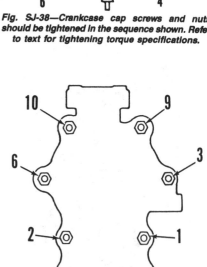

Fig. SJ-39—Cylinder head cap screws should be tightened in the sequence shown. Refer to text for tightening torque specifications.

lbs.) is obtained on 8 mm cap screws and starter bracket nuts. Rotate crankshaft to make sure components rotate freely. Check crankshaft end play. Maximum allowable crankshaft end play is 0.8 mm (0.031 in.). Increase thickness of shim (4—Fig. SJ-37) if crankshaft end play is beyond 0.8 mm (0.031 in.). Cylinder head gasket should be installed with a light coat of Three Bond 1215 or a suitable equivalent applied on both sides. Using tightening sequence shown in Fig. SJ-39, tighten the cylinder head cap screws in 1.36 N·m (1.0 ft.-lb.) increments until a final torque of 17.7-23.1 N·m (13-17 ft.-lbs.) is obtained. Complete the remainder of reassembly in the reverse order of disassembly while noting the following: Tighten flywheel nut to 43.5-49.0 N·m (32-36 ft.-lbs.). Apply a thin coating of a RTV silicone sealer on both sides of gasket (4—Fig. SJ-35) prior to assembly. Apply a bead of a RTV silicone sealer around threads at head end of engine mounting cap screws and tighten to 18.4 N·m (14 ft.-lbs.). Wipe off excess sealer. Apply RTV 102 or a suitable equivalent to mounting flange of exhaust pipe (7) prior to installation. Apply a bead of a RTV silicone sealer between mounting surfaces of exhaust housing (6) and jet pump housing (2—Fig. SJ-48). Install shim (5) removed during disassembly

and rotate impeller (6) clockwise to screw impeller onto engine crankshaft end. Apply a bead of a RTV silicone sealer around outlet nozzle (12) where nozzle mates with jet pump housing (2) and jet pump cover (8). Install gasket (7) dry. Using tightening sequence shown in Fig. SJ-49, tighten jet pump cover (8—Fig. SJ-48) cap screws to 9.1 N·m (7 ft.-lbs.). Seal area between outlet nozzle (12) and exhaust housing (6—Fig. SJ-35) with a RTV silicone sealer. Apply a coating of a RTV silicone sealer on both sides of gaskets (4 and 9—Fig. SJ-48).

RINGS, PISTONS AND CYLINDERS. The pistons are fitted with two piston rings. Piston rings are retained in position by locating pins. The chrome plated piston ring must be installed in top piston ring groove. Piston-to-cylinder wall clearance should be 0.10-0.14 mm (0.0039-0.0054 in.) with a maximum allowable clearance of 0.25 mm (0.0098 in.). Pistons and rings are available in standard size as well as 0.25 mm (0.010 in.) and 0.50 mm (0.020 in.) oversizes. Cylinder should be bored to an oversize if cylinder is out-of-round or taper exceeds 0.10 mm (0.004 in.). Install piston on connecting rod so "F" on piston crown will point towards flywheel end of crankshaft.

CONNECTING RODS, BEARINGS AND CRANKSHAFT. Connecting rods, bearings and crankshaft are a pressed together unit. Crankshaft should be disassembled ONLY by experienced service personnel and with proper service equipment.

Caged needle bearings are used at both large and small ends of the connecting rod. Maximum allowable limit of crankshaft runout is 0.12 mm (0.0047 in.) measured at bearing surfaces with crankshaft ends supported.

When installing crankshaft, lubricate pistons, rings, cylinders and bearings with engine oil and refer to ASSEMBLY section.

MANUAL STARTER

Breaker Point Ignition Models

Refer to Fig. SJ-42 for exploded view of manual rewind starter assembly. Starter cup (13) is mounted on magneto flywheel.

Starter can be removed and disassembled as follows: Untie starter rope (4) in starter handle. Slowly allow rope to wind onto rope pulley (3). Remove starter housing (1) from power head. Invert starter housing (1) and remove clip (12) and washer (11). Withdraw friction plate (10) and remove pawls (8) and pawl return springs (9). Carefully remove rope pulley assembly (3) to prevent dislodging of rewind spring (2) from housing. Any part of the starter can be serviced or renewed at this point.

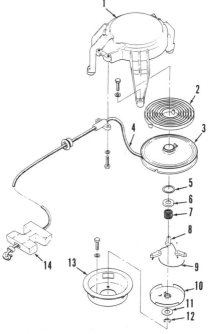

Fig. SJ-42—Exploded view of manual rewind starter used on models equipped with breaker point ignition.

1. Housing
2. Rewind spring
3. Pulley
4. Starter rope
5. Thrust washer
6. Spring seat
7. Friction spring
8. Pawls
9. Return springs
10. Friction plate
11. Washer
12. Clip
13. Cup
14. Handle

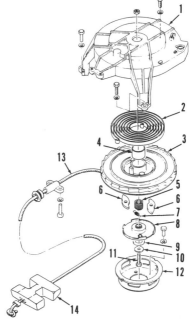

Fig. SJ-43—Exploded view of manual rewind starter used on models equipped with CD ignition.

1. Housing
2. Rewind spring
3. Pulley
4. Bushing
5. Friction spring
6. Pawls
7. Return spring
8. Friction plate
9. Thrust washer
10. Washer
11. Bolt
12. Cup
13. Starter rope
14. Handle

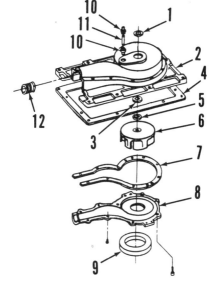

Fig. SJ-48—Exploded view of jet pump assembly.

1. Seal
2. Housing
3. Seal
4. Gasket
5. Shim
6. Impeller
7. Gasket
8. Cover
9. Gasket
10. Fittings
11. Tube
12. Outlet nozzle

Reassemble as follows: Install rewind spring (2) in housing (1) beginning with outside coil of spring. Wind starter rope on pulley (3) counterclockwise as viewed from bottom leaving approximately three feet of rope extending from pulley (3). Bring rope through notch in pulley and rotate pulley four turns counterclockwise as viewed from flywheel side. Feed end of rope through starter housing and tie a slip-knot in rope to retain tension. Release rope from notch in pulley. Assemble parts (5 through 9) and hook friction plate (10) in return springs (9). Turn friction plate approximately one-half turn counterclockwise and position on rope pulley. Install thrust washer (11) and snap ring (12). Install rewind starter assembly onto power head. Untie starter rope slip-knot and feed rope end through belly pan. Attach handle onto starter rope and position in control panel.

NOTE: Do not apply any more tension on rewind spring (2) than is required to draw starter handle (14) back into the proper released position.

CD Ignition Models

Refer to Fig. SJ-43 for exploded view of manual rewind starter assembly. Starter cup (12) is mounted on magneto flywheel.

Starter can be removed and disassembled as follows: Untie starter rope (13) in starter handle. Slowly allow rope to wind onto rope pulley (3). Remove starter housing (1) from power head. Invert starter housing (1) and remove bolt (11), washer (10) and thrust washer (9). Withdraw friction plate (8) and remove

pawls (6) and pawl return spring (7). Carefully remove rope pulley assembly (3) to prevent dislodging of rewind spring (2) from housing. Any part of the starter can be serviced or renewed at this point.

Reassemble as follows: Install rewind spring (2) in housing (1) beginning with outside coil of spring. Wind starter rope on pulley (3) counterclockwise as viewed from bottom leaving approximately three feet of rope extending from pulley (3). Bring rope through notch in pulley and rotate pulley four turns counterclockwise as viewed from flywheel side. Feed end of rope through starter housing and tie a slip-knot in rope to retain tension. Release rope from notch in pulley. Assemble parts (5 through 8). Hook friction plate (8) in return spring (7). Install thrust washer (9) and washer (10). Apply a suitable thread locking solution on threads of bolt (11) prior to assembly. Install bolt (11) and securely tighten. Install rewind starter assembly onto power head. Untie starter rope slip-knot and feed rope end through belly pan. Attach handle onto starter rope and position in control panel.

NOTE: Do not apply any more tension on rewind spring (2) than is required to draw starter handle (14) back into the proper released position.

JET PUMP

All Models

REMOVE AND REINSTALL. The engine and jet pump assembly must be removed as a complete unit. Remove fuel supply line (L—Fig. SJ-32) from fitting on fuel tank and primer hose (P) from primer button. Remove hydraulic throttle system reservoir and install a 1/8 inch brass plug (B—Fig. SJ-33) into tee fitting opening. On models with a fixed magneto base plate, remove "S" bracket (4) from cylinder actuator rod. On nonupgraded 1980 and 1981 models, remove magneto base plate linkage from cylinder actuator rod. On all models, remove nut (N) and grommet (G—Fig. SJ-32). Remove starter handle from starter rope (R) and allow starter rope to slowly rewind onto starter pulley. Pull end of starter rope through belly pan opening (O) and tie a slip-knot in starter rope. Disconnect tether switch wires from engine harness and feed wires through belly pan or remove tether switch from control panel. Remove four mounting screws (S—Fig. SJ-30). Break seal between exhaust housing and hull and jet pump water intake and hull, then use a suitable lifting device to hoist complete unit from hull. Feed hydraulic

throttle system line (H—Fig. SJ-32) and cylinder (C—Fig. SJ-33) through opening in belly pan as engine and jet pump assembly is being withdrawn. Place complete unit on a clean work bench.

Prior to reinstalling complete unit, apply RTV silicone sealer to both sides of gasket located between exhaust housing and hull and jet pump water intake and hull. Use a suitable lifting device to hoist complete unit into hull. Guide hydraulic throttle system line (H—Fig. SJ-32) and cylinder (C—Fig. SJ-33) through opening in belly pan as unit is being installed. Install four mounting screws (S—Fig. SJ-30) and tighten to 24.5-27.2 N·m (18-20 ft.-lbs.) on models prior to 1984 and 13.6-14.9 N·m (10-11 ft.-lbs.) on models after 1983. Complete reinstallation in reverse order of removal. Refer to BLEEDING under HYDRAULIC THROTTLE section to remove any trapped air within system.

OVERHAUL. Remove jet pump cover (8—Fig. SJ-48). Rotate impeller (6) counterclockwise to remove from engine crankshaft. Note shims (5) located above impeller and retain for reassembly.

NOTE: If impeller cannot be rotated off of engine crankshaft, place a blunt-end brass punch at base of an impeller blade and strike punch with a suitable mallet (driving impeller counterclockwise) to break impeller loose from crankshaft.

Inspect impeller (6) for cracked or broken blades or any other damage. Inspect housing (2) and cover (8) for excessive wear or any other damage. Renew any component that is excessively worn or is diagnosed with any other damage. Renew all gaskets during reassembly.

To reassemble, install shim (5) removed during disassembly and rotate impeller (6) clockwise to screw impeller onto engine crankshaft end. Apply a bead of a RTV silicone sealer around outlet nozzle (12) where nozzle mates with jet pump cover (8). Install gasket (7) dry. Using tightening sequence shown in Fig. SJ-49, tighten jet pump cover (8—Fig. SJ-48) cap screws to 9.1 N·m (7 ft.-lbs.). Measure clearance between impeller (6) blades and jet pump cover (8) through water intake opening. Clearance should be 0.25 mm (0.010 in.) or less. If clearance is more than 0.25 mm (0.010 in.), increase thickness of shim (5) to bring clearance within recommended specification. Shim (5) is available in thicknesses of 0.25 mm (0.010 in.), 0.76 mm (0.030 in.) and 1.14 mm (0.045 in.). Apply a coating of a RTV silicone sealer on both sides of gaskets (4 and 9).

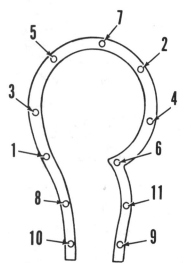

Fig. SJ-49—Jet pump cover cap screws should be tightened in the sequence shown.

WETBIKE

ULTRANAUTICS
620 W. Hueneme Road
Oxnard, CA 93033

MODELS 1978-1984, MODEL 800 (1985-1987), SILVER STREAK (1987-1988) AND TOM CAT (1988)

NOTE: Metric fasteners are used throughout engine and jet pump.

General

Engine Make	Suzuki
Engine Type	Two-Stroke; Water-Cooled
HP/Rated Rpm:	
Prior to 1985	50/5300
After 1984	60/5300
Number of Cylinders	2
Bore:	
50 HP Models	80 mm (3.15 in.)
60 HP Models	84 mm (3.31 in.)
Stroke	72 mm (2.83 in.)
Displacement:	
50 HP Models	723 cc (44.12 cu. in.)
60 HP Models	798 cc (48.7 cu. in.)
Compression Ratio:	
50 HP Models	7.0:1
60 HP Models	6.5:1
Engine Lubrication	Pre-Mix
Fuel:Oil Ratio	50:1
Engine Oil Recommendation	Two-Stroke; BIA Certified TC-W

Tune-Up

Engine Idle Speed	600-650 rpm*
Spark Plug:	
NGK	BR8HS
Champion	RL78C
Electrode Gap	0.6-0.7 mm (0.024-0.028 in.)
Ignition:	
Type	CDI
Timing	8° BTDC @ 1000 rpm 25° BTDC @ 5000 rpm
Carburetor:	
Make	Mikuni
Model	B40-32
Bore Size	40 mm (1.57 in.)
Main Jet	155
Air Jet	1.2
Pilot Jet	70
Idle Mixture Setting	1-3/4 Turns
Float Height:	
50 HP Models	15.4-17.5 mm (0.60-0.68 in.)
60 HP Models	16.5-18.5 mm (0.65-0.73 in.)

Tune-Up (Cont.)

*Engine must stop when throttle twist grip is released to complete closed position. If not, engine idle speed should be adjusted to a lower rpm. A slight rotation of throttle twist grip must be required to keep engine running.

Sizes—Clearances

Cylinder Wear Limit:	
50 HP Models	80.1 mm (3.153 in.)
60 HP Models	84.1 mm (3.314 in.)
Piston-to-Cylinder Wall Clearance:	
50 HP Models	0.078-0.092 mm (0.0031-0.0036 in.)
60 HP Models	0.112-0.127 mm (0.0044-0.0050 in.)
Piston Pin Diameter	19.995-20.000 mm (0.7872-0.7874 in.)
Piston Pin Bore Diameter	19.998-20.006 mm (0.7873-0.7876 in.)
Piston Ring End Gap:	
Top and Second	0.2-0.4 mm (0.008-0.016 in.)
Service Limit	0.8 mm (0.031 in.)
Maximum Connecting Rod Small End Side Shake	5.0 mm (0.20 in.)
Maximum Crankshaft Runout at Main Bearing Journal	0.05 mm (0.002 in.)
Maximum Reed Stopper Opening:	
50 HP Models	8.8 mm (0.346 in.)
60 HP Models	7.95 mm (0.313 in.)
Maximum Reed Valve Stand Open	0.2 mm (0.008 in.)

Capacities

Fuel Tank:	
Models 1978-1985	30 L (8 gal.)
Models 1986-1988	34 L (9 gal.)

Tightening Torques

Carburetor Mounting Nuts	10-13 N·m (7-10 ft.-lbs.)

Tightening Torques (Cont.)
Cylinder Head Cap Screws—
50 HP Models:
    6 mm..................................7-9 N·m
                    (5-7 ft.-lbs.)
    8 mm................................34-39 N·m
                  (25-29 ft.-lbs.)
60 HP Models:
    6 mm..................................7-9 N·m
                    (5-7 ft.-lbs.)
    8 mm................................34-39 N·m
                  (25-29 ft.-lbs.)
    10 mm..............................39-58 N·m
                  (29-43 ft.-lbs.)
Crankcase Cap Screws...................36-39 N·m
                  (26-29 ft.-lbs.)
Engine Exhaust Cover Cap Screws..........8-11 N·m
                  (6-8 ft.-lbs.)
Reed Plate Cap Screws...................4-7 N·m
                  (3-5 ft.-lbs.)

Tightening Torques (Cont.)
Spark Plug...........................25-27 N·m
                  (18-20 ft.-lbs.)
Flywheel Nut...........................196 N·m
                  (144 ft.-lbs.)
Exhaust Chamber Base..................19-24 N·m
                  (14-18 ft.-lbs.)
Engine Mounting Nuts..................21-24 N·m
                  (15-18 ft.-lbs.)
Pinion Gear Nut.......................22-26 N·m
                  (16-19 ft.-lbs.)
Pinion Shaft Cover....................19-23 N·m
                  (14-17 ft.-lbs.)
Impeller Shaft Nut......................68 N·m
                  (50 ft.-lbs.)
Jet Pump Front Cover Cap Screws........19-23 N·m
                  (14-17 ft.-lbs.)
Jet Pump Nozzle Nuts..................30-39 N·m
                  (22-29 ft.-lbs.)
Jet Pump Mounting Cap Screws..........34-39 N·m
                  (25-29 ft.-lbs.)

LUBRICATION

All Models

The engine is lubricated by oil mixed with the fuel. Fuel:oil ratios should be 25:1 during break-in of a new or rebuilt engine and 50:1 for normal service when using a BIA certified two-stroke TC-W engine oil. When using any other type of two-stroke engine oil, fuel:oil ratios should be 20:1 during break-in and 30:1 for normal service. Manufacturer recommends regular or no-lead automotive gasoline having an 85-95 octane rating. Gasoline and oil should be thoroughly mixed.

The jet pump gears and bearings are lubricated by oil contained in the gearcase. SAE 90 hypoid marine gear oil should be used. The gearcase is drained and filled through the same plug port (D—Fig. WB-1). To drain the oil, place the Wetbike so gearcase is parallel to a flat, level surface. Remove "OIL FILL" plug (D) and "OIL CHECK" plug (V). Allow lubricant to drain into a suitable container. To fill gearcase, add oil through "OIL FILL" plug (D) opening until oil begins to flow from "OIL CHECK" plug (V) opening. Reinstall "OIL CHECK" plug (V) with a new gasket, if needed, and tighten plug. Reinstall "OIL FILL" plug (D) with a new gasket, if needed, and tighten plug.

During winterizing or more frequent if needed, grease jet pump output nozzle bushing by injecting a water-resistant grease into grease fitting at rear of jet pump output nozzle.

FUEL SYSTEM

All Models

CARBURETOR. Mikuni type B40-32 carburetors are used on all models. Refer to Fig. WB-3 for an exploded view of carburetor assemblies. Initial setting of idle mixture screw (7—Fig. WB-3) from a lightly seated position should be 1-3/4 turns. Final carburetor adjustment should be made with engine at normal operating temperature and running. Make sure cooling system will receive an adequate supply of water prior to operating engine. Rotate throttle twist grip to slightly accelerate engine.

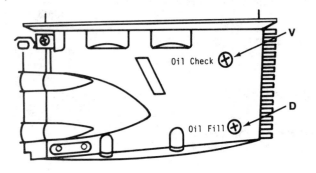

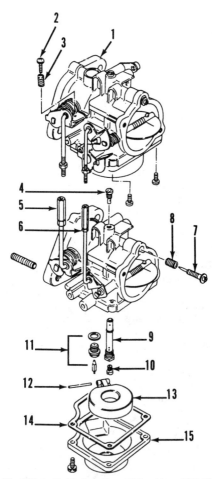

Fig. WB-1—View identifying jet pump gearcase "OIL FILL" plug (D) and "OIL CHECK" plug (V).

Fig. WB-3—Exploded view of Mikuni type B40-32 carburetors.

1. Body
2. Throttle stop screw
3. Spring
4. Pilot jet
5. Throttle shaft connector
6. Choke shaft connector
7. Idle mixture screw
8. Spring
9. Main nozzle
10. Main jet
11. Inlet valve assy.
12. Float pin
13. Float
14. Gasket
15. Float bowl

NOTE: Engine must stop when throttle twist grip is released to complete closed position.

Adjust idle mixture screw (7) so engine idles smoothly and will accelerate cleanly without hesitation. If necessary, readjust throttle stop screw (2) so engine stops when throttle twist grip is released (approximately 600-650 rpm).

Main fuel metering is controlled by main jet (10). Standard main jet size for normal operation is number 155.

To check float height, remove float bowl and invert carburetor. Distance (A—Fig. WB-4) between main jet (10) and bottom of float (13) should be 15.4-17.5 mm (0.60-0.68 in.) on 50 hp models and 16.5-18.5 mm (0.65-0.73 in.)

on 60 hp models. Adjust float height by bending float tang (T).

To synchronize throttle plate opening of top carburetor with bottom carburetor, use Suzuki carburetor balancer tool 09913-13121 or equivalent and make adjustment at throttle shaft connector (5—Fig. WB-3).

Synchronize upper and lower carburetor choke plates, then adjust choke solenoid actuating arm so choke plates fully close when solenoid plunger is fully retracted.

REED VALVES. The inlet reed valves (Fig. WB-6) are located on a reed plate between inlet manifold and crankcase. Models prior to 1985 are equipped with steel reed valves. Models after 1984 are equipped with fiberglass reed valves. The reed petals should seat very lightly against the reed plate throughout their entire length with the least possible tension. Tip of reed petal must not stand open more than 0.2 mm (0.008 in.) from contact surface. Reed stopper opening should not exceed 8.8 mm (0.346 in.) on 50 hp models and 7.95 mm (0.313 in.) on 60 hp models.

Renew reeds if petals are broken, cracked, warped, rusted or bent. Never attempt to bend a reed petal or to straighten a damaged reed. Never install a bent or damaged reed. Seating surface of reed plate should be smooth and flat. When installing reeds or reed stopper, make sure that petals are centered over the inlet holes in reed plate and that the reed stoppers are centered over reed petals. Apply a suitable thread locking solution on reed stopper mounting screws and securely tighten. Apply a thin coating of a form-in-place gasket compound on both sides of reed plate prior to assembling reed plate and intake manifold to crankcase.

FUEL PUMP. A diaphragm type fuel pump is mounted on the side of engine cylinder block and is actuated by pressure and vacuum pulsations from the engine crankcases. Refer to Fig. WB-8 for exploded view of fuel pump assembly used on models prior to 1985. Refer to Fig. WB-9 for exploded view of fuel pump used on models after 1984.

When servicing pump, scribe reference marks across pump body to aid in

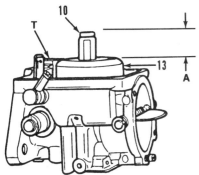

Fig. WB-4—Float height (A) should be 15.4-17.5 mm (0.60-0.68 in.) on 50 hp models and 16.5-18.5 mm (0.65-0.73 in.) on 60 hp models measured between main jet (10) and bottom of float (13). Bend float tang (T) to adjust.

Fig. WB-8—Exploded view of diaphragm type fuel pump used on models prior to 1985.

1. Cover
2. Diaphragm
5. Body
6. Spring
8. Diaphragm
10. Base
11. "O" rings
12. Insulator block

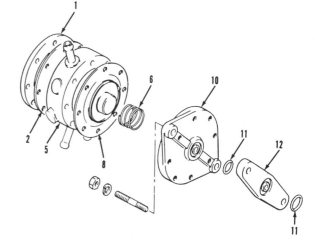

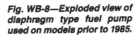

Fig. WB-9—Exploded view of diaphragm type fuel pump used on models after 1984.

1. Cover
2. Diaphragm
3. Gasket
4. Check valves
5. Body
6. Spring
7. Spring seat
8. Diaphragm
9. Gasket
10. Base

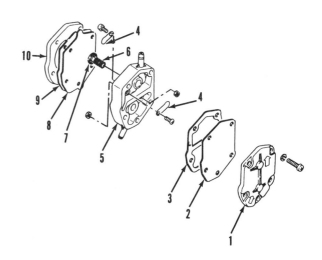

Fig. WB-6—Exploded view of intake manifold and reed valve assembly.

1. Intake manifold
2. Reed plate
3. Reed petals
4. Reed stopper

Wetbike

reassembly. Defective or questionable parts should be renewed. Diaphragm should be renewed if air leaks or cracks are found, or if deterioration is evident.

FUEL TANK AND FUEL FILTER. Fuel strainer (2—Fig. WB-11 and Fig.

WB-12) is attached on the bottom of the fuel tank pickup line and an inline fuel filter (4) is used on all models. Periodically remove inline fuel filter (4) and blow through inlet side of filter with low air pressure to check for blockage. Very little restriction should

be noted. Renew fuel filter (4) if excessive restriction is noted. Fuel tank strainer (2) should not need to be removed and cleaned unless contamination is suspected.

An anti-siphon valve (3) is used on all models to prevent fuel from being siphoned out fuel tank (1) should fuel line become damaged.

PERSONAL WATER VEHICLE

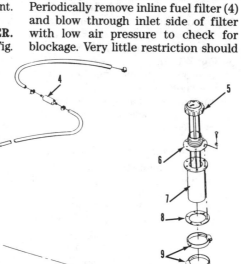

Fig. WB-11—Exploded view of fuel tank and fuel supply line on models prior to 1986.
1. Fuel tank
2. Fuel strainer
3. Anti-siphon valve
4. Fuel filter
5. Fuel level gage & cap
6. Filler neck
7. Filler tube
8. Plate
9. Clamps

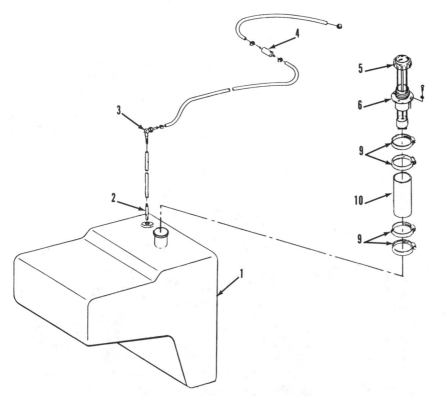

Fig. WB-12—Exploded view of fuel tank and fuel supply line on models after 1985.
1. Fuel tank
2. Fuel strainer
3. Anti-siphon valve
4. Fuel filter
5. Fuel level gage & cap
6. Filler neck
9. Clamps
10. Filler hose

IGNITION

All Models

All models are equipped with a simultaneous capacitor discharge ignition system. The ignition timing is electronically advanced as the magneto base plate is fixed. Ignition timing should not require adjustment, after first being correctly set, unless magneto base plate is moved or an ignition component is renewed.

Ignition timing should be 8 degrees BTDC at 1000 rpm and 25 degrees BTDC at 5000 rpm. Ignition timing can be checked using a suitable power timing light. Immerse vehicle in water so jet pump is submerged or connect a supplemental water supply to flush inlet after removing plug (P—Fig. WB-14) and using adapter 0510-503.

NOTE: When using a supplemental water supply, do not turn on water until engine is ready to be started as exhaust flooding could occur. Manufacturer recommends using only medium water pressure. Operate engine only at low rpm and for short periods of time.

To check ignition timing, start engine and accelerate to 1000 rpm. Note flywheel timing marks (M—Fig. WB-15) in relation to index mark (I) on flywheel housing. If ignition timing is incorrect, stop engine and reposition magneto base plate. Make sure supplemental water supply is turned off at approximately same time engine is stopped.

50 HP Models

TROUBLE-SHOOTING. If ignition malfunction occurs, use only approved procedures to prevent damage to the components. The fuel system should be checked first to make certain that faulty running is not caused by incorrect mixture or contaminated fuel. Make sure malfunction is not due to spark plug, wiring or wiring connection failure. Trouble-shoot ignition circuit using Suzuki pocket tester number 09900-25002 or a suitable ohmmeter as follows:

Check condition of low-speed capacitor charge coil by separating the red/black wire connector at magneto

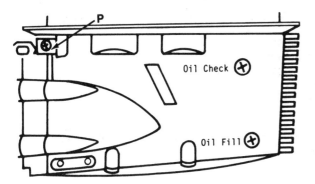

Fig. WB-14—Remove jet pump plug (P) and use adapter 0510-503 to attach a supplemental water supply.

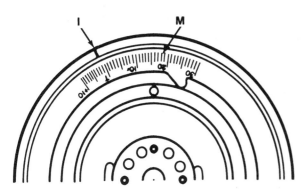

Fig. WB-15—Recommended flywheel timing mark (M) should align with index mark (I) on flywheel housing when engine is operated at recommended speed for correct ignition timing.

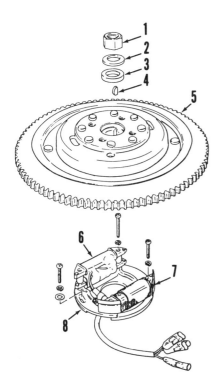

Fig. WB-16—Exploded view of magneto and case components used on models prior to 1985.

1. Nut
2. Lockwasher
3. Flat washer
4. Key
5. Flywheel
6. High/low-speed coil assy.
7. Lighting coil
8. Magneto base plate

coil resistance reading should be within the limits of 0.28-0.38 ohm. Attach a tester lead to each high tension wire. Secondary coil resistance reading should be within the limits of 2980-4030 ohms.

To check condition of CDI module, use tester or ohmmeter in conjunction with test chart shown in Fig. WB-17. Renew CDI module if required.

60 HP Models

TROUBLE-SHOOTING. If ignition malfunction occurs, use only approved procedures to prevent damage to the components. The fuel system should be checked first to make certain that faulty running is not caused by incorrect mixture or contaminated fuel. Make sure malfunction is not due to spark plug, wiring or wiring connection failure. Trouble-shoot ignition circuit using Suzuki pocket tester number 09900-25002 or a suitable ohmmeter as follows:

Check condition of low-speed capacitor charge coil by separating the blue/red wire connector and black wire connector at magneto base plate and attach a tester lead to each wire. Low-speed charge coil can be considered satisfactory if resistance reading is within the limits of 135-165 ohms. Check condition of high-speed charge coil (pulser coil) by separating the white/red connector and black wire connector at magneto base plate and attach a tester lead to each wire. High-speed charge coil can be considered satisfactory if resistance reading is within the limits of 7.29-8.91 ohms.

To check condition of ignition coil, separate the black/white wire connector at coil and remove high tension wires from spark plugs. Attach one tester lead to black/white wire and other tester lead to coil ground. Primary coil resistance reading should be within

base plate and attach a tester lead. Attach the other tester lead to engine ground. Low-speed charge coil can be considered satisfactory if resistance reading is within the limits of 112-149 ohms. Check condition of high-speed charge coil by separating the red/black connector and blue/red wire connector at magneto base plate and attach a tester lead to each wire. High-speed charge coil can be considered satisfactory if resistance reading is within the limits of 1.62-1.98 ohms.

To check condition of ignition coil, separate the white/black wire connector at coil and remove high tension wires from spark plugs. Attach one tester lead to white/black wire and other tester lead to coil ground. Primary

Fig. WB-17—Use adjacent chart and values listed below to test condition of CDI module on 50 hp models.

A. Tester needle should show deflection then return toward infinite resistance.*
B. Infinite
C. Continuity
*Momentarily touch blue/red and white/black wires together prior to performing test.

+ Tester Lead / − Tester Lead	Blue /Red	Red /Black	Black	White /Black
Blue /Red		A	A	A
Red /Black	B		B	B
Black	C	C		A
White /Black	C	C	C	

the limits of 0.076-0.104 ohm. Attach a tester lead to each high tension wire. Secondary coil resistance reading should be within the limits of 2980-4030 ohms.

To check condition of CDI module, use tester or ohmmeter in conjunction with test chart shown in Fig. WB-20. Renew CDI module if required.

CHARGING SYSTEM

All Models

All models are equipped with a lighting coil, rectifier, 20 ampere fuse and battery. Standard battery has a 32 ampere hour, 12 volt rating. The lighting coil should produce 6 amperes at 5000 rpm.

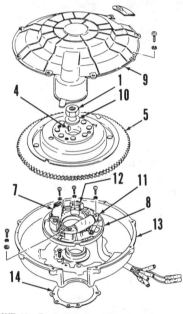

Fig. WB-19—Exploded view of magneto and case components used on models after 1984.

1. Nut
4. Key
5. Flywheel
7. Lighting coil
8. Magneto base plate
9. Cover
10. Spacer
11. Low-speed coil
12. High-speed coil
13. Magneto case
14. Gasket

The battery electrolyte level should be checked periodically and filled to maximum level with distilled water if required. The battery should be removed from the vehicle and the battery caps removed when charging. Maximum charging rate should not exceed 4 amperes.

NOTE: Remove 20 ampere fuse prior to removing battery to prevent possible damage to CDI module. Make sure battery charging area is well ventilated.

The lighting coil can be statically testing using a suitable ohmmeter. Refer to Fig. WB-22. Separate yellow wire and red wire leading from lighting coil to rectifier assembly at connectors. Measure resistance between the two wires leading to lighting coil. Resistance reading should be 0.41-0.50 ohms on 50 hp models and 0.33-0.41 ohms on 60 hp models. Check for continuity between each of the lighting coil wires and ground. Tester should show infinite resistance at each wire. To check rectifier assembly, first make sure battery is fully charged, lighting coil and in-line 20 ampere fuse test good, all wiring is in good condition and all connectors fit tightly or are securely fastened. Connect a supplemental water supply to flush inlet after removing plug (P—Fig. WB-14) and using adapter 0510-503.

NOTE: Do not turn on water until engine is ready to be started as exhaust flooding could occur. Manufacturer recommends using only medium water pressure.

Start and run engine. Attach a suitable ammeter between terminal end of fuse and positive battery lead.

NOTE: If a center function type ammeter is NOT being used, make sure ammeter is connected after engine is started or damage to ammeter could result.

Accelerate engine to 5000 rpm while observing ammeter.

NOTE: Do not hold engine speed at 5000 rpm for longer than 10 seconds. Allow engine to return to idle and stabilize before repeating test.

The ammeter should show approximately 6 amperes. Make sure supplemental water supply is turned off at approximately same time engine is stopped.

COOLING SYSTEM

All Models

All models are water-cooled. Forced water is supplied to the engine through holes at the top, rear of jet pump wear ring. As jet pump impeller rpm increases, so does water circulation through cooling system.

Make sure jet pump water intake is kept clean. Inspect all hoses periodically for cracks, kinks or any other damage. The cooling system should be flushed out after each operating period when vehicle is used in contaminated or salt water. The cooling system should be flushed out prior to extended periods of storage and prior to usage after extended periods of storage.

To flush the cooling system, connect a supplemental water supply to flush inlet after removing plug (P—Fig. WB-14) and using adapter 0510-503. Use only clean, fresh water.

NOTE: Do not turn on water until engine is ready to be started as exhaust flooding

+ Tester Lead − Tester Lead	Blue /Red	White /Red	Black	Black /White
Blue /Red		B	A	A
White /Red	C		C	A
Black	C	B		A
Black /White	C	B	C	

Fig. WB-20—Use adjacent chart and values listed below to test condition of CDI module on 60 hp models.

A. Tester needle should show deflection then return toward infinite resistance
B. Infininte
C. Continuity

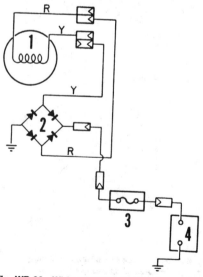

Fig. WB-22—Wiring diagram of charging system used on all models.

1. Lighting coil
2. Rectifier
3. Fuse (20 ampere)
4. Battery
R. Red
Y. Yellow

could occur. Manufacturer recommends using only medium water pressure.

Operate engine at low rpm for a short period of time to flush system. Make sure supplemental water supply is turned off at approximately same time engine is stopped.

ENGINE

All Models

REMOVE AND REINSTALL. Disconnect battery cables from battery and remove battery from vehicle. Detach engine wiring harness from control panel harness at connector. Disconnect fuel supply line from fuel pump and plug fuel line. Disconnect bilge pump leads. Disconnect throttle control cable from upper carburetor. Remove the eight nuts and lockwashers retaining the engine mounting plate to the jet pump housing. Use a suitable lifting device to hoist engine assembly from vehicle. Place engine assembly on a clean work bench.

Prior to reinstalling engine assembly, apply a form-in-place gasket compound on both sides of gasket located between engine mounting plate and jet pump housing, grease rubber hull seal and apply a light coating of a water-resistance grease on drive shaft splines. Use a suitable lifting device to hoist engine assembly into vehicle. Align eight engine mounting plate studs with holes in jet pump housing. Make sure engine assembly properly seats.

NOTE: Rotate drive shaft, if needed, to align drive shaft and crankshaft splines.

Install the eight lockwashers and nuts and tighten to 34-39 N·m (25-29 ft.-lbs.). Complete reinstallation in reverse order of removal.

DISASSEMBLY. Remove the nine nuts, flat washers and lockwashers retaining the engine mounting plate to the engine assembly. Use a suitable lifting device to hoist engine assembly from engine mounting plate. Remove engine base gasket, then set engine assembly on a clean work area for complete disassembly.

Remove the air intake silencer. Disconnect the fuel lines and choke solenoid actuator from the carburetors. Remove the nuts and lockwashers retaining the carburetors. Slide carburetors and gaskets off intake manifold

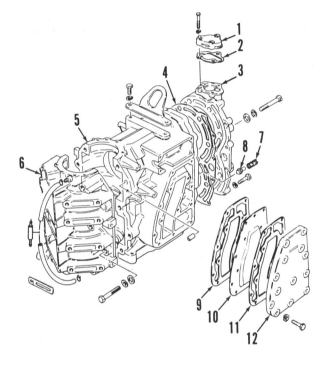

Fig. WB-24—Exploded view of cylinder block and related components used on 50 hp models.

1. Cover
2. Gasket
3. Cylinder head
4. Gasket
5. Cylinder block
6. Crankcase
7. Spring
8. Valve
9. Gasket
10. Inner exhaust cover
11. Gasket
12. Outer exhaust cover

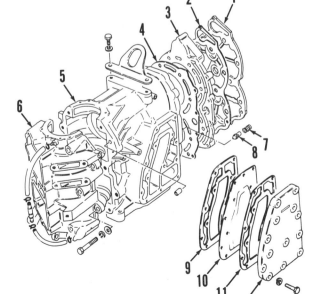

Fig. WB-25—Exploded view of cylinder block and related components used on 60 hp models.

1. Cylinder head cover
2. Gasket
3. Cylinder head
4. Gasket
5. Cylinder block
6. Crankcase
7. Spring
8. Valve
9. Gasket
10. Inner exhaust cover
11. Gasket
12. Outer exhaust cover

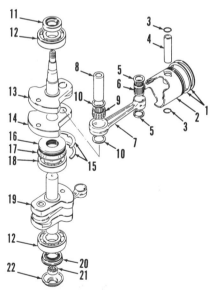

Fig. WB-26—Exploded view of crankshaft assembly used on 50 hp models.

1. Piston rings
2. Piston
3. Piston pin clips
4. Piston pin
5. Thrust washers
6. Needle bearing
7. Connecting rod
8. Crankpin
9. Needle bearing
10. Thrust washers
11. Upper crankshaft seal
12. Ball bearings
13. Upper crank half
14. Upper crank half
15. Thrust rings
16. Labyrinth seal
17. "O" ring
18. Ball bearing
19. Lower crank assy.
20. Lower crankshaft seal
21. Drive shaft seal
22. Drive shaft seal housing

studs. Remove starter motor, ignition components, fuel pump, rectifier, flywheel and magneto base plate assembly. Remove magneto case with base gasket and upper crankshaft seal (11—Fig. WB-26 or Fig. WB-27). Remove outer exhaust cover (12—Fig. WB-24 or Fig. WB25), gasket (11), inner exhaust cover (10) and gasket (9). Remove intake manifold (1—Fig. WB-6) and reed plate (2) with reed valve assemblies. Remove cylinder head cover (1—Fig. WB24 or Fig. WB-25), gasket (2), cylinder head (3) and gasket (4). Clean carbon from combustion chamber and any foreign material accumulation in water passages. Withdraw spring (7) and valve (8) from cylinder block. Remove crankcase retaining cap screws and separate crankcase (6) from cylinder block (5). Remove drive shaft seal housing (22—Fig. WB-26 or Fig. WB-27). Crankshaft and piston assembly can now be removed from cylinder block.

Engine components are now ready for overhaul as outlined in the appropriate following paragraphs. Refer to the following section for assembly procedure.

ASSEMBLY. Refer to specific service sections when assembling crankshaft, connecting rod, piston and reed valves. Make sure all joint and gasket surfaces are clean, free from nicks and burrs and hardened cement or carbon.

Whenever the engine is disassembled, it is recommended that all gasket surfaces and mating surfaces without gaskets be carefully checked for nicks, burrs and warped surfaces which might interfere with a tight seal. Cylinder head, head end of cylinder block and some mating surfaces of manifold and crankcase should be checked on a surface plate and lapped, if necessary, to provide a smooth surface. Do not remove any more metal than is necessary.

When assembling engine, first lubricate all friction surfaces and bearings with engine oil. Place thrust rings (15—Fig. WB-26 or Fig. WB-27) in cylinder block, then install crankshaft assembly. Make certain main bearing locating pins engage notches (N—Fig. WB-28) in cylinder block. Apply a suitable high temperature grease to lip portion of crankshaft and drive shaft seals, then install lower crankshaft seal (20—Fig. WB-26 or Fig. WB-27) ensuring seal flange properly engages groove in cylinder block. Install drive shaft seal or seals (21) into seal housing (22). Apply a sufficient amount of water-resistant grease on seal housing (22) to fill area between lower crankshaft seal and drive shaft seal, then install seal housing to cylinder block. Apply a coat of a form-in-place gasket compound on mating surfaces of crankcase and cylinder block and position crankcase on cylinder block. Using tightening sequence shown in Fig. WB-29, tighten the crankcase screws in 11 N·m (8 ft.-lbs.) increments until a final torque of 36-39 N·m (26-29 ft.-lbs.) is obtained. Install upper crankshaft seal (11—Fig. WB-26 or Fig. WB-27) into magneto case with open side towards cylinder block, then install magneto case with gasket on cylinder block assembly.

Cylinder head gasket should be installed with a light coating of a form-in-place gasket compound applied on both sides. With valve (8—Fig. WB-24 or Fig. WB-25) and spring (7) installed in cylinder block, position cylinder head, cylinder head cover and related gaskets on cylinder block. Use tightening sequence shown in Fig. WB-30 and tighten cylinder head cap screws to the following torque values. On 50 hp models, tighten 6 mm cap screws to 8-12 N·m (6-9 ft.-lbs.) and 10 mm cap screws to 40-60 N·m (29-44 ft.-lbs.). On 60 hp models, tighten 6 mm cap screws to 7-9 N·m (5-7 ft.-lbs.), 8 mm cap screws to 34-39 N·m (25-29 ft.-lbs.) and 10 mm cap screws to 39-58 N·m (29-43 ft.-lbs.).

RINGS, PISTONS AND CYLINDERS. The pistons are fitted with two piston rings. Piston rings are interchangeable in grooves but must be installed with manufacturer's marking facing towards closed end (top) of piston. Piston ring end gap should be 0.2-0.4 mm (0.008-0.016 in.) with a maximum allowable ring end gap of 0.8 mm (0.031 in.). Piston-to-cylinder wall clearance should be 0.097-0.112 mm (0.0038-0.0044 in.) on 50 hp models and 0.112-0.127 mm (0.0044-0.0050 in.) on 60 hp models. Pistons and rings are available in standard size as well as 0.25 mm (0.010 in.) and 0.50 mm (0.020 in.) oversizes. Cylinder should be bored to an oversize if cylinder is out-of-round or taper exceeds 0.10 mm (0.004 in.). Install piston on connecting rod so arrow on piston crown will point towards exhaust port when piston is in cylinder.

CONNECTING RODS, BEARINGS AND CRANKSHAFT. Connecting rods, bearings and crankshaft are a pressed together unit. Crankshaft should be disassembled ONLY by experienced service personnel and with proper service equipment.

Caged needle bearings are used at both large and small ends of the connecting rod. Determine rod bearing

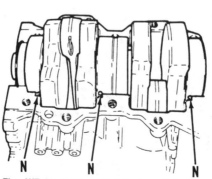

Fig. WB-27—Exploded view of crankshaft assembly used on 60 hp models.

1. Piston rings	14. Upper crank half
2. Piston	15. Thrust rings
3. Piston pin clips	16. Labyrinth seal
4. Piston pin	18. Ball bearing
5. Thrust washers	19. Lower crank assy.
6. Needle bearing	20. Lower crankshaft
7. Connecting rod	seal
8. Crankpin	21. Drive shaft seals
9. Needle bearing	22. Drive shaft seal
10. Thrust washers	housing
11. Upper crankshaft	23. Seal
seal	24. Ball bearing
12. Ball bearing	25. "O" ring
13. Upper crank half	

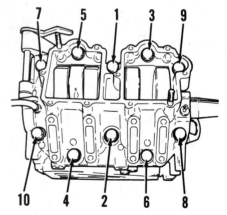

Fig. WB-28—View of installed crankshaft assembly showing main bearing locating notches.

Fig. WB-29—Crankcase cap screws should be tightened in the sequence shown above.

wear by measuring connecting rod small end side-to-side movement as shown at (A—Fig. WB-31). Normal side-to-side movement is 5 mm (0.20 in.) or less. Maximum allowable limit of crankshaft runout is 0.05 mm (0.002 in.) measured at bearing surfaces with crankshaft ends supported.

When installing crankshaft, lubricate pistons, rings, cylinders and bearings with engine oil and refer to ASSEMBLY section.

ENGINE MOUNTING PLATE AND MUFFLER

All Models

R&R AND OVERHAUL. Disconnect battery cables from battery and remove battery from vehicle. Detach engine wiring harness from control panel harness at connector. Disconnect fuel supply line from fuel pump and plug fuel line. Disconnect bilge pump leads. Disconnect throttle control cable from upper carburetor. Remove the eight nuts and lockwashers retaining the engine mounting plate to the jet pump housing. Use a suitable lifting device to hoist engine assembly from vehicle. Place

engine assembly on a clean work bench. Remove the nine nuts, flat washers and lockwashers retaining the engine mounting plate to the engine assembly. Use a suitable lifting device to hoist engine assembly from engine mounting plate.

Refer to Fig. WB-33 for an exploded view of engine mounting plate and muffler components. Disassemble components after reference to exploded view. Clean any foreign material accumulation in water passages and blow clear with clean compressed air. Check all gasket surfaces for nicks, burrs and warped surfaces which might interfere with a tight seal. Inspect all hoses for

cracks, swollen areas or any other signs of damage or deterioration. Renew all gaskets and any other components diagnosed with damage. Apply a form-in-place gasket compound on both sides of gaskets (6, 12, 15, 19 and 26) prior to assembly. Tighten exhaust chamber base (16) retaining nuts (17) to 19-24 N·m (14-18 ft.-lbs.). Tighten exhaust diffuser (13) retaining screws (14) to 16-19 N·m (12-14 ft.-lbs.). Tighten cooling chamber (10) retaining screws (11) to 19-24 N·m (14-18 ft.-lbs.). Securely tighten nuts retaining exhaust neck (25) and screws retaining plate (7). Make sure all hose clamps are securely tightened.

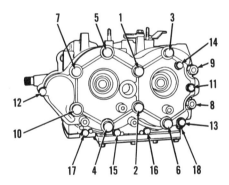

Fig. WB-30—Cylinder head cap screws should be tightened in the sequence shown. Refer to text for tightening torque specifications.

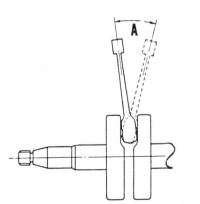

Fig. WB-31—Maximum side-to-side shake (A) at small end of connecting rod should be 5 mm (0.20 in.) or less.

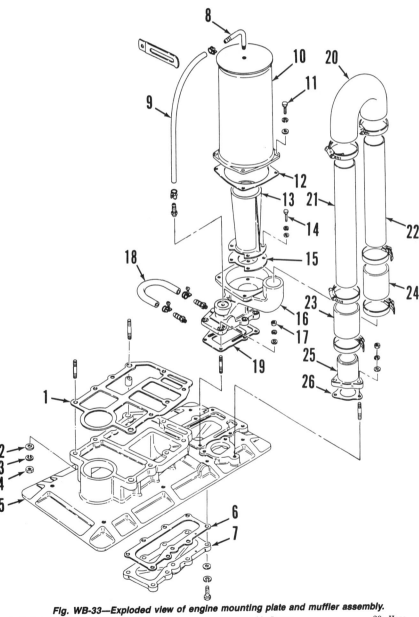

Fig. WB-33—Exploded view of engine mounting plate and muffler assembly.

1. Gasket
2. Flat washers
3. Lockwashers
4. Nuts
5. Engine mounting plate
6. Gasket
7. Plate
8. Fitting
9. Hose
10. Cooling chamber
11. Screws
12. Gasket
13. Exhaust diffuser
14. Screws
15. Gasket
16. Exhaust chamber base
17. Nuts
18. Hose
19. Gasket
20. Hose
21. Exhaust tube
22. Exhaust tube
23. Hose
24. Hose
25. Exhaust neck
26. Gasket

Apply a form-in-place gasket compound on both sides of gasket (1). Use a suitable lifting device to hoist engine assembly onto engine mounting plate. Install the nine flat washers (2), lockwashers (3) and nuts (4) retaining the engine mounting plate to the engine assembly and tighten to 20-24 N·m (15-18 ft.-lbs.).

Prior to reinstalling engine assembly, apply a form-in-place gasket compound on both sides of gasket located between engine mounting plate and jet pump housing, grease rubber hull seal and apply a light coating of a water-resistant grease on drive shaft splines. Use a suitable lifting device to hoist engine assembly into vehicle. Align eight engine mounting plate studs with holes in jet pump housing. Make sure engine assembly properly seats.

NOTE: Rotate drive shaft, if needed, to align drive shaft and crankshaft splines.

Install the eight lockwashers and nuts and tighten to 34-39 N·m (25-29 ft.-lbs.). Complete reassembly in reverse order of disassembly.

ELECTRIC STARTER

All Models

All models are equipped with electric starter shown in Fig. WB-35. Disas-sembly is evident after inspection of unit and reference to exploded view. When servicing starter motor, scribe reference marks across motor frame to aid in reassembly. Starter brushes have a standard length of 16 mm (0.63 in.) and should be renewed if worn to 12 mm (0.47 in.). Commutator has a standard diameter of 33 mm (1.30 in.) and should be renewed if worn to a diameter of 31 mm (1.22 in.). Commutator undercut should be 0.5-0.8 mm (0.02-0.03 in.). If undercut is 0.2 mm (0.007 in.) or less, then use a suitable tool to remove the mica between commutator sections until undercut between each section is within the recommended range. After reassembly, bench test starter motor before installing on engine.

BILGE PUMP

All Models

All models are equipped with an electric bilge pump located at stern of vehicle. A toggle switch located on vehicle control panel is used to supply electrical power to bilge pump. All 1986 and later models are equipped with a float switch to activate bilge pump. Make sure pickup area at base of bilge pump is kept clean of all foreign debris. Inspect bilge pump discharge hose for cracks or any other signs of damage or deterioration and renew if needed. Make sure hose fits tightly on bilge pump outlet and on fitting in side of hull.

If bilge pump malfunctions, first make sure toggle switch, wiring, inline fuse and on later models, float switch, are in good condition and properly operate prior to renewing bilge pump.

JET PUMP

All Models

REMOVE AND REINSTALL. Position suitable lifting fixtures on vehicle portion of Wetbike so vehicle can be raised off the ground.

NOTE: Make sure vehicle will not tip to one side when raised; otherwise, damage to engine or vehicle hull could result.

Attach fixtures to a suitable hoist. Remove the eight nuts and lockwashers retaining the engine mounting plate to the jet pump housing. Raise vehicle off the ground until engine mounting plate clears jet pump drive shaft. Place jet pump assembly on a clean work bench.

Prior to reinstalling jet pump assembly, apply a form-in-place gasket compound on both sides of gasket located between engine mounting plate and jet pump housing, grease rubber hull seal and apply a light coating of a water-resistant grease on drive shaft splines. Slowly lower vehicle onto jet pump assembly. Align eight engine mounting plate studs with holes in jet pump housing. Make sure jet pump assembly properly seats against engine mounting plate.

NOTE: Rotate jet pump drive shaft or engine flywheel, if needed, to align drive shaft and crankshaft splines.

Install the eight lockwashers and nuts and tighten to 34-39 N·m (25-29 ft.-lbs.).

OVERHAUL. Remove the four countersunk screws retaining rear ski to jet pump housing, then lift jet pump assembly free from rear ski. Remove fill plug (20—Fig. WB-37) and check plug (19) and allow lubricant to drain into a suitable container.

Remove outlet nozzle (45) and wear ring (43). Prevent impeller shaft rotation, then use a suitable spanner wrench and rotate impeller (37) clockwise to remove. Note thrust washer (36) located in front of impeller (37). Remove front cover (21) and "O" ring (26). Prevent impeller shaft rotation, then use a suitable tool to remove nut (22) and withdraw lockwasher (23) and flat washer (24). Slide impeller shaft (35) out rear of jet pump housing (17). Scribe a reference mark on the forward

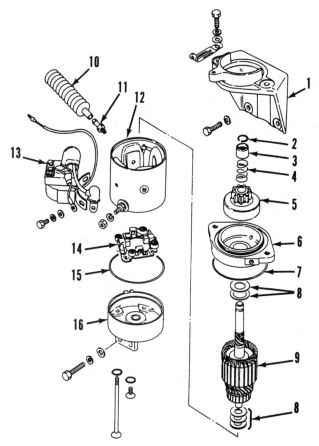

Fig. WB-35—Exploded view of electric starter motor.

1. Bracket
2. "C" ring
3. Stop
4. Spring
5. Drive
6. Frame head
7. "O" ring
8. Thrust washers
9. Armature
10. Bellows
11. Vent fitting
12. Frame
13. Starter solenoid
14. Brush assy.
15. "O" ring
16. End housing

portion of pinion housing (1). Mark should face forward when reassembling pinion housing (1) to jet pump housing (17). Remove the four cap screws, lockwashers and flat washers securing pinion housing (1), then carefully withdraw pinion housing (1) and gasket (2). Grasp pinion shaft (7) and lift upward to withdraw components (3 through 13) from housing (17). Separate components (3 through 13), if needed, with reference to Fig. WB-37. Remove components (25 and 27 through 31) by

inserting impeller shaft (35) into housing (17) and driving components outward from housing. Use a soft-faced mallet to tap on impeller shaft end. Remove snap ring (32). Remove bearing (33) and seals (34) by using suitable tools and driving components out front of housing or by using a suitable slide-hammer puller assembly.

Inspect gears for excessive wear or any other damage on teeth and splines. Inspect shafts for wear on splined and friction surfaces of bearings and oil

seals. Inspect impeller (37) and wear ring (43) for excessive wear or any other damage. Inspect all bearings for freedom of rotation and damaged components. Inspect bearing carrier (5), bearing carrier (27), jet pump housing (17), front cover (21) and outlet nozzle (45) for damage. Make sure water inlet holes at rear of housing (17) are clean of any foreign matter. Use clean compressed air to check for obstruction. Renew all gaskets, "O" rings and seals during reassembly. Renew any other components that are excessively worn

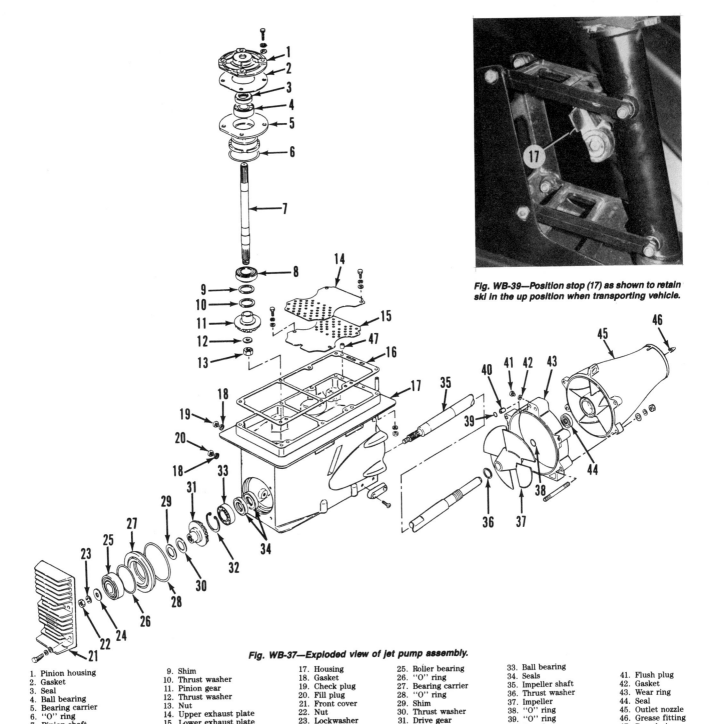

Fig. WB-39—Position stop (17) as shown to retain ski in the up position when transporting vehicle.

Fig. WB-37—Exploded view of jet pump assembly.

1. Pinion housing	9. Shim	17. Housing	25. Roller bearing	33. Ball bearing	41. Flush plug
2. Gasket	10. Thrust washer	18. Gasket	26. "O" ring	34. Seals	42. Gasket
3. Seal	11. Pinion gear	19. Check plug	27. Bearing carrier	35. Impeller shaft	43. Wear ring
4. Ball bearing	12. Thrust washer	20. Fill plug	28. "O" ring	36. Thrust washer	44. Seal
5. Bearing carrier	13. Nut	21. Front cover	29. Shim	37. Impeller	45. Outlet nozzle
6. "O" ring	14. Upper exhaust plate	22. Nut	30. Thrust washer	38. "O" ring	46. Grease fitting
7. Pinion shaft	15. Lower exhaust plate	23. Lockwasher	31. Drive gear	39. "O" ring	47. Dowel pin
8. Tapered roller bearing	16. Gasket	24. Flat washer	32. Snap ring	40. Dowel pin	

or are diagnosed with any other damage.

Reassemble components (1 through 13) and (21 through 34) with the exception of "O" rings (6 and 26).

NOTE: Apply an industrial blueing on drive gear teeth (31) prior to installation. The blueing is used to check gear tooth contact pattern.

Install components into housing (17). Tighten pinion gear nut (13) to 22-26 N·m (16-19 ft.-lbs.). Tighten impeller shaft nut (22) to 68 N·m (50 ft.-lbs.). Tighten pinion housing (1) cap screws to 22-26 N·m (16-19 ft.-lbs.). Tighten front cover (21) cap screws to 19-23 N·m (14-17 ft.-lbs.).

Position a suitable dial indicator and related tools on pinion shaft so backlash between pinion gear (11) and drive gear (31) can be measured. Push impeller shaft (35) inward, then grasp pinion shaft (7) and pull upward. Check backlash between teeth of gears. Backlash should be between 0.15-0.30 mm (0.006-0.012 in.). If not, remove and separate components (1 through 13) and adjust thickness of shim (9) to obtain recommended backlash. Reassemble and install components, then verify recommended backlash has been obtained. Push impeller shaft (35) inward, then grasp pinion shaft (7) and pull upward. Maintain pressure on impeller shaft and rotate pinion shaft a few turns clockwise while maintaining upward pressure. Remove front cover (21) and components (22 through 31). Check drive gear tooth contact pattern on drive side of gear. If pattern is in center of tooth, then no shim adjustment is required. If pattern is towards toe of tooth (center of gear), then shim (9) must be decreased and shim (29) must be increased in equal amounts to maintain correct backlash. If pattern is towards heel of tooth (outside of gear), then shim (9) must be increased and shim (29) must be decreased in equal amounts to maintain correct backlash. Continue procedure until pattern is in center of tooth and backlash is correct.

Remove front cover (21) and install "O" ring (26). Remove pinion components (1 through 13) and install "O" ring (6). Complete reassembly in reverse order of disassembly. Make sure pinion housing (1) is installed with reference mark facing towards front of housing. Apply a water-resistant grease on impeller shaft (35) threads, then install and rotate impeller (37) counterclockwise to thread onto impeller shaft. Use spanner wrench and securely tighten impeller on impeller shaft. Apply a water-resistant grease on lip portion of seal (44) and outlet nozzle bushing. Refer to LUBRICATION section for procedure to fill jet pump gearcase with oil. Refer to previous REMOVE AND REINSTALL section for procedure to reinstall jet pump assembly.

STEERING

All Models

A front ski via a steering tube and handlebar is used to steer vehicle. Minimal steering control is available when vehicle is in complete down position. Maximum steering control is available when vehicle is in complete up position. When transporting vehicle, position stop (17—Fig. WB-39) as shown to retain ski in the up position.

OVERHAUL. Overhaul of steering components is evident after referral to Fig. WB-40. Upper swivel bushing (12) and lower swivel bushing (13) are self-lubricating. On 50 hp models, tighten swivel arm cap screws to 30-34 N·m (22-25 ft.-lbs.). On 60 hp models, tighten swivel arm nuts (21) to 20-24 N·m (15-18 ft.-lbs.). Tighten stop screw (16) to 7-9 N·m (5-7 ft.-lbs.). Tighten front ski retaining screws to 27-34 N·m (20-25 ft.-lbs.). Recheck torque on front ski retaining screws after a short operation period.

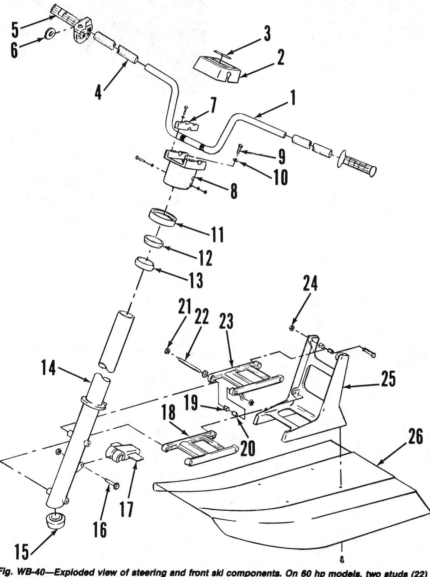

Fig. WB-40—Exploded view of steering and front ski components. On 60 hp models, two studs (22) are used. On 50 hp models, four cap screws are used in place of studs (22). Flat washer (10) and steering spacer (11) are used on models after 1985. Foam spacer (6) is used models after 1986.

1. Handlebar
2. Cover
3. Decal
4. Pad
5. Grip & throttle assy.
6. Foam spacer
7. Crown clamps
8. Crown
9. Cap screw
10. Flat washer
11. Spacer
12. Upper swivel bushing
13. Lower swivel bushing
14. Steering tube
15. Cushion
16. Bolt
17. Stop
18. Lower swing arm
19. Plastic bushing
20. Sleeve
21. Nut
22. Studs
23. Upper swing arm
24. Nut
25. Foot
26. Front ski

WETJET

WETJET INTERNATIONAL LTD.
108 Mill St. E.
Paynesville, MN 56362

428 (1985-EARLY 1986), 428 L/C (LATE 1986-1987) AND 432 (1988)

NOTE: Metric fasteners are used throughout engine.

General

Engine Make	Cuyuna
Engine Type	Two-Stroke; Water-Cooled
HP/Rated Rpm	40/6250
Number of Cylinders	2
Bore	2.658 in. (67.5 mm)
Stroke	2.362 in. (60.0 mm)
Displacement	26.1 cu. in. (428 cc)
Compression Ratio	7.2:1
Engine Lubrication	Pre-Mix
Fuel:Oil Ratio	40:1
Engine Oil Recommendation	Wetjet or Two-Stroke; BIA Certified TC-W

Tune-Up

Engine Idle Speed	900-1000 rpm
Spark Plug:	
NGK	BR8ES
Champion	RN3C
Electrode Gap	0.035-0.040 in. (0.9-1.0 mm)
Ignition:	
Type	Nippondenso CDI
Timing	28° BTDC or 0.174 in. (4.4 mm) @ 1800 rpm
Carburetor:	
Make	Mikuni
Model	BN38 Diaphragm
Bore Size	1.3 in. (34 mm)
Low Speed Needle Setting	3/4 Turn
High Speed Needle Setting	3/4 Turn

Sizes—Clearances

Cylinder Wear Limit	2.660 in. (67.55 mm)
Piston-to-Cylinder Wall Clearance	0.005-0.010 in. (0.13-0.25 mm)
Piston Pin Diameter	0.6298-0.6299 in. (15.996-16.000 mm)
Piston Pin Bore Diameter	0.6301-0.6311 in. (16.004-16.030 mm)

Sizes—Clearances (Cont.)

Connecting Rod Small End Diameter	0.8661-0.8667 in. (22.000-22.013 mm)
Piston Ring End Gap—Top and Second	0.007-0.031 in. (0.18-0.79 mm)
Maximum Crankshaft Runout	0.003 in.* (0.08 mm)

*Refer to text for measuring procedures.

Capacities

Fuel Tank:	
Models 1985 and Early 1986	3 gal. (11.4 L)
Models Late 1986-1988	5 gal. (18.9 L)

Tightening Torques

Cylinder Head Cap Screws	16-18 ft.-lbs. (22-24 N·m)
Crankcase Base Nuts	16-18 ft.-lbs. (22-24 N·m)
Intake Manifold Cap Screws	20-22 ft.-lbs. (27-30 N·m)
Exhaust Manifold Cap Screws	30 ft.-lbs. (41 N·m)
Spark Plug	20-22 ft.-lbs. (27-30 N·m)
Flywheel Nut	46-50 ft.-lbs. (63-68 N·m)
Engine-to-Mounting Plate Cap Screws	45 ft.-lbs. (61 N·m)
Engine Mounting Plate-to-Vehicle Cap Screws	30 ft.-lbs. (41 N·m)
Drive Flange-to-Crankshaft Cap Screw	55 ft.-lbs. (75 N·m)
Drive Flange-to-Jet Pump Cap Screw	30 ft.-lbs. (41 N·m)
Standard Screws:	
5 mm	40-50 in.-lbs. (4.5-5.6 N·m)
6 mm	6-8 ft.-lbs. (8-11 N·m)

LUBRICATION

All Models

The engine is lubricated by oil mixed with the fuel. Fuel:oil ratios should be 20:1 during break-in (first three gallons) of a new or rebuilt engine and 40:1 for normal service when using Wetjet oil or a BIA certified two-stroke TC-W engine oil. Manufacturer recommends regular or no-lead automotive gasoline having a minimum octane rating of 88. Gasoline and oil should be thoroughly mixed.

On Wetjet 428 models, consult a Wetjet dealer for recommended jet pump lubricating intervals and procedures. On Wetjet 428 L/C and 432 models, a Brut type jet pump is used. After every 10 hours of operation in fresh water or after each operation in salt water, grease jet pump front bearing and rear bushing with white lithium grease. Inject grease into grease fitting at rear of jet pump outlet body to grease rear bushing. Raise passenger seat and inject grease into grease fitting beneath rear of seat to grease front ball bearing.

FUEL SYSTEM

All Models

CARBURETOR. Refer to Fig. WJ-1 for an exploded view of Mikuni type BN38 diaphragm carburetor used on all models. On Wetjet 428 models, a primer system is used for cold engine starts. On all other models, choke plate (21—Fig. WJ-1) is actuated by choke knob (K—Fig. WJ-2) on control panel via a cable and linkage.

Initial setting of low speed mixture needle (22—Fig. WJ-3) and high speed mixture needle (30—Fig. WJ-4) is ¾ turn out from a lightly seated position. Final carburetor adjustments must be made with engine at normal operating temperature and running. Clockwise rotation of either needle leans the mixture. Adjust low speed mixture needle (22—Fig. WJ-3) until smooth acceleration from the idle position is noted.

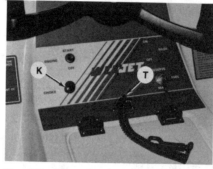

Fig. WJ-2—Figure identifying choke knob (K) and ignition tether switch (T). Choke is actuated by pulling knob (K) outward. The tether switch cap must be snapped onto tether switch prior to attempting starting of engine.

After adjusting low speed mixture needle, adjust idle speed screw (26) until engine idle speed is between 900-1000 rpm with throttle lever completely released. To adjust high speed fuel:air mixture, the engine spark plugs must be removed and their insulator tip color noted.

NOTE: Make sure that fuel tank contains a 40:1 fuel mixture.

Make sure cooling system will receive an adequate supply of water, then operate and sustain engine at wide-open throttle for a suitable test period. Stop the engine with throttle in wide-open position. Remove spark plugs and note insulator tip color. Normal insulator tip color is brown to light tan. If insulator tip appears to be light tan to white in color, then mixture is too lean and high speed mixture needle (30—Fig. WJ-4) should be rotated outward (counterclockwise) ¼ turn to richen mixture. If insulator tip appears to be dark brown to black in color, then mixture is too rich and high speed mixture needle (30) should be rotated inward (clockwise) ¼ turn to lean mixture. Clean, regap and reinstall spark

Fig. WJ-3—View identifies location of low speed mixture needle (22) and idle speed screw (26).

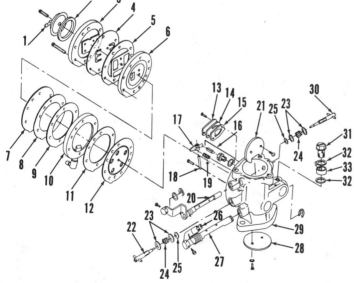

Fig. WJ-1—Exploded view of Mikuni type BN38 diaphragm carburetor used on all models.

1. Fuel inlet cover	9. Gasket	18. Pivot shaft	26. Idle speed screw
2. Gasket	10. Diaphragm cover	19. Spring	27. Throttle shaft
3. Inlet body	11. Gasket	20. Choke shaft	28. Throttle plate
4. Check valve diaphragm	12. Regulating diaphragm	21. Choke plate	29. Body
5. Gasket	13. Plate	22. Low speed mixture needle	30. High speed mixture needle
6. Pump body	14. Diaphragm	23. Washers	31. Banjo bolt
7. Diaphragm	15. Gasket	24. Springs	32. Gaskets
8. Gasket	16. Inlet valve assy.	25. "O" rings	33. Return line fitting
	17. Valve lever		

Fig. WJ-4—View identifies location of high speed mixture needle (30).

plugs and continue test procedures until spark plug insulator tips are a normal color.

The fuel pump and regulating diaphragm (12—Fig. WJ-1) can be removed after removing the six through-bolts. Note that alignment tabs on components (3 through 12) are provided to assist in proper alignment during reassembly.

Do not remove choke plate, throttle plate or shafts unless necessary. The choke and throttle plate retaining screws are either staked or retained with a thread locking solution to prevent loosening. If screws are removed, properly stake or apply a suitable thread locking solution on threads prior to assembly. Inlet needle valve lever (17) must be flush with floor of housing recess when needle valve is seated. Refer to Fig. WJ-5. If lever must be adjusted, push down on lever immediately above spring to collapse spring, then bend the end which contacts needle valve.

FUEL PUMP. The fuel pump is an integral part of the carburetor. The fuel pump assembly can be overhauled without overhauling the complete carburetor.

With reference to Fig. WJ-1, disassemble the fuel pump assembly. Inspect all components for excessive wear or any other damage and renew if needed. Clean components as needed with a suitable cleaning solution. Blow dry with clean compressed air. If compressed air is not available, use only lint-free cloths to wipe dry. Make sure all passages are clear of any obstructions.

Fig. WJ-7—Remove three through-bolts (B) to withdraw flame arrestor (F).

With reference to Fig. WJ-1, reassemble the fuel pump assembly with new gaskets. Securely tighten the six through-bolts.

FUEL TANK AND FUEL FILTER (Wetjet 428 L/C and 432 Models). A check valve and fuel strainer assembly (5—Fig. WJ-6) is attached on the bottom of the fuel tank pickup line and an inline fuel filter (1) is used on all models. Periodically remove inline fuel filter (1) and blow through inlet side of filter with low air pressure to check for blockage. Very little restriction should be noted. Renew fuel filter (1) if excessive restriction is noted. Fuel tank strainer (5) should not need to be removed and cleaned unless contamination is suspected.

FLAME ARRESTOR. Periodically remove flame arrestor (F—Fig. WJ-7) and clean assembly with a suitable cleaning solution. Blow dry with clean compressed air. Inspect assembly for any damage and renew if needed. Install flame arrestor and make sure assembly fits tightly around neck of carburetor. Securely tighten three through-bolts (B).

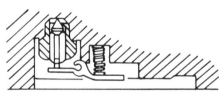

Fig. WJ-5—Inlet needle valve lever should be flush with floor of housing recess as shown.

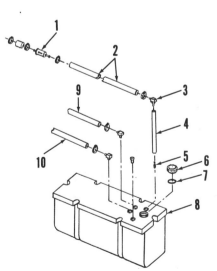

Fig. WJ-6—Exploded view of fuel tank and related components used on Wetjet 428 L/C and 432 models.

1. Fuel filter	6. Cap
2. Supply hose	7. Gasket
3. Elbow	8. Fuel tank
4. Clear hose	9. Return hose
5. Check valve & strainer	10. Vent hose

Fig. WJ-9—Exploded view of ignition system components and housing components. View identifies location of lighting coil, rectifier/regulator assembly and electric starter.

1. Ignition housing	5. Rectifier/regulator	8. Charge & trigger coil	12. Gasket
2. Electric starter	6. Magneto base plate	9. Flywheel	13. Ignition housing cover
3. CDI module	7. Lighting coil	10. Lockwasher	14. Access plug
4. Ignition coil		11. Nut	

IGNITION

All Models

All models are equipped with a simultaneous capacitor discharge ignition system. The ignition timing is electronically advanced as the magneto base plate is fixed. Ignition timing should not require adjustment, after first being correctly set, unless magneto base plate is moved or an ignition component is renewed.

IGNITION TIMING. Ignition timing should be 28 degrees BTDC or 0.174 inch (4.4 mm) at 1800 rpm. Ignition timing can be checked using a suitable power timing light.

Timing marks must be placed on flywheel (9—Fig. WJ-9) and ignition housing (1). Remove both spark plugs and ground spark plug leads to engine. Position a suitable dial indicator assembly so indicator needle projects through spark plug hole into number two cylinder head (cylinder towards front of vehicle). Remove ignition housing cover (13) and gasket (12). Position a suitable tool on nut (11) and rotate crankshaft clockwise (viewed from front of engine) until piston in number two cylinder is at top dead center (TDC). Zero dial indicator, then rotate crankshaft counterclockwise until dial indicator reads 0.174 inch (4.4 mm) before top dead center (BTDC). Use a suitable marking device and place marks on ignition housing and flywheel so marks are aligned. Remove dial indicator assembly and install spark plugs. Tighten spark plugs to 20-22 ft.-lbs. (27-30 N·m) and attach spark plug leads.

NOTE: Some models where equipped with access plug (14) in ignition housing cover (13). On these models, the plug can be removed and the flywheel and ignition housing marked without removing ignition housing cover. If this procedure is used, the power take-off end of the crankshaft must be used to rotate crankshaft. When reinstalling access plug, make sure a suitable sealant is used around access plug to prevent water from seeping into ignition housing.

Immerse vehicle in water so jet pump pickup is properly submerged or connect a supplemental water supply to cooling system supply hose after removing hose from jet pump outlet fitting (F—Fig. WJ-10) and using a suitable adapter.

To check ignition timing, start engine and accelerate to 1800 rpm. Note flywheel timing mark in relation to mark on ignition housing. If ignition timing is incorrect, magneto base plate (6—Fig. WJ-9) must be repositioned. Stop engine, then rotate flywheel until openings are aligned with the two magneto base plate retaining screws. Use a suitable tool and reach through flywheel openings. Loosen magneto base plate screws. Rotate magneto base plate clockwise to retard ignition timing and counterclockwise to advance ignition timing. Tighten magneto base plate screws, then recheck ignition timing. Continue procedure until correct ignition timing is obtained.

Install a new ignition housing gasket (12). Install ignition housing (13) and securely tighten retaining cap screws.

TROUBLE-SHOOTING. If ignition malfunction occurs, use only approved procedures to prevent damage to the components. The fuel system should be checked first to make certain that faulty running is not caused by incorrect mixture or contaminated fuel. Make sure malfunction is not due to spark plug, wiring or wiring connection failure. Trouble-shoot ignition circuit using a suitable ohmmeter as follows:

Separate the three-wire and two-wire connector between magneto components and CDI module. Refer to Fig. WJ-11. Check condition of charge coil by attaching one tester lead to red/black wire leading to magneto assembly and attaching other tester lead to black/red wire leading to magneto assembly. Charge coil can be considered satisfactory if resistance reading is within the limits of 16,200-19,800 ohms. Check condition of trigger coil by attaching one tester lead to black/red wire leading to magneto assembly and attaching other tester lead to black/white wire leading to magneto assembly. Trigger coil can be considered satisfactory if resistance reading is within the limits of 2.0-2.4 ohms.

To check condition of ignition coil, separate the white/blue wire and black wire at connector and remove high tension wires from spark plugs. Attach one tester lead to terminal end of white/blue wire leading to coil and other tester lead to terminal end of black wire leading to coil. Primary coil resistance reading should be within the limits of 0.28-0.38 ohms. Attach a tester lead to each high tension wire. Secondary coil resistance reading should be within the limits of 3120-4680 ohms.

If no components are found defective in the previous tests and ignition malfunction is still suspected, then install a known good CDI module and recheck engine operation.

Fig. WJ-10—Water for engine cooling system is supplied through jet pump outlet fitting (F).

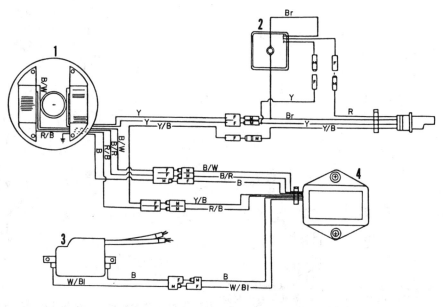

Fig. WJ-11—View showing ignition system and charging system wiring schematic.

1. Magneto assy.		
2. Rectifier/regulator	B. Black	Br. Brown	R/B. Red/black
3. Ignition coil	R. Red	B/R. Black/red	W/Bl. White/blue
4. CDI module	Y. Yellow	B/W. Black/white	Y/B. Yellow/black

CHARGING SYSTEM

All Models

All models are equipped with a lighting coil, rectifier/regulator, battery and ignition switch. Standard battery has a 16 ampere hour, 12 volt rating. The lighting coil should produce 32 ac volts at 6000 rpm.

The battery electrolyte level should be checked periodically and filled to maximum level with distilled water if required. The battery should be removed from the vehicle and the battery caps removed when charging. The manufacturer recommends charging the battery at a rate of 1.6 amperes for a period of four to five hours. Do not exceed maximum charging rate of two amperes.

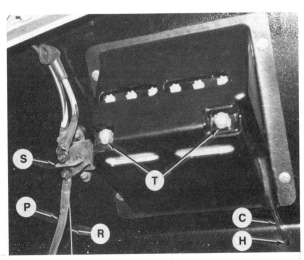

Fig. WJ-12—Battery is located at fore of vehicle's hull. Make sure battery cables are correctly connected to terminal ends (T) of battery. Make sure clear overflow tube (C) is routed into hole (H) in hull. Tube (C) must be free from any kinks or contaminates that would restrict the flow of electrolyte or dangerous gases. Starter solenoid is identified at (S). Electric starter power supply cable (P) and ground strap (R), if so equipped, must be removed from starter solienoids (S) when removing engine.

NOTE: Make sure battery charging area is well ventilated.

The lighting coil can be statically tested using a suitable ohmmeter. Refer to Fig. WJ-11. Separate two yellow wires leading from lighting coil to rectifier/regulator assembly at connector block. Measure resistance between the two yellow wires leading to lighting coil. Resistance reading should be 0.16-0.20 ohms. Check for continuity between each of the lighting coil wires and ground. Tester should show infinite resistance at each wire. To check rectifier/regulator assembly, first make sure battery is fully charged, lighting coil test good and all wiring is in good condition and all connectors fit tightly or are securely fastened. Attach a suitable voltmeter directly on battery terminals. Immerse vehicle in water so jet pump pickup is properly submerged or connect a supplemental water supply to cooling system supply hose after removing hose from jet pump outlet fitting (F—Fig. WJ-10) and using a suitable adapter. Start and run engine while observing voltmeter. The voltmeter should show approximately 13.5 dc volts.

COOLING SYSTEM

All Models

All models are water-cooled. Forced water is supplied to the engine through jet pump outlet fitting (F—Fig. WJ-10). As jet pump impeller rpm increases, so does water circulation through cooling system.

Make sure jet pump water intake grill (G—Fig. WJ-14) is kept clean. Inspect all hoses periodically for cracks, kinks or any other damage. The cooling system should be flushed out after each operating period when vehicle is used in contaminated or salt water. The cooling system should be flushed out prior to extended periods of storage and prior to usage after extended periods of storage.

To flush the cooling system, connect a supplemental water supply to cooling system supply hose after removing hose from jet pump outlet fitting (F—Fig. WJ-10) and using a suitable adapter. Use only clean, fresh water. Allow water to circulate through system for approximately five minutes. Disconnect supplemental water supply and reattach cooling system supply hose to jet pump outlet fitting (F). If vehicle is to be

Fig. WJ-14—Jet pump water intake grill (G) must be kept clean of all foreign debris.

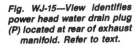

Fig. WJ-15—View identifies power head water drain plug (P) located at rear of exhaust manifold. Refer to text.

stored for an extended period, start the engine and allow to run for a maximum of 5 to 10 seconds. All water remaining in exhaust system will be forced out, preventing damage from developing contaminates or freezing.

NOTE: Make sure engine is not operated without a supply of water longer than 5 to 10 seconds or damage to exhaust hoses and muffler could result.

To drain water from engine, remove plug (P—Fig. WJ-15) at rear of exhaust manifold and hose (H—Fig. WJ-16) from fitting at base of exhaust header pipe (D). Use clean compressed air and blow through hose (H) to force water out through plug (P—Fig. WJ-15) opening. Tilt vehicle to the starboard side to completely drain cooling system. Reinstall manifold plug (P) and securely tighten. Reattach hose (H—Fig. WJ-16) and securely tighten clamp.

ENGINE

All Models

REMOVE AND REINSTALL. Disconnect battery cables from battery and remove battery from vehicle. Detach engine wiring harness from control panel harness at connector. Disconnect

fuel supply line and return line from fuel pump and plug fuel lines. On Wetjet 428 models, remove carry-on fuel tank. On Wetjet 428 L/C and 432 models, remove fuel tank mounting screws, then lift fuel tank onto left body channel with fuel hoses still connected. Remove fuel tank support straps. Disconnect throttle control cable and choke cable (if equipped) from carburetor and remove cables from mounting bracket. Remove ground strap (G—Fig. WJ-17), on models so equipped, located between crankshaft drive flange and drive shaft. Remove exhaust hose (H) from muffler (M) inlet and base of expansion chamber (B—Fig. WJ-18). Remove cooling system supply hose from exhaust manifold inlet fitting (F). Remove electric starter power supply cable (P—Fig. WJ-12) and ground strap (R), if so equipped, from starter solenoid (S). Remove ground straps (T—Fig. WJ-19) attached on engine mounting plate that will restrict removal of engine assembly. Remove four cap screws (W), flat washers and lockwashers retaining the engine mounting plate to the vehicle hull. Use a suitable lifting device to hoist engine assembly from vehicle. Place engine assembly on a clean work bench.

To reinstall engine assembly, use a suitable lifting device to hoist engine assembly into vehicle. On models equip-

Fig. WJ-18—View identifies expansion chamber (B) and exhaust manifold cooling system inlet fitting (F).

ped with drive shaft ground strap (G—Fig. WJ-17), position ground strap mounting holes 90 degrees apart and 180 degrees opposite of ground strap on rear of drive shaft and jet pump input flange. This is to make sure drive shaft balance is maintained.

Apply a suitable thread locking solution on the threads of the four cap screws (W—Fig. WJ-19). Install cap screws with lockwashers and flat washers. Tighten cap screws to 30 ft.-lbs. (41 N·m). Complete reassembly in reverse order of disassembly while noting the following. Apply a suitable thread locking solution on threads of ground strap (G—Fig. WJ-17) and

threads of ground straps (T—Fig. WJ-19) screws prior to installation. After connecting, coat starter power supply cable (P—Fig. WJ-12) connector end on solenoid (S) with liquid neoprene or liquid tape.

DISASSEMBLY. Remove the four cap screws and lockwashers retaining the engine mounting plate to the engine assembly. Use a suitable lifting device to hoist engine assembly from engine mounting plate. Set engine assembly on a clean work area for complete disassembly.

Remove the flame arrestor. Remove expansion chamber, header pipe and exhaust manifold. Disconnect pulse line from fitting (23—Fig. WJ-20). Remove intake manifold with carburetor assembly. Remove water manifold (24). Detach spark plug leads from spark plugs, then remove spark plugs. Remove electric starter (2—Fig. WJ-9). Remove ignition housing cover (13) and gasket (12). Remove flywheel retaining nut (11) and lockwasher (10), then use a suitable

Fig. WJ-16—To drain water from power head, refer to text and remove hose (H) from fitting on exhaust header pipe (D).

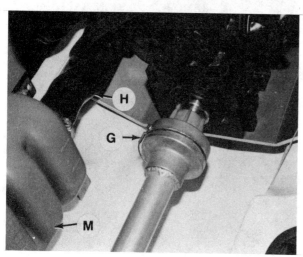

Fig. WJ-17—View identifies ground strap (G), exhaust hose (H) and muffler (M).

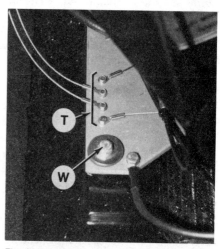

Fig. WJ-19—Remove ground straps (T) attached on engine mounting plate that will restrict removal of engine assembly. Four cap screws (W), one at each corner of engine mounting plate, secures engine assembly to vehicle hull.

puller and withdraw flywheel (9). Withdraw key (18—Fig. WJ-20) from slot in crankshaft end. Remove the two magneto base plate (6—Fig. WJ-9) mounting screws, then position magneto base plate assembly to the side to allow access to ignition housing (1) mounting screws. Remove the four ignition housing mounting screws, then withdraw ignition housing with ignition system and charging system components. Remove cylinder heads (1—Fig. WJ-20). Lift "O" rings (2 and 3) from grooves in top of cylinders. Invert engine assembly so base of crankcase is facing upward. Remove crankcase base nuts and washers. Securely hold assembled components together, then invert assembly so top of cylinders are facing upward. Identify pistons and cylinders for correct reassembly. Use a soft-faced mallet and lightly tap on side of cylinders to break cylinders loose from crankcase. Lift cylinders off pistons while supporting each piston as cylinder slides clear of piston. Separate pistons from connecting rods. Make sure piston components for each cylinder are kept together.

NOTE: Piston pin puller 11-48-307 or a suitable equivalent must be used to remove piston pin (7) from piston (6). Damage to connecting rod may result if correct tools are not used.

Use a soft-faced mallet and lightly tap upper crankcase half (10) to break crankcase halves apart. Lift upper crankcase half (10) off lower crankcase half (22). Crankshaft and piston assembly can now be removed from lower crankcase half (22).

Engine components are now ready for overhaul as outlined in the appropriate following paragraphs. Refer to the following section for assembly procedure.

ASSEMBLY. Refer to specific service sections when assembling the crankshaft, connecting rod and piston. Make sure all joint and gasket surfaces are clean, free from nicks and burrs and hardened cement or carbon.

Whenever the engine is disassembled, it is recommended that all gasket surfaces and mating surfaces without gaskets be carefully checked for nicks, burrs and warped surfaces which might interfere with a tight seal. Cylinder head, head end of cylinder and mating surfaces of crankcase should be checked on a surface plate and lapped, if necessary, to provide a smooth surface. Do not remove any more metal than is necessary.

When assembling engine, first lubricate all friction surfaces and bear-

ings with engine oil. Place collar (13—Fig. WJ-20) and thrust ring (12) onto pto end of crankshaft. Lubricate lip of seal (11) with a suitable high-temperature grease, then install seal (11) onto pto end of crankshaft. Make certain seal (11) is installed with open side (spring side) towards bearing (14). Install crankshaft assembly (15) into lower crankcase half (22). Rotate center seal on crankshaft until outer pinch line is aligned with crankcase halves mating surface on either side of lower crankcase half. Apply a coat of a form-in-place gasket compound on mating surfaces of lower crankcase half and upper crankcase half, then position upper crankcase half on lower crankcase half.

Position stop plates (16) on outside of connecting rods and lubricate needle bearing (17) with engine oil. Position piston assemblies over connecting rods, then install piston pins (7). Retain piston pins with new retaining clips (8). Position open end of clips (8) to face 12 o'clock or 6 o'clock position. Lubricate pistons and piston rings with engine oil. Install new cylinder base gaskets (9), then use suitable tools to install cylinders (4). Securely hold assembled components together, then invert

assembly so base of crankcase is facing upward. Mount intake manifold (27) on cylinders (4) with new gaskets (28) and insulator plates (29). Tighten intake manifold cap screws to 20-22 ft.-lbs. (27-30 N·m) using a crisscross pattern. Using tightening sequence shown in Fig. WJ-21, tighten the crankcase base nuts in 5 ft.-lbs. (7 N·m) increments until a final torque of 16-18 ft.-lbs. (22-24 N·m) is obtained. Invert assembly so top of cylinders are facing upward. Install "O" rings (2 and 3—Fig. WJ-20) into grooves on top of cylinders (4). Position cylinder heads (1) on cylinders. Using tightening sequence shown in Fig. WJ-22, tighten the cylinder head cap screws in 5 ft.-lbs. (7 N·m) increments until a final torque of 16-18 ft.-lbs. (22-24 N·m) is obtained. Mount exhaust manifold (31—Fig. WJ-20) with gaskets (30) on cylinders. Tighten exhaust manifold cap screws to 30 ft.-lbs. (41 N·m) using a crisscross pattern.

Install seal (21) into ignition housing (1—Fig. WJ-9). Make certain seal (21—Fig. WJ-20) is installed with open side (spring side) towards bearing (19). Install "O" ring (20) onto outside of ignition housing neck. Lubricate lip of seal (21) with a suitable high-

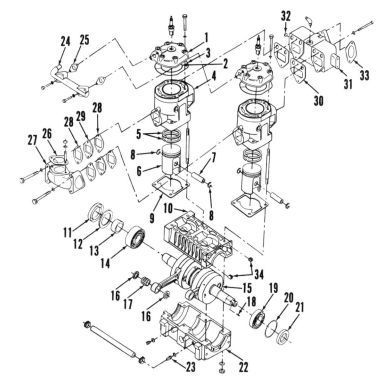

Fig. WJ-20—Exploded view of engine assembly. All models are equipped with thrust ring (12). A center thrust ring is used on Cuyuna Engine Model 21330 and later. Seal (11) and collar (13) on Cuyuna Engine Model 22037 and earlier differs in collar outside diameter and seal opening diameter from later models.

1. Cylinder head	10. Upper crankcase half	18. Key	26. Gasket
2. "O" ring	11. Seal	19. Ball bearing	27. Intake manifold
3. "O" ring	12. Thrust ring	20. "O" ring	28. Gasket
4. Cylinder	13. Collar	21. Seal	29. Insulator plate
5. Piston rings	14. Ball bearing	22. Lower crankcase half	30. Gasket
6. Piston	15. Crankshaft assy.	23. Pulse fitting	31. Exhaust manifold
7. Piston pin	16. Stop plates	24. Water manifold	32. Drain plug
8. Retaining clips	17. Needle bearing	25. Gasket	33. Gasket
9. Cylinder base gasket			34. Grommets

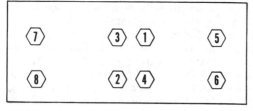

Magneto End

Fig. WJ-21—Crankcase base nuts should be tightened in the sequence shown. Refer to text for tightening torque specifications.

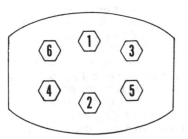

Fig. WJ-22—Cylinder head cap screws should be tightened in the sequence shown. Refer to text for tightening torque specifications.

temperature grease. Lubricate "O" ring (20) with a thin coating of a water-resistant grease. Install grommets (34) into upper crankcase half (10) slots. Reassemble ignition housing to crankcase assembly. Tighten the four ignition housing mounting screws to 16-18 ft.-lbs. (22-24 N·m) using a crisscross pattern. Align mark at base of magneto base plate (6—Fig. WJ-9) with long mark at bottom of ignition housing (1) and install magneto base plate. Apply Loctite 222 or a suitable equivalent thread locking solution on threads of magneto base plate retaining screws, then install screws with flat washers and lockwashers and securely tighten. Install flywheel key (18—Fig. WJ-20) in slot of crankshaft, then install flywheel (9—Fig. WJ-9). Apply a few drops of Loctite 242 or a suitable equivalent thread locking solution to threads on crankshaft end, then install lockwasher (10) and flywheel retaining nut (11). Tighten nut (11) to 46-50 ft.-lbs. (63-68 N·m).

RINGS, PISTONS, CYLINDERS AND CYLINDER HEADS. The pistons are fitted with two piston rings. Piston rings are interchangeable in grooves but must be installed with manufacturer's marking facing towards closed end (top) of piston. Piston ring end gap should be 0.007-0.031 inch (0.18-0.79 mm). Piston-to-cylinder wall clearance should be 0.005-0.010 inch (0.13-0.25 mm). Pistons and rings are available in standard size as well as 0.020 inch (0.5 mm) oversize. Cylinder should be bored to an oversize if cylinder is out-of-round or taper exceeds 0.002 in (0.05 mm). Install piston on connecting rod so arrow on piston

crown will point towards exhaust port when piston is in cylinder.

When installing cylinders, lubricate piston rings and cylinders and refer to ASSEMBLY section.

CONNECTING RODS, BEARINGS AND CRANKSHAFT. Connecting rods, bearings and crankshaft are a pressed together unit. Crankshaft should be disassembled ONLY by experienced service personnel and with proper service equipment.

Caged needle bearings are used at piston end of connecting rod. Maximum allowable limit of crankshaft runout is 0.003 inch (0.08 mm). Measure magneto end of crankshaft 0.7 inch (17.78 mm) from crankshaft end and pto end of

crankshaft 1.0 inch (25.4 mm) from crankshaft end.

When installing crankshaft, lubricate bearings with engine oil and refer to ASSEMBLY section.

ELECTRIC STARTER

All Models

All models are equipped with electric starter shown in Fig. WJ-24. Disassembly is evident after inspection of unit and reference to exploded view. When servicing starter motor, scribe reference marks across motor frame to aid in reassembly. Inspect all components for excessive wear or any other damage and renew if needed.

During reassembly, apply a light coat of a form-in-place gasket compound on frame head (5—Fig. WJ-24) and end cap (12) where caps mate with frame (8). After reassembly, bench test starter motor before installing on engine. Prior to installation, apply a light coat of a form-in-place gasket compound around outside of frame head (5) where frame head mates with ignition housing.

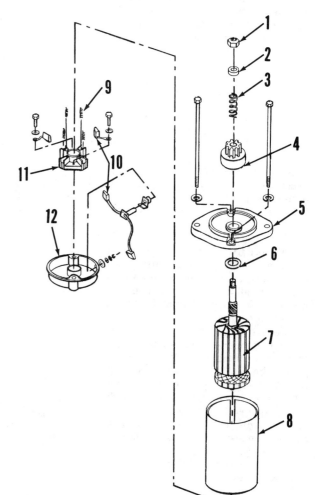

Fig. WJ-24—Exploded view of electric starter assembly used on all models.

1. Nut
2. Spring seat
3. Spring
4. Starter drive
5. Frame head
6. Thrust washer
7. Armature
8. Frame
9. Spring
10. Brushes
11. Brush holder
12. End cap

BILGE PUMP

All Models

When the vehicle is operated, the jet pump forces water past siphon tube (T—Fig. WJ-26). The passing force of water creates a vacuum effect, thus drawing (siphoning) any water out of vehicle bilge. Make sure all hoses, strainer (1—Fig. WJ-27) and one-way check valve (9) are kept clean of all foreign debris. Disassemble and clean or renew components if needed. Check operation of one-way check valve (9) as follows. Remove one-way check valve from hoses. Use low air pressure and blow through one-way check valve openings. Air should flow freely through one-way check valve in the direction indicated by arrow on outside of valve. Air should not pass through valve when applied to opposite end. Make sure one-way check valve is installed with outside arrow pointing towards jet pump. Make sure all hose connections are tight or vacuum loss will result in siphoning system malfunction.

DRIVE SHAFT

All Models

REMOVE AND REINSTALL. Disconnect battery cables from battery and remove battery from vehicle. On Wetjet 428 models, remove carry-on fuel tank. On Wetjet 428 L/C and 432 models, remove fuel tank mounting screws, then lift fuel tank onto left body channel with fuel hoses still connected. Remove fuel tank support straps. Remove ground strap (F—Fig. WJ-29), on models so equipped, located between crankshaft drive flange and drive shaft. Remove ground strap (R), on models so equipped, located between jet pump drive flange and drive shaft. Remove exhaust hose (H—Fig. WJ-17) from muffler (M) inlet and base of expansion chamber (B—Fig. WJ-18). Remove ground straps (T—Fig. WJ-19) attached on engine

mounting plate that will prevent engine from being slid forward. Remove four cap screws (W), flat washers and lockwashers retaining the engine mounting plate to the vehicle hull. Slide engine assembly forward 3-4 inches (76-101 mm).

NOTE: If care is exercised, engine wiring harness, fuel supply line, fuel return line, throttle control cable, choke cable (if equipped) and cooling system supply hose need not be disconnected.

Lift drive shaft from vehicle.

Install drive shaft with soft (black) coupler (B—Fig. WJ-29) in jet pump drive flange and hard (white) coupler (W) in crankshaft drive flange. On models equipped with drive shaft ground straps (F and R), position ground strap mounting holes 90 degrees apart and 180 degrees opposite of ground strap on front or rear of drive shaft. This is to make sure drive shaft balance is maintained.

Apply a suitable thread locking solution on the threads of the four cap screws (W—Fig. WJ-19). Install cap screws with lockwashers and flat washers. Tighten cap screws to 30 ft.-lbs. (41 N·m). Complete reassembly in reverse order of disassembly while

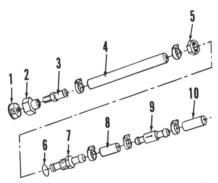

Fig. WJ-27—Exploded view of bilge siphoning system components.

1. Strainer	6. "O" ring
2. Strainer housing	7. Fitting
3. Fitting	8. Hose
4. Hose	9. One-way check valve
5. Nut	10. Hose

noting the following. Apply a suitable thread locking solution on threads of ground straps (F and R—Fig. WJ-29) and threads of ground straps (T—Fig. WJ-19) screws prior to installation.

INSPECTION. Inspect crankshaft drive flange, coupler (W—Fig. WJ-29), coupler (B), jet pump drive flange and drive shaft for excessive wear or any other damage and renew if needed. Tighten drive flange-to-crankshaft cap screw to 55 ft.-lbs. (75 N·m) and drive flange-to-jet pump cap screw to 30 ft.-lbs. (41 N·m).

JET PUMP

Wetjet 428 Models

Jet pump used on Wetjet 428 models differs from jet pump used on Wetjet 428 L/C and 432 models. Consult a Wetjet dealer for recommended jet pump servicing procedures.

Wetjet 428 L/C And 432 Models

DISASSEMBLY AND INSPECTION. Disconnect battery cables from battery. Remove jet pump guard and disconnect steering cable from outlet nozzle (1—Fig. WJ-31). Remove cooling system supply hose from fitting on top of outlet body (4). Disconnect clear bilge siphon hose from side of outlet body (4). Loosen band clamp (5), then withdraw outlet body (4) and band clamp (5). Withdraw impeller (9), pin (10), shims (11) and nose cone (12) out rear of jet pump.

Remove battery from vehicle. Remove fuel tank mounting screws, then lift fuel tank onto left body channel with fuel hoses still connected. Remove fuel tank support straps. Remove ground strap (F—Fig. WJ-29), on models so equipped, located between crankshaft drive flange and drive shaft. Remove ground strap (R), on models so equipped, located between jet pump drive flange and drive shaft. Remove exhaust hose (H—Fig.

Fig. WJ-26—View identifies location of siphon tube (T) in rear of jet pump.

Fig. WJ-29—Some models are equipped with ground strap (F) between crankshaft drive flange and drive shaft and ground strap (R) between jet pump drive flange and drive shaft. Position soft (black) coupler (B) between jet pump drive flange and drive shaft and hard (white) coupler (W) between crankshaft drive flange and drive shaft.

WJ-17) from muffler (M) inlet and base of expansion chamber (B—Fig. WJ-18). Remove ground straps (T—Fig. WJ-19) attached on engine mounting plate that ill prevent engine from being slid forward. Remove four cap screws (W), flat washers and lockwashers retaining the engine mounting plate to the vehicle hull. Slide engine assembly forward 3-4 inches (76-101 mm).

NOTE: If care is exercised, engine wiring harness, fuel supply line, fuel return line, throttle control cable, choke cable (if equipped) and cooling system supply hose need not be disconnected.

Lift drive shaft from vehicle. Remove hex head screw retaining jet pump drive flange. Reinstall pin (10—Fig. WJ-31) into impeller shaft. Install tool 11-40-303 over impeller shaft and position tool slots to engage pin. Place a chain wrench on jet pump drive flange, then rotate drive flange counterclockwise while preventing impeller shaft rotation with tool 11-40-303. Completely unscrew propeller shaft from threaded adapter (23) and withdraw out rear of jet pump. Withdraw jet pump drive flange with adapter (23). Use a suitable tool and pry out seal (22). Remove snap ring (21). Use a suitable punch and hammer and drive bearing (20) out front of

intake housing. Pry out seal (19). Remove sixteen screws from bottom of hull to withdraw intake housing (16) with grill (25) and anode (26).

Inspect impeller shaft for wear on friction surfaces of bearings and oil seals. Inspect impeller (9) and wear ring (14) for excessive wear or any other damage. Inspect all bearings for freedom of rotation and damaged components. Inspect outlet body (4) and intake housing (16) for damage. Renew all gaskets, "O" ring and seals during reassembly. Renew any other components that are excessively worn or are diagnosed with any other damage.

ASSEMBLY. Apply a 3/16 inch (4.7 mm) bead of RTV silicone sealer around gasket (24—Fig. WJ-31) where gasket mates with hull. Apply a 1/4 inch (6.35 mm) bead of RTV silicone sealer at base and back side of "O" ring (15). Install intake housing (16) with grill (25) and anode (26) into vehicle. Apply a drop of a suitable thread locking solution on threads of sixteen intake housing screws and evenly tighten all sixteen screws. Wipe all excess RTV silicone sealer from outside of hull. Apply additional RTV silicone sealer, if needed, around mating area of intake housing (16) and hull to ensure no water leakage will result. Apply a white lithium grease on seals

(19 and 22) and install seal (19), bearing (20), snap ring (21) and seal (22) into front of intake housing (16). Install threaded adapter (23) and jet pump drive flange into front of intake housing (16). Apply a suitable thread seizure preventing solution to threads on end of impeller shaft (13). Reach impeller shaft through intake housing (16) and thread into adapter (23). Hold jet pump drive flange and hand tighten impeller shaft using tool 11-40-303 to secure impeller shaft against bearing (20). Install hex head retaining screw in jet pump drive flange. Place a chain wrench on drive flange and use the correct sized hex head socket and tool to tighten retaining screw to 30 ft.-lbs. (41 N·m).

Install drive shaft with soft (black) coupler (B—Fig. WJ-29) in jet pump drive flange and hard (white) coupler (W) in crankshaft drive flange. On models equipped with drive shaft ground straps (F and R), position ground strap mounting holes 90 degrees apart and 180 degrees opposite of ground strap on front or rear of drive shaft. This is to make sure drive shaft balance is maintained.

Apply a suitable thread locking solution on the threads of the four cap screws (W—Fig. WJ-19). Install cap screws with lockwashers and flat washers. Tighten cap screws to 30 ft.-

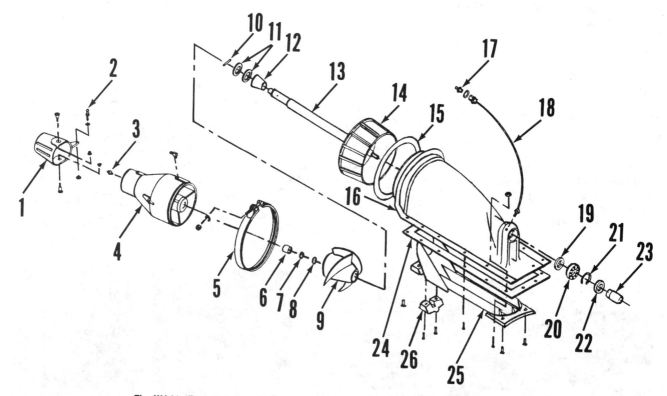

Fig. WJ-31—Exploded view of jet pump assembly used on Wetjet 428 L/C and 432 models.

1. Outlet nozzle				
2. Ball fitting	6. Bushing	10. Pin	14. Wear ring	18. Grease supply line	22. Seal
3. Grease fitting	7. Seal	11. Shims	15. "O" ring	19. Seal	23. Threaded adapter
4. Outlet body	8. Seal	12. Nose cone	16. Intake housing	20. Bearing	24. Gasket
5. Band clamp	9. Impeller	13. Impeller shaft	17. Grease fitting	21. Snap ring	25. Grill
					26. Anode

lbs. (41 N·m). Complete reassembly of internal vehicle components in reverse order of disassembly while noting the following: Apply a suitable thread locking solution on threads of ground straps (F and R—Fig. WJ-29) and threads of ground straps (T—Fig. WJ-19) screws prior to installation.

Remove pin (10—Fig. WJ-31). Install nose cone (12), shims (11), pin (10) and impeller (9). Align and seat impeller (9) on pin (10). Hold pressure against impeller and measure clearance between impeller blades and wear ring (14). Clearance should be 0.012-0.018 inch (0.30-0.46 mm). If clearance is too low, then add one shim (11). If clearance is too high, then remove one shim (11). Adjust shim (11) thickness until correct clearance is obtained. Grease bushing (6) with white lithium grease. Install outlet body (4) on impeller shaft (13). Align tab at front of outlet body (4) with notch in intake housing (16) and assemble components. Install band clamp (5) with adjusting nut on top and tighten nut until ¾ inch (19.05 mm) of stud protrudes through nut. Install clear bilge siphon hose, cooling system supply hose and connect steering cable end on outlet nozzle ball fitting (2). Install jet pump guard. Inject white lithium grease into grease fitting (3) at rear of outlet body (4) and grease fitting (17) beneath rear of passenger seat.

STEERING

All Models

ADJUSTMENT. With steering wheel in straight ahead position, jet pump outlet nozzle (1—Fig. WJ-31) should be centered or at a 90 degree angle to stern of vehicle. If not, secure steering wheel in a straight ahead position. Remove jet pump guard and detach cable end (33—Fig. WJ-33) from outlet nozzle ball fitting (2—Fig. WJ-31). Loosen locknut (32—Fig. WJ-33) and rotate cable end (33) in direction required to center outlet nozzle. Reattach cable end and check outlet nozzle setting. Tighten

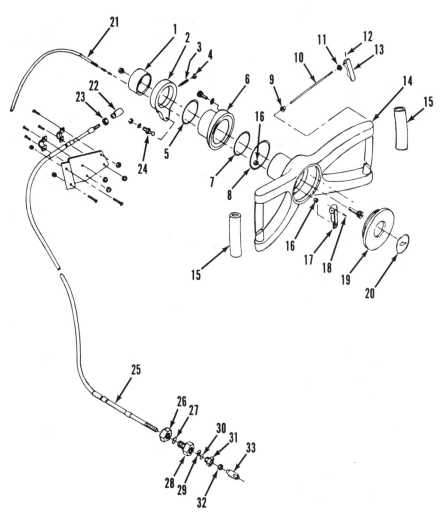

Fig. WJ-33—Exploded view of steering and related components.

1. Adjustment cap
2. Lever
3. Set screw
4. Nut
5. Teflon ring
6. Mount
7. Teflon ring
8. "O" ring
9. Grommet
10. Throttle shaft
11. Grommet
12. Pin
13. Throttle lever
14. Steering wheel
15. Grips
16. Jam nuts
17. Pull lever
18. Pin
19. Cover
20. Button
21. Throttle cable
22. Cable end
23. Locknut
24. Ball fitting
25. Steering cable
26. Nut
27. "O" ring
28. Adapter
29. Clip
30. "O" ring
31. Inverted flare nut
32. Locknut
33. Cable end

locknut (32) after correct adjustment is obtained. Reinstall jet pump guard.

OVERHAUL. Overhaul of steering components is evident after referral to Fig. WJ-33. Grease "O" ring (8) and Teflon ring (7) with a suitable water-resistant grease during reassembly.

YAMAHA

YAMAHA MOTOR CORPORATION U.S.A.
Marine Division
6555 Katella Avenue
Cypress, CA 90630

WAVEJAMMER AND WAVERUNNER (1987 AND 1988)

NOTE: Metric fasteners are used throughout vehicle.

General

Engine Make	Own
Engine Type	Two-Stroke; Water-Cooled
HP/Rated Rpm	30/4500-5500
Number of Cylinders	2
Bore	72 mm (2.84 in.)
Stroke	61 mm (2.40 in.)
Displacement	496 cc (30.3 cu. in.)
Compression Ratio	7.0:1
Engine Lubrication	Pre-Mix
Fuel:Oil Ratio	50:1
Engine Oil Recommendation	Yamalube or Two-Stroke; BIA Certified TC-W

Tune-Up

Engine Idle Speed	1500 rpm
Spark Plug:	
NGK	B7HS
Champion	L82C
Electrode Gap	0.5-0.6 mm (0.020-0.024 in.)
Ignition:	
Type	CDI
Timing	9°-11° @ 1000 rpm
	18°-22° @ 3000 rpm
	25°-29° @ 5500 rpm
Carburetor:	
Make	Mikuni
Model	BN34 Diaphragm
Bore Size	28 mm (1.1 in.)
Low Speed Needle Setting	9/16—1-1/16 Turns
High Speed Needle Setting	5/8—1-1/8 Turns

Sizes—Clearances

Cylinder Out-of-Round Limit	0.05 mm (0.002 in.)
Cylinder Taper Limit	0.08 mm (0.003 in.)
Piston-to-Cylinder Wall Clearance	0.060-0.065 mm (0.0024-0.0026 in.)
Piston Ring End Gap:	
Top	0.2-0.4 mm (0.008-0.016 in.)
Second	0.20-0.35 mm (0.008-0.014 in.)

Sizes—Clearances (Cont.)

Piston Ring Side Clearance:	
Top	0.02-0.06 mm (0.0008-0.0024 in.)
Second	0.04-0.08 mm (0.0016-0.0032 in.)
Maximum Crankshaft Runout	0.03 mm (0.0012 in.)
Maximum Connecting Rod Small End Shake	2.0 mm (0.08 in.)
Maximum Cylinder Head Warp	0.1 mm (0.004 in.)

Capacities

Fuel Tank:	
WaveJammer	13 L (3.4 gal.)
WaveRunner	22 L (5.8 gal.)

Tightening Torques

Cylinder Head Cap Screws	28 N·m (20 ft.-lbs.)
Crankcase Cap Screws	28 N·m (20 ft.-lbs.)
Exhaust Cover Cap Screws	8 N·m (71 in.-lbs.)
Engine Mounting Cap Screws	17 N·m (12 ft.-lbs.)
Flywheel	140 N·m (103 ft.-lbs.)
Spark Plug	20 N·m (14 ft.-lbs.)
Drive Shaft Couplings	37 N·m (27 ft.-lbs.)
Jet Pump Mounting Cap Screws	34 N·m (24 ft.-lbs.)
Impeller	18 N·m (13 ft.-lbs.)
Standard Screws:	
5 mm	5 N·m (44 in.-lbs.)
6 mm	8 N·m (71 in.-lbs.)
8 mm	18 N·m (13 ft.-lbs.)
10 mm	36 N·m (25 ft.-lbs.)
12 mm	43 N·m (31 ft.-lbs.)

LUBRICATION

All Models

The engine is lubricated by oil mixed with the fuel. Fuel:oil ratios should be 25:1 during break-in (first tankful) of a new or rebuilt engine and 50:1 for normal service when using Yamalube Two-Cycle Lubricant For Outboards or a BIA certified two-stroke TC-W engine oil. Manufacturer recommends no-lead automotive gasoline having a minimum octane rating of 84. Gasoline and oil should be thoroughly mixed.

Grease intermediate housing through grease fitting (G—Fig. Y-32) with a water-resistant grease every six months or more frequent if needed.

FUEL SYSTEM

All Models

CARBURETOR. Refer to Fig. Y-1 for an exploded view of Mikuni type BN34 diaphragm carburetor used on all models. A choke plate (21—Fig. Y-1) is actuated by choke knob (K—Fig. Y-2 or Fig. Y-3) on control panel via a cable and linkage. Initial setting of low speed mixture needle (22—Fig. Y-1) is 9/16—1-1/16 turns out from a lightly seated position and high speed mixture needle (29) is 5/8 to 1-1/8 turns out from a lightly seated position. Final carburetor adjustments must be made with engine at normal operating temperature and running. Clockwise rotation of either needle

leans the mixture. Adjust low speed mixture needle (22) until smooth acceleration from the idle position is noted. After adjusting low speed mixture needle, adjust idle speed screw (37—Fig. Y-4) until engine idle speed is approximately 1500 rpm with throttle lever completely released. To adjust high speed fuel:air mixture, the engine spark plugs must be removed and their insulator tip color noted.

NOTE: Make sure that fuel tank contains a 50:1 fuel mixture.

Fig. Y-2—View identifies location of choke knob (K) on WaveJammer.

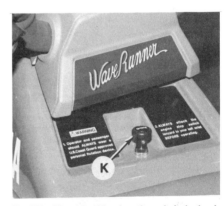

Fig. Y-3—View identifies location of choke knob (K) on WaveRunner.

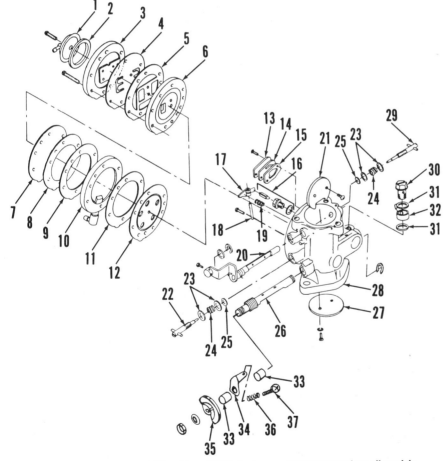

Fig. Y-1—Exploded view of Mikuni type BN34 diaphragm carburetor used on all models.

1. Fuel inlet cover
2. Gasket
3. Inlet body
4. Check valve diaphragm
5. Gasket
6. Pump body
7. Diaphragm
8. Gasket
9. Gasket
10. Diaphragm cover
11. Gasket
12. Regulating diaphragm
13. Plate
14. Diaphragm
15. Gasket
16. Inlet valve assy.
17. Valve lever
18. Pivot shaft
19. Spring
20. Choke shaft
21. Choke plate
22. Low speed mixture needle
23. Washers
24. Springs
25. "O" rings
26. Throttle shaft
27. Throttle plate
28. Body
29. High speed mixture needle
30. Banjo bolt
31. Gaskets
32. Return line fitting
33. Spacers
34. Bracket
35. Cable lever
36. Spring
37. Idle screw

Fig. Y-4—View identifies location of idle speed screw (37).

Make sure cooling system will receive an adequate supply of water, then operate and sustain engine at wide-open throttle for a suitable test period. Stop the engine with throttle in wide-open position. Remove spark plugs and note insulator tip color. Normal insulator tip color is brown to light tan. If insulator tip appears to be light tan to white in color, then mixture is too lean and high speed mixture needle (29—Fig. Y-1) should be rotated outward (counterclockwise) ¼ turn to richen mixture. If insulator tip appears to be dark brown to black in color, then mixture is too rich and high speed mixture needle (29) should be rotated inward (clockwise) ¼ turn to lean mixture. Clean, regap and reinstall spark plugs and continue test procedures until spark plug insulator tips are a normal color.

The fuel pump and regulating diaphragm (12) can be removed after removing the six through-bolts. Note that alignment tabs on components (3 through 12) are provided to assist in proper alignment during reassembly.

Do not remove choke plate, throttle plate or shafts unless necessary. The choke and throttle plate retaining screws are either staked or retained with a thread locking solution to prevent loosening. If screws are removed,

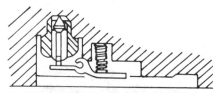

Fig. Y-5—Inlet needle valve lever should be flush with floor of housing recess as shown.

properly stake or apply a suitable thread locking solution on threads prior to assembly. Inlet needle valve lever (17) must be flush with floor of housing recess when needle valve is seated. Refer to Fig. Y-5. If lever must be adjusted, push down on lever immediately above spring to collapse the spring, then bend the end which contacts needle valve.

REED VALVES. Two vee type reed valve assemblies (one for each cylinder) are located between the intake manifold and crankcase. Remove intake manifold for access to reed valve assemblies.

Renew reeds if petals are broken, cracked, warped or bent. Do not attempt to bend or straighten reeds. Reed seating surface on reed blocks should be smooth and flat. Maximum allowable reed petal stand open is 0.9 mm (0.04 in.). Reed stop setting should be 6.0 mm (0.24 in.).

FUEL PUMP. The fuel pump is an integral part of the carburetor. The fuel pump assembly can be overhauled without overhauling the complete carburetor.

With reference to Fig. Y-1, disassemble the fuel pump assembly. Inspect all components for excessive wear or any other damage and renew if needed. Clean components as needed with a suitable cleaning solution. Blow dry with clean compressed air. If compressed air is not available, use only lint-free cloths to wipe dry. Make sure all passages are clear of any obstructions.

With reference to Fig. Y-1, reassemble the fuel pump assembly with new gaskets. Securely tighten the six through-bolts.

FUEL TANK AND FUEL FILTER. A fuel strainer assembly is attached on the bottom of "ON" fuel tank pickup line (O—Fig. Y-6) and on the bottom of "RES" fuel tank pickup line (R). An in-line fuel filter (I) is located between fuel

selector valve (V—Fig. Y1-7) and carburetor fuel pump intake. Periodically unscrew cup on bottom of fuel filter (I—Fig. Y-6) and withdraw sealing ring and filter element from base. Clean cup and inspect filter element for excessive contamination or damage. Renew sealing ring and any damaged components. Renew filter element if excessive contamination is noted. Reassembly is reverse order of disassembly. Fuel tank strainers should not need to be removed and renewed unless contamination is suspected.

THROTTLE LEVER FREE PLAY. Throttle lever should have 2-5 mm (0.08-0.20 in.) free play measured between lever stop (S—Fig. Y-8) and end of throttle lever (L). To adjust, loosen locknut (N) and rotate cable adjuster (A) until the recommended free play is obtained. Tighten locknut (N) to retain adjustment.

FLAME ARRESTOR. Flame arrestor (F—Fig. Y-9) is located beneath cover (C). Periodically remove four screws retaining cover (C) and withdraw cover and flame arrestor (F). Inspect flame arrestor for contamination or damage and renew if needed. When installing flame arrestor (F), make sure a tight seal is formed between mounting base and flame arrestor. Securely tighten the four cap screws retaining cover (C).

IGNITION

All Models

All models are equipped with a simultaneous capacitor discharge ignition system. The ignition timing is electronically advanced as the magneto base plate is fixed.

TROUBLE-SHOOTING. If ignition malfunction occurs, use only approved procedures to prevent damage to the components. The fuel system should be checked first to make certain that faulty running is not caused by incorrect

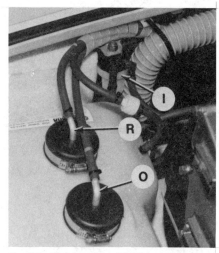

Fig. Y-6—View identifies "ON" fuel tank pickup line (O), "RES" fuel tank pickup line (R) and in-line fuel filter (I).

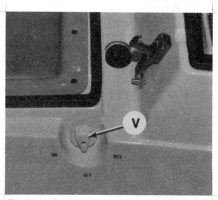

Fig. Y-7—View identifies fuel selector valve (V).

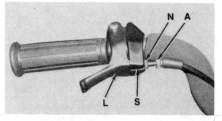

Fig. Y-8—Throttle lever free play should be 2-5 mm (0.08-0.20 in.) measured between lever stop (S) and end of throttle lever (L). To adjust, loosen locknut (N) and rotate cable adjuster (A).

mixture or contaminated fuel. Make sure malfunction is not due to spark plug, wiring or wiring connection failure. Trouble-shoot ignition circuit using a suitable ohmmeter as follows:

Separate the wires at the connectors between magneto components and CDI module. Refer to Fig. Y-11. Check condition of charge coil (3) by attaching one tester lead to brown wire leading to magneto assembly and attaching other tester lead to black wire leading to magneto assembly. Charge coil can be considered satisfactory if resistance reading is within the limits of 81-99 ohms. Check condition of pulser coil (2) by attaching one tester lead to white/red wire leading to magneto assembly and attaching other tester lead to black wire leading to magneto assembly. Pulser coil can be considered satisfactory if resistance reading is within the limits of 92-112 ohms. Charge coil (3) and pulser coil (2) are serviceable after removing flywheel cover and flywheel. Make sure a suitable puller is used to withdraw flywheel. Tighten flywheel nut to 140 N·m (103 ft.-lbs.).

To check condition of ignition coil, separate the orange wire and black wire connector at coil and remove high tension wires from spark plugs. Attach one tester lead to terminal end of orange wire and other tester lead to terminal end of black wire. Primary coil resistance reading should be within the limits of 0.12-0.18 ohms. Attach a tester lead to each high tension wire. Secondary coil resistance reading should be within the limits of 2800-4200 ohms.

If no components are found defective in the previous tests and ignition

malfunction is still suspected, then install a known good CDI module and recheck engine operation.

CHARGING SYSTEM

All Models

All models are equipped with a lighting coil, rectifier/regulator, 20 ampere fuse and battery. Standard battery has a 19 ampere hour, 12 volt rating. The lighting coil should produce at least 11.5 ac volts at 3000 rpm and 13.5-16.5 ac volts at 5500 rpm. Rectifier/regulator assembly should regulate voltage between 14.3-15.3 dc volts.

The battery electrolyte level should be checked periodically and filled to maximum level with distilled water if required. The battery should be removed from the vehicle and the battery caps removed when charging. The manufacturer recommends charging the battery at a rate of 1.9 amperes for a period of 10 hours. Do not exceed recommended charging rate.

NOTE: Make sure battery charging area is well ventilated.

The lighting coil can be statically tested using a suitable ohmmeter. Refer to Fig. Y-11. Separate two green wires leading from lighting coil to rectifier/regulator assembly at connectors. Measure resistance between the two

green wires leading to lighting coil. Resistance reading should be 0.9-1.1 ohms. Check for continuity between each of the lighting coil wires and ground. Tester should show infinite resistance at each wire. To check rectifier/regulator assembly, refer to chart shown in Fig. Y-12. To check rectifier/regulator during operation, first make sure battery is fully charged, lighting coil test good and all wiring is in good condition and all connectors fit tightly or are securely fastened. Attach a suitable voltmeter directly to battery terminals. Remove wash port plug (P—Fig. Y-13) located on top of exhaust guide plate. Install Yamaha flush kit ABA-FLUSH-KT-01 (K—Fig. Y-14) or a suitable equivalent. Connect a supplemental water supply to flush kit inlet.

NOTE: Do not turn on water until engine is ready to be started as exhaust flooding could occur.

Start and run engine while observing voltmeter. The voltmeter should show

+Tester Lead / -Tester Lead	Green 1	Green 2	Red	Black
Green 1		A	B	C
Green 2	A		B	C
Red	D	D		D
Black	B	B	E	

Fig. Y-12—Use chart shown above and values listed below to test condition of rectifier/regulator assembly.

A. 3,000-30,000 ohms
B. 1,000-10,000 ohms
C. 2,000-15,000 ohms
D. Infinite resistance
E. 2,000-20,000 ohms

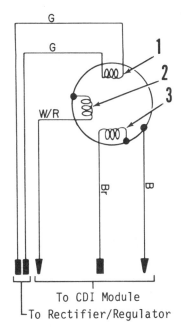

Fig. Y-11—View identifying magneto components and color of leads.

1. Lighting coil
2. Pulser coil
3. Charge coil
B. Black

G. Green
Br. Brown
W/R. White with red tracer

To CDI Module
To Rectifier/Regulator

Fig. Y-13—View identifies cooling system wash port plug (P) located on top of exhaust guide plate and jet pump cooling system supply hose (W).

Fig. Y-9—Flame arrestor (F) is located beneath cover (C).

approximately 14.3-15.3 dc volts. Make sure supplemental water supply is turned off at approximately same time engine is stopped.

COOLING SYSTEM

All Models

All models are water-cooled. Forced water is supplied to the engine by the jet pump. As jet pump impeller rpm increases, so does water circulation through cooling system.

Make sure jet pump water intake grill (G—Fig. Y-15) is kept clean. Inspect all hoses periodically for cracks, kinks or any other damage. The cooling system should be flushed out after each operating period when vehicle is used in contaminated or salt water. The cooling system should be flushed out prior to extended periods of storage and prior to usage after extended periods of storage.

To flush the cooling system, remove wash port plug (P—Fig. Y-13) located on top of exhaust guide plate. Install Yamaha flush kit ABA-FLUSH-KIT-01 (K—Fig. Y-14) or a suitable equivalent. Connect a supplemental water supply to flush kit inlet. Use only clean, fresh water.

NOTE: Do not turn on water until engine is ready to be started as exhaust flooding could occur.

Allow water to circulate through system for 10-15 minutes with engine operating at fast idle. Make sure supplemental water supply is turned off at approximately same time engine is stopped. If vehicle is to be stored for an extended period, start the engine and operate the throttle in quick bursts between idle position and ¾ throttle for a maximum of 10-15 seconds. All water remaining in exhaust system will be forced out, preventing damage from developing contaminates or freezing.

NOTE: Make sure engine is not operated without a supply of water longer than 10-15 seconds or damage to engine and/or exhaust components could result.

Spray clean, fresh water into jet pump intake grill (G) to wash contaminates or salt from jet pump components.

ENGINE

All Models

REMOVE AND REINSTALL. Disconnect battery cables from battery and remove battery from vehicle. Remove throttle cable and choke cable from carburetor. Remove hoses from carburetor and label if needed. Remove the two carburetor mounting nuts, then withdraw the carburetor. Cover intake manifold passage to prevent entrance of foreign debris. Disconnect stop switch and starter switch from main engine wiring harness at connectors. Remove cooling system supply hose (W—Fig. Y-17) and exhaust hose (H). Remove drive coupler shield. Remove four cap screws (C) and washers retaining front and rear engine mounting plates to vehi-

cle hull. Note shims (S) located under mounting plates and identify each shim for installation in original location. Remove any other components that will interfere with engine removal. Use a suitable lifting device to hoist engine assembly from vehicle. Place engine assembly on a clean work bench.

To reinstall, position Yamaha tool YW-6367, with stamped side facing upward, to underside of engine flywheel cover. Use a suitable adhesive to retain rubber mount damper in place. If Yamaha special tool is not available, use a rubber damper 19.5 mm (0.77 in.) in thickness.

Use a suitable lifting device to hoist engine assembly into vehicle. Make sure coupler is located between engine drive flange (E—Fig. Y-18) and intermediate housing drive flange (I). A jackscrew hole is provided directly above each engine mounting hole in front and rear engine mounting plates. Install shims (S—Fig. Y-17) into original locations. Lay a straightedge across top of engine drive flange (E—Fig. Y-18) and intermediate housing drive flange (I). Engine drive flange (E) should be 0-0.6 mm (0-0.024 in.) higher (H) than intermediate drive

Fig. Y-15—Jet pump water intake grill (G) is located on bottom of hull.

Fig. Y-17—View identifying cooling system supply hose (W) and exhaust hose (H). Two cap screws (C) and washers are located on port and starboard side of vehicle to retain front and rear engine mounting plates to vehicle hull. Note shims (S) located under mounting plates and identify each shim for installation in original location.

Fig. Y-14—View identifies Yamaha flush kit ABA-FLUSH-KT-01 (K).

Fig. Y-18—Refer to text for measuring height (H) and clearance (C) between engine drive flange (E) and intermediate housing drive flange (I).

flange (I). Measure clearance between engine drive flange (E) and base of intermediate housing drive flange (I). Clearance (C) should be 2-4 mm (0.079-0.157 in.). If recommended settings are not measured, then adjust jackscrews in front and rear engine mounting plates until recommended settings are obtained. Then measure clearance between shim (S—Fig. Y-17) and engine mounting plate for required shim (S) thickness. Measure clearance for all four engine mounts. Install recommended shims and remove jackscrews. Remove Yamaha tool YW-6367 or suitable equivalent. Apply Loctite 242 or a suitable equivalent on threads of four cap screws (C) and tighten cap screws to 17 N·m (12 ft.-lbs.). Remeasure as previously outlined to verify engine drive flange to intermediate housing drive flange settings are as recommended. Adjust shim thickness if needed.

Complete reassembly in reverse order of disassembly.

DISASSEMBLY. Remove muffler, exhaust guide plate outer and inner covers and exhaust guide plate. Engine drive flange and shaft are withdrawn with exhaust guide plate. Remove flywheel cover, flywheel, magneto components and front oil seal housing. Remove electric starter and overheat sensor (R—Fig. Y-19). Remove intake manifold, exhaust cover, exhaust inner plate and gaskets. Remove cylinder head. Remove front and rear engine mounting plates. Remove remaining crankcase cover cap screws, then separate crankcase cover from cylinder block. Crankshaft and piston assembly can now be removed from cylinder block.

Engine components are now ready for overhaul as outlined in the appropriate following paragraphs. Refer to the following section for assembly procedure.

ASSEMBLY. Refer to specific service sections when assembling the crankshaft, connecting rod and piston. Make sure all joint and gasket surfaces are clean, free from nicks and burrs and hardened cement or carbon.

Whenever the engine is disassembled, it is recommended that all gasket surfaces and mating surfaces without gaskets be carefully checked for nicks, burrs and warped surfaces which might interfere with a tight seal. Cylinder head, head end of cylinder and mating surfaces of crankcase should be checked on a surface plate and lapped, if necessary, to provide a smooth surface. Do not remove any more metal than is necessary.

When assembling engine, first lubricate all friction surfaces and bearings with engine oil. Install crankshaft assembly and make certain main bearing locating pins engage notches in cylinder block. Apply Yamaha Gasket Maker or a suitable equivalent on mating surfaces of crankcase and cylinder block, then position crankcase cover on cylinder block. Install front and rear engine mounting plates with spacers. Spacers are located under cap screws (3, 4, 5 and 6) as identified in Fig. Y-20. Apply Loctite PST Pipe Sealant or a suitable equivalent on threads of crankcase cap screws. Using tightening sequence shown in Fig. Y-20, tighten the crankcase-to-cylinder block cap screws first to 15 N·m (11 ft.-lbs.) then to a final torque of 28 N·m (20 ft.-lbs.). Install cylinder head gasket and cylinder head. Apply Loctite PST Pipe Sealant or a suitable equivalent on threads of cylinder head cap screws. Using tightening sequence shown in Fig. Y-21, tighten the cylinder head cap screws to 15 N·m (11 ft.-lbs.) with the exception of cap screws (1, 5 and 9). Leave cap screws (1, 5 and 9) loose until muffler and overheat sensor (R—Fig. Y-19) are installed. Install exhaust cover, exhaust inner plate and gaskets. Apply Loctite PST Pipe Sealant or a suitable equivalent on threads of exhaust cover cap screws. Using tightening sequence shown in Fig. Y-22, tighten the exhaust cover cap screws first to 4 N·m (3 ft.-lbs.) then to a final torque of 8 N·m (6 ft.-lbs.). Note that cap screw (3—Fig. Y-22) is shorter than all other exhaust cover cap screws. Apply Loctite 242 or a suitable equivalent on reed valve assembly mounting screws. Install intake manifold gasket and reed valve assemblies on intake manifold. Apply Loctite PST Pipe Sealant or a suitable equivalent on threads of intake manifold cap screws. Tighten intake manifold cap screws to 8 N·m (6 ft.-lbs.). Install front oil seal housing. Apply Loctite PST Pipe Sealant or a suitable equivalent on threads of cap screws retaining front oil seal housing and securely tighten. Install magneto assembly. Install starter motor and

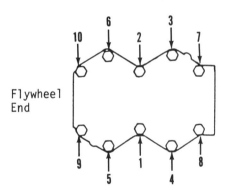

Fig. Y-20—Tighten crankcase cap screws in sequence shown to torque specified in text.

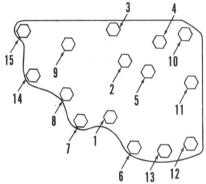

Fig. Y-22—Tighten exhaust cover cap screws in sequence shown to torque specified in text.

Fig. Y-19—View identifies location of engine overheat sensor (R).

Fig. Y-21—Tighten cylinder head cap screws in sequence shown to torque specified in text.

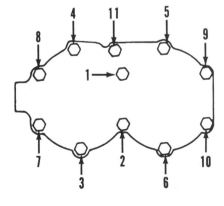

apply Loctite PST Pipe Sealant or a suitable equivalent on threads of retaining cap screws and securely tighten. Install flywheel and tighten retaining nut to 140 N·m (103 ft.-lbs.). Install flywheel cover and apply Loctite PST Pipe Sealant or a suitable equivalent on threads of retaining cap screws and tighten M6 cap screws to 8 N·m (6 ft.-lbs.) and M8 cap screws to 18 N·m (13 ft.-lbs.). Install engine drive flange and shaft with exhaust guide plate, outer and inner covers and related gaskets onto engine. Apply Loctite PST Pipe Sealant or a suitable equivalent on threads of mounting cap screws and tighten cap screws to 10 N·m (7 ft.-lbs.). Install overheat sensor (R—Fig. Y-19) and muffler assembly. Tighten cylinder head mounting cap screws to 15 N·m (11 ft.-lbs.). Apply Loctite PST Pipe Sealant or a suitable equivalent on cap screws retaining muffler to exhaust guide plate and tighten cap screws to 10 N·m (7 ft.-lbs.). Using tightening sequence shown in Fig. Y-21, tighten the cylinder head cap screws to a final torque of 28 N·m (20 ft.-lbs.). Using tightening sequence shown in Fig. Y-23, tighten the exhaust guide plate and exhaust guide plate outer cover cap screws to a final torque of 20 N·m (14 ft.-lbs.).

PISTONS, PINS, RINGS AND CYLINDERS. Cylinder bore should be measured in several different locations to determine if an out-of-round or tapered condition exists. Cylinder out-of-round limit is 0.05 mm (0.002 in.) and taper limit is 0.08 mm (0.003 in.). Bore cylinder to 0.50 mm (0.020 in.) oversize if measured cylinder out-of-round or taper is beyond limit. Inspect cylinder wall for scoring. If minor scoring is noted, cylinders should be honed to smooth out cylinder wall.

Recommended piston skirt-to-cylinder clearance is 0.060-0.065 mm (0.0024-0.0026 in.). Recommended piston ring end gap is 0.2-0.4 mm (0.008-0.016 in.) for top ring and 0.20-0.35 mm (0.008-0.014 in.) for second ring. The recommended piston ring side clearance is 0.02-0.06 mm (0.0008-0.0024 in.) for top ring and 0.04-0.08 mm (0.0016-0.0032 in.) for second ring. The top piston ring is semi-keystone shaped. Make sure piston rings properly align with locating pins in ring grooves.

When reassembling, install new piston pin retaining clips (4—Fig. Y-24) and make sure that "UP" on dome of piston is towards flywheel end of engine. Coat bearings, pistons, rings and cylinder bores with engine oil during assembly.

CONNECTING RODS, CRANKSHAFT AND BEARINGS. The crankshaft assembly should only be disassembled if the necessary tools and experience are available to service this type of crankshaft.

Maximum crankshaft runout measured at bearing outer races with crankshaft ends supported in lathe centers is 0.03 mm (0.0012 in.). Connecting rod big end side clearance should be 0.15-0.65 mm (0.006-0.026 in.). Side-to-side shake of connecting rod small end measured as shown in Fig. Y-25 should be a maximum of 2.0 mm (0.08 in.).

Crankshaft, connecting rods and center section components are available only as a unit assembly. Outer main bearings (17 and 19—Fig. Y-24) are available individually.

Thirty-four needle bearings (7) are used in each connecting rod small end. Rollers can be held in place with petroleum jelly while installing piston.

Lubricate bearings, pistons, rings and cylinders with engine oil prior to installation. Tighten crankcase and cylinder head screws as outlined in ASSEMBLY section.

ELECTRIC STARTER

All Models

All models are equipped with electric starter shown in Fig. Y-27. Disassembly is evident after inspection of unit and reference to exploded view. When servicing starter motor, scribe reference marks across motor frame to aid in reassembly.

NOTE: An impact driver should be used to remove through-bolts (13). A thread locking solution is placed on through-bolt threads at the factory.

Starter brushes have a standard length of 17 mm (0.67 in.) and should be renewed if worn to 13 mm (0.51 in.).

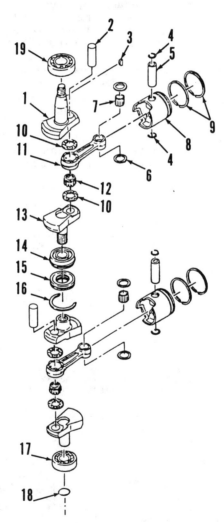

Fig. Y-24—Exploded view of crankshaft assembly.

1. Crank half
2. Crankpin
3. Key
4. Clip
5. Piston pin
6. Thrust washer
7. Needle bearings
8. Piston
9. Piston rings
10. Thrust washers
11. Connecting rod
12. Roller bearing
13. Crank half
14. Bearing & snap ring
15. Labyrinth seal
16. Snap ring
17. Bearing
18. "O" ring
19. Bearing

Fig. Y-23—Tighten exhaust guide plate and exhaust guide plate outer cover cap screws in sequence shown to torque specified in text.

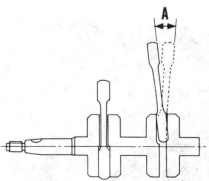

Fig. Y-25—Side shake (A) at small end of connecting rod should be a maximum of 2.0 mm (0.08 in.).

Commutator has a standard diameter of 33 mm (1.30 in.) and should be renewed if worn to a diameter of 31 mm (1.22 in.). Commutator undercut should be 0.5-0.8 (0.02-0.03 in.). If undercut is 0.2 mm (0.007 in.) or less, then use a suitable tool to remove the mica between commutator sections until undercut between each section is within the recommended range. Apply a water-resistant grease to lip of seal in frame head (6). Apply a suitable thread locking solution on threads of through-bolts (13) during reassembly. After reassembly, bench test starter motor before installing on engine.

BILGE PUMP

All Models

When the vehicle is operated, the jet pump forces water through hose (T—Fig. Y-29) and past siphon hose (S) opening. The passing force of water creates a vacuum effect, thus drawing (siphoning) any water out of vehicle bilge. Make sure all hoses and strainer (R—Fig. Y-30) are kept clean of all foreign debris. Disassemble and clean or renew components if needed. Make sure all hose connections are tight or vacuum loss will result in siphoning system malfunction. An antisiphon loop is positioned at rear of engine to prevent water from being drawn into hull when engine is not being operated.

ENGINE DRIVE FLANGE

All Models

R&R AND OVERHAUL. Disconnect battery cables from battery and remove battery from vehicle. Remove throttle cable and choke cable from carburetor. Remove hoses from carburetor and label if needed. Remove the two carburetor mounting nuts, then withdraw the carburetor. Cover intake manifold passage to prevent entrance of foreign debris. Disconnect stop switch and starter switch from main engine wiring harness at connectors. Remove cooling system supply hose (W—Fig. Y-17) and exhaust hose (H). Remove drive coupler shield. Remove four cap screws (C) and washers retaining front and rear engine mounting plates to vehicle hull. Note shims (S) located under mounting plates and identify each shim for installation in original location. Remove any other components that will interfere with engine removal. Use a suitable lifting device to hoist engine assembly from vehicle. Place engine assembly on a clean work bench.

Remove exhaust guide plate outer and inner covers and exhaust guide plate. Engine drive flange (E—Fig. Y-18) and shaft are withdrawn with exhaust guide plate. Place flange drive shaft into a suitable soft-jawed vise and use Yamaha tool YW-6365 with a suitable tool to rotate drive flange off shaft. Withdraw shaft out rear of exhaust guide plate. In-spect all components for excessive wear or any other damage and renew if needed. Renew exhaust guide plate shaft seal during reassembly. Apply a water-resistant grease on flange drive shaft, bearing and seal. Apply Loctite PST Pipe Sealant or a suitable equivalent on threads of flange drive shaft. Place shaft with assembled components into a suitable soft-jawed vise. Screw drive flange onto threaded shaft and use Yamaha tool YW-6365 with a suitable torque wrench and tighten drive flange to 37 N·m (27 ft.-lbs.). Install engine drive flange and shaft with exhaust guide plate, outer and inner covers and related gaskets onto engine. Apply Loctite PST Pipe Sealant or a suitable equivalent on threads of mounting cap screws. Using tightening sequence shown in Fig. Y-23, tighten the exhaust guide plate and exhaust guide plate outer cover cap screws first to a torque of 10 N·m (7 ft.-lbs.), then to a final torque of 20 N·m (14 ft.-lbs.).

To reinstall engine, position Yamaha tool YW-6367, with stamped side facing upward, to underside of engine flywheel cover. Use a suitable adhesive to retain rubber mount damper in place. If Yamaha special tool is not available, use a rubber damper 19.5 mm (0.77 in.) in thickness.

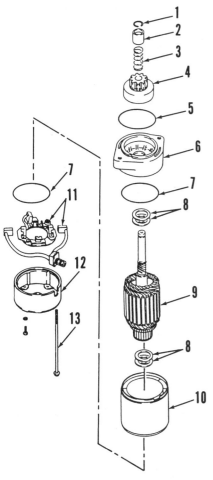

Fig. Y-30—View identifies bilge strainer (R).

Fig. Y-29—The jet pump forces water through hose (T) and past bilge siphon hose (S) opening when the vehicle is operated.

Fig. Y-27—Exploded view of typical electric starter.

1. "C" ring
2. Stop
3. Spring
4. Drive
5. "O" ring
6. Frame head & seal
7. "O" ring
8. Thrust washers
9. Armature
10. Frame
11. Brush assy.
12. End housing
13. Through-bolt

Use a suitable lifting device to hoist engine assembly into vehicle. Make sure coupler is located between engine drive flange (E—Fig. Y-18) and intermediate housing drive flange (I). A jackscrew hole is provided directly above each engine mounting hole in front and rear engine mounting plates. Install shims (S—Fig. Y-17) into original locations. Lay a straightedge across top of engine drive flange (E—Fig. Y-18) and intermediate housing drive flange (I). Engine drive flange (E) should be 0-0.6 mm (0-0.024 in.) higher (H) than intermediate drive flange (I). Measure clearance between engine drive flange (E) and base of intermediate housing drive flange (I). Clearance (C) should be 2-4 mm (0.079-0.157 in.). If recommended settings are not measured, then adjust jackscrews in front and rear engine mounting plates until recommended settings are obtained. Then measure clearance between shim (S—Fig. Y-17) and engine mounting plate for required shim (S) thickness. Measure clearance for all four engine mounts. Install recommended shims and remove jackscrews. Remove Yamaha tool YW-6367 or suitable equivalent. Apply Loctite 242 or a suitable equivalent on threads of four cap screws (C) and tighten cap screws to 17 N·m (12 ft.-lbs.). Remeasure as previously outlined to verify engine drive flange to intermediate housing drive flange settings are as recommended. Adjust shim thickness if needed.

Complete reassembly in reverse order of disassembly.

INTERMEDIATE HOUSING AND DRIVE FLANGE

All Models

R&R AND OVERHAUL. Disconnect battery cables from battery and remove battery from vehicle. Remove throttle cable and choke cable from carburetor. Remove hoses from carburetor and label if needed. Remove the two carburetor mounting nuts, then withdraw the carburetor. Cover intake manifold passage to prevent entrance of foreign debris. Disconnect stop switch and starter switch from main engine wiring harness at connectors. Remove cooling system supply hose (W—Fig. Y-17) and exhaust hose (H). Remove drive coupler shield. Remove four cap screws (C) and washers retaining front and rear engine mounting plates to vehicle hull. Note shims (S) located under mounting plates and identify each shim for installation in original location. Remove any other components that will interfere with engine removal. Use a suitable lifting device to hoist engine assembly from

vehicle. Place engine assembly on a clean work bench.

Remove intermediate housing (I—Fig. Y-32) three mounting cap screws. Withdraw intermediate housing with drive flange. Position Yamaha tool YW-6355 in a vise with splined-end and shaft facing upward. Place intermediate housing assembly on Yamaha tool YW-6355 with drive flange facing upward. Use Yamaha tool YW-6365 with a suitable tool to rotate drive flange off shaft. Remove oil seal housing cap screws (S) and withdraw oil seal housing with oil seal and "O" ring. Press shaft out front of intermediate housing. Inspect all components for excessive wear or any other damage and renew if needed. Renew all seals and "O" rings during reassembly. Press shaft with bearings into intermediate housing from front of housing. Apply Loctite 242 or a suitable equivalent on threads of oil seal housing cap screws (S) and securely tighten. Screw drive flange onto threaded shaft and use Yamaha tools YW-6355 and YW-6365 with a suitable torque wrench and tighten drive flange to 37 N·m (27 ft.-lbs.). Apply Loctite 242 or a suitable equivalent on threads of intermediate housing mounting cap screws and securely tighten. Inject a water-resistant grease into intermediate housing grease fitting (G).

To reinstall engine, position Yamaha tool YW-6367, with stamped side facing upward, to underside of engine flywheel cover. Use a suitable adhesive to retain rubber mount damper in place. If Yamaha special tool is not available, use a rubber damper 19.5 mm (0.77 in.) in thickness.

Use a suitable lifting device to hoist engine assembly into vehicle. Make sure

Fig. Y-32—Grease intermediate housing (I) through grease fitting (G) with a marine type water-resistant grease. Cap screws (S) retain oil seal housing to intermediate housing.

coupler is located between engine drive flange (E—Fig. Y-18) and intermediate housing drive flange (I). A jackscrew hole is provided directly above each engine mounting hole in front and rear engine mounting plates. Install shims (S—Fig. Y-17) into original locations. Lay a straightedge across top of engine drive flange (E—Fig. Y-18) and intermediate housing drive flange (I). Engine drive flange (E) should be 0-0.6 mm (0-0.024 in.) higher (H) than intermediate drive flange (I). Measure clearance between engine drive flange (E) and base of intermediate housing drive flange (I). Clearance (C) should be 2-4 mm (0.079-0.157 in.). If recommended settings are not measured, then adjust jackscrews in front and rear engine mounting plates until recommended settings are obtained. Then measure clearance between shim (S—Fig. Y-17) and engine mounting plate for required shim (S) thickness. Measure clearance for all four engine mounts. Install recommended shims and remove jackscrews. Remove Yamaha tool YW-6367 or suitable equivalent. Apply Loctite 242 or a suitable equivalent on threads of four cap screws (C) and tighten cap screws to 17 N·m (12 ft.-lbs.). Remeasure as previously outlined to verify engine drive flange to intermediate housing drive flange settings are as recommended. Adjust shim thickness if needed.

Complete reassembly in reverse order of disassembly.

JET PUMP

All Models

R&R AND OVERHAUL. Disconnect battery cables from battery and remove battery from vehicle. Turn fuel control valve to "OFF" position and rotate vehicle on either side. Remove six screws retaining jet pump cover and lower cover to allow access to hoses. Remove bilge siphon hose and jet pump supply hose from fittings on cover. Remove cooling system supply hose from jet pump fitting. Detach steering linkage joint (L—Fig. Y-34) at ball joint on output nozzle. Remove four jet pump mounting cap screws (C) (two at front and two at rear) and four through-bolts (B) (two on top and two on bottom). Use a suitable tool and separate impeller housing from intake housing. Withdraw jet pump assembly with impeller drive shaft out rear of vehicle.

Place Yamaha tool YB-6079 on impeller drive shaft splines and position in a vise. Use a suitable tool and rotate impeller clockwise to remove (impeller has left-hand threads).

Fig. Y-34—View identifies jet pump mounting cap screws (C) (two at front and two at rear), through-bolts (B) (two on top and two on bottom), outlet nozzle (N) and steering linkage joint (L).

Fig. Y-36—View identifies steering cable linkage joint (S) at steering shaft lever. Linkage joint is located under tower access cover on Wave-Jammer models.

Inspect impeller drive shaft bearing in intake housing for excessive wear and freedom of rotation. The intake housing must be removed to service bearing. Remove cap screw on side of housing and withdraw spacer. Use Yamaha tools YB-6229 and YB-6364 and drive bearing, washer and seals rearward into jet pump intake. Apply a water-resistant grease on bearing and seal lips, then drive components into intake housing from jet pump intake side using Yamaha tools YB-6229 and YW-6356. Secure spacer with retaining cap screw.

Inspect impeller and impeller housing for excessive wear or any other damage. Impeller drive shaft runout should not exceed 0.5 mm (0.02 in.) measured 371 mm (14.6 in.) from front of shaft with impeller drive shaft supported in V-blocks. Inspect all jet pump bearings for freedom of rotation and damaged components. Inspect jet pump outlet body and intake housing for damage. Renew any seals that are damaged during reassembly. Renew any other components that are excessively worn or are diagnosed with any other damage.

Apply Loctite PST Pipe Sealant or a suitable equivalent on impeller threads of impeller shaft. Install impeller onto impeller drive shaft with original shim. Rotate impeller counterclockwise and tighten to 18 N·m (13 ft.-lbs.). Apply Yamabond 4 or a suitable equivalent on mating surfaces between outlet nozzle, outlet body, impeller housing and intake housing during assembly.

Measure impeller blades clearance to impeller housing after assembly. Recommended clearance is 0.3 mm (0.012 in.). Add clearance measurement from all three blades together, then divide the total by three to obtain the average for all three blades. If recommended clearance is not measured, the shim thickness behind the impeller must be adjusted to obtain optimum performance. Increase shim thickness if average of measured clearances is above 0.3 mm (0.012 in.) and decrease shim thickness if average of measured clearances is below 0.3 mm (0.012 in.). Shims are available in thicknesses of 0.1 mm (0.004 in.), 0.3 mm (0.012 in.), 0.5 mm (0.020 in.) and 1.0 mm (0.040 in.). If required shim thickness exceeds 5.1 mm (0.20 in.), then impeller and impeller housing should be renewed.

Reinstall jet pump assembly in reverse order of removal. Apply Loctite PST Pipe Sealant or a suitable equivalent on threads of four through-bolts (B) and securely tighten. Tighten four jet pump mounting cap screws (C) to 34 N·m (24 ft.-lbs.). Complete reassembly in reverse order of disassembly. Apply a RTV silicone sealer around mounting surface of jet pump cover, then install cover and securely tighten six screws.

STEERING

All Models

ADJUSTMENT. When steering handlebar is rotated from side-to-side, there should be a minimum of 18 mm (0.71 in.) clearance between edge of outlet nozzle (N—Fig. Y-34) and each side of hull. If not, remove steering linkage joint (S—Fig. Y-36) from ball joint on steering shaft lever. If port side clearance is greater than starboard side, rotate linkage joint (S) outward on cable. If starboard side clearance is greater than port side, rotate linkage joint (S) inward on cable. Reattach steering linkage joint (S) on ball joint and recheck steering clearance. Repeat adjustment procedure if needed.

NOTE: If linkage joint (S) must be rotated out beyond the black threaded area (8 mm [0.3 in.]) on cable, then linkage joint (S) must be rotated inward beyond 8 mm (0.3 in.) mark and the remainder of the adjustment performed on jet pump linkage joint (L—Fig. Y-34).

NOTES